"No fiction is worth reading except for entertainment. If it entertains and is clean, it is good literature, or its kind. If it forms the habit of reading, in people who might not read otherwise, it is the best literature."

—EDGAR RICE BURROUGHS,
Tarzan of the Apes

EDGAR RICE BURROUGHS'

Jungle Tales of Tarzan®

To Linda, Dejah, and Jane Burroughs,
who continue the ERB legacy and have made
me feel like part of their illustrious family.

—MARTIN POWELL

To Anita Haskins, who believed in me
when I didn't believe in myself.

—MICHAEL HUDSON

To my sister, Elizabeth, and my brother, Michael, whose
faith and fortitude inspire me every day. You and your
generation are the future, and these stories are for you.

—DIANA LETO

Publisher **MIKE RICHARDSON**   *Producer* **MICHAEL HUDSON**   *Editor* **PATRICK THORPE**
Digital Art and Production **CHRISTINA McKENZIE**   *Collection Designer* **DIANA LETO**

Published by Dark Horse Books, a division of Dark Horse Comics, Inc., 10956 SE Main Street, Milwaukie, Oregon 97222
DarkHorse.com / SequentialPulpComics.com

First edition: June 2015 / ISBN 978-1-61655-744-7
Signed limited edition: June 2015 / ISBN 978-1-61655-745-4
10 9 8 7 6 5 4 3 2 1
PRINTED IN CHINA

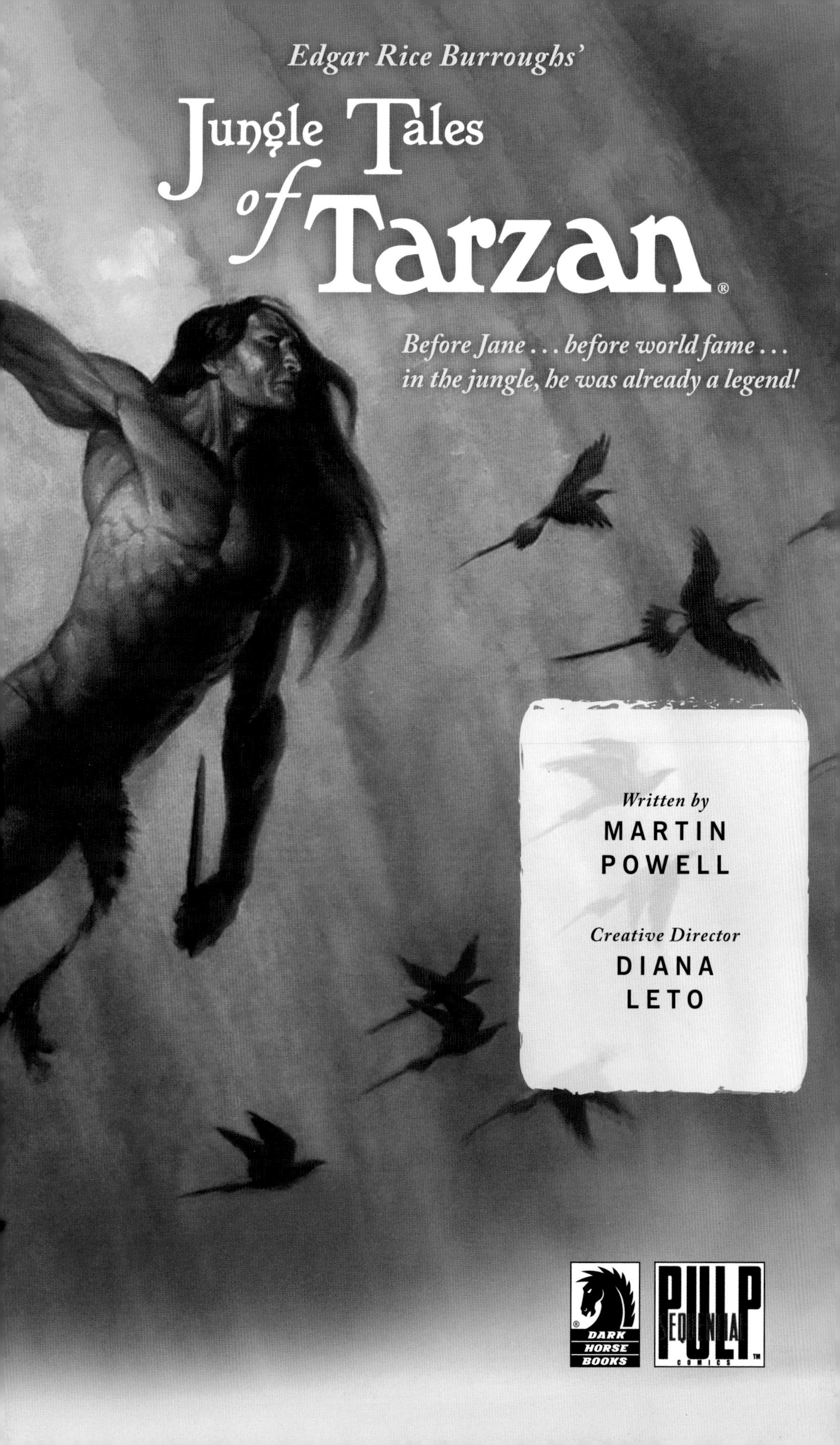

Edgar Rice Burroughs'

Jungle Tales of Tarzan®

Before Jane . . . before world fame . . .
in the jungle, he was already a legend!

Written by
MARTIN POWELL

Creative Director
DIANA LETO

DARK HORSE BOOKS

PULP SEQUENTIAL COMICS™

BACK TO THE JUNGLE

Tarzan may be the most recognizable figure in the history of literature, with a mind-boggling readership of two billion, but he is also the most misunderstood. The nearly one hundred movies and countless television series produced during the century of his existence have profoundly warped the original intent of Edgar Rice Burroughs' twenty-four novels. We think we know all there is to know about Tarzan and his beloved Jane, but unless we have read the original books, we know next to nothing.

At the beginning of the twentieth century ERB created an astonishingly exotic world, one as richly detailed and complex as anything written by George R. R. Martin. In the first of Burroughs' novels, *Tarzan of the Apes*, we learned the origin story of Tarzan's aristocratic parents stranded on the wild shores of Africa. But before long we were introduced to a cast of outrageous characters that included cannibal tribes, animals both friend and foe, Belgian slave traders, international spies, gorgeous (and next to naked) pagan priestesses, and chimerical creatures living in mystal lost cities.

But Burroughs' greatest invention, aside from Tarzan himself, was the band of anthropoid apes called "Mangani" who snatched the infant Lord Greystoke and raised him through a childhood as idyllic as it was savage. What makes the Mangani unique among literary creations is the conceit that these primates had the ability to speak in words—a complete language which, if nothing else, would make the species the missing link in human evolution.

It is this Tarzan still living among the Mangani as a feral man-child of almost twenty that you will meet in this graphic novel based on ERB's *Jungle Tales of Tarzan*, a collection of twelve linked short stories. It is Tarzan before Jane. Tarzan before the moment of consciousness that he is, in fact, human and not Mangani. Tarzan, through his adventures, creating the legend that precedes the coming of the white man into his jungle.

What Sequential Pulp has done so brilliantly is bring together the greatest living *Tarzan* artists to illustrate, in very different styles, each of the *Jungle* tales. While staying as faithful to the hundred-year-old source material as possible, they have breathed fresh life into it, tailoring the stories to a twenty-first-century audience. Whether they tell of the ape-man's first, bestial romance with a young female Mangani, his clash with a leprous witch doctor and his razor-fanged pet hyenas, his dreams, his hallucinations, or even his search for God, the stories will illuminate the remarkable inner workings of Tarzan's mind as he pits himself against the elements and the human and nonhuman denizens of the jungle.

Read on and learn how the myth began . . .

ROBIN MAXWELL
January 2014

ROBIN MAXWELL IS THE NATIONALLY BEST-SELLING AUTHOR OF EIGHT NOVELS OF HISTORICAL FICTION FEATURING POWERFUL WOMEN. IN 2012, HER CRITICALLY ACCLAIMED *JANE: THE WOMAN WHO LOVED TARZAN* WAS PUBLISHED, A RETELLING OF THE TARZAN MYTH FROM JANE'S POINT OF VIEW. SHE LIVES IN THE DESERT OF CALIFORNIA WITH HER HUSBAND, YOGI MAX THOMAS.

VISIT MS. MAXWELL ONLINE AT ROBINMAXWELL.COM.

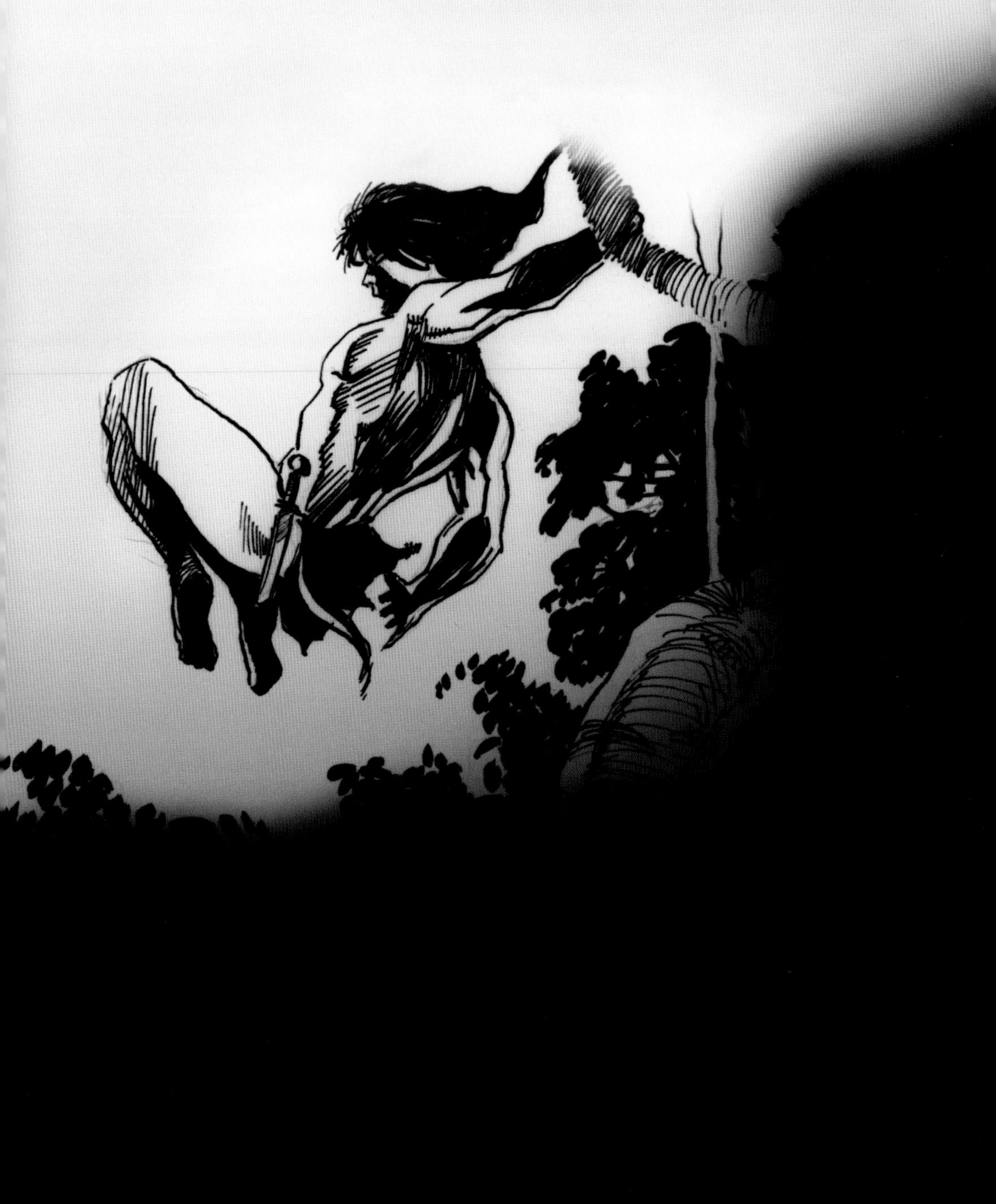

CONTENTS

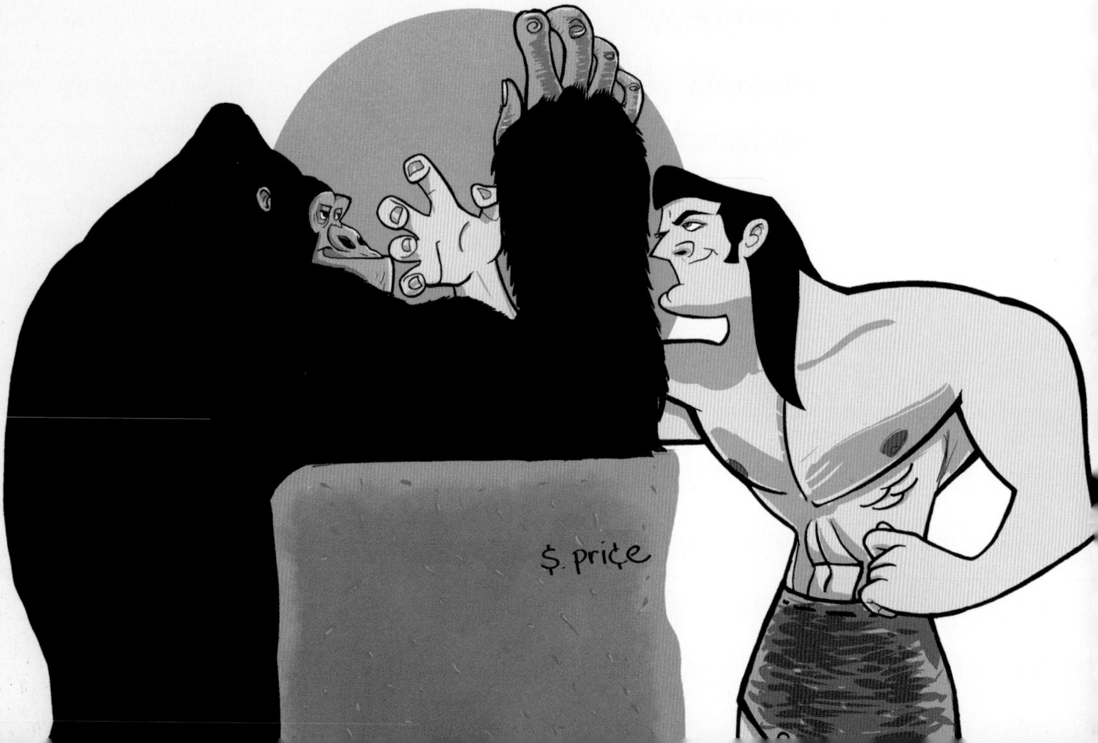
$. price

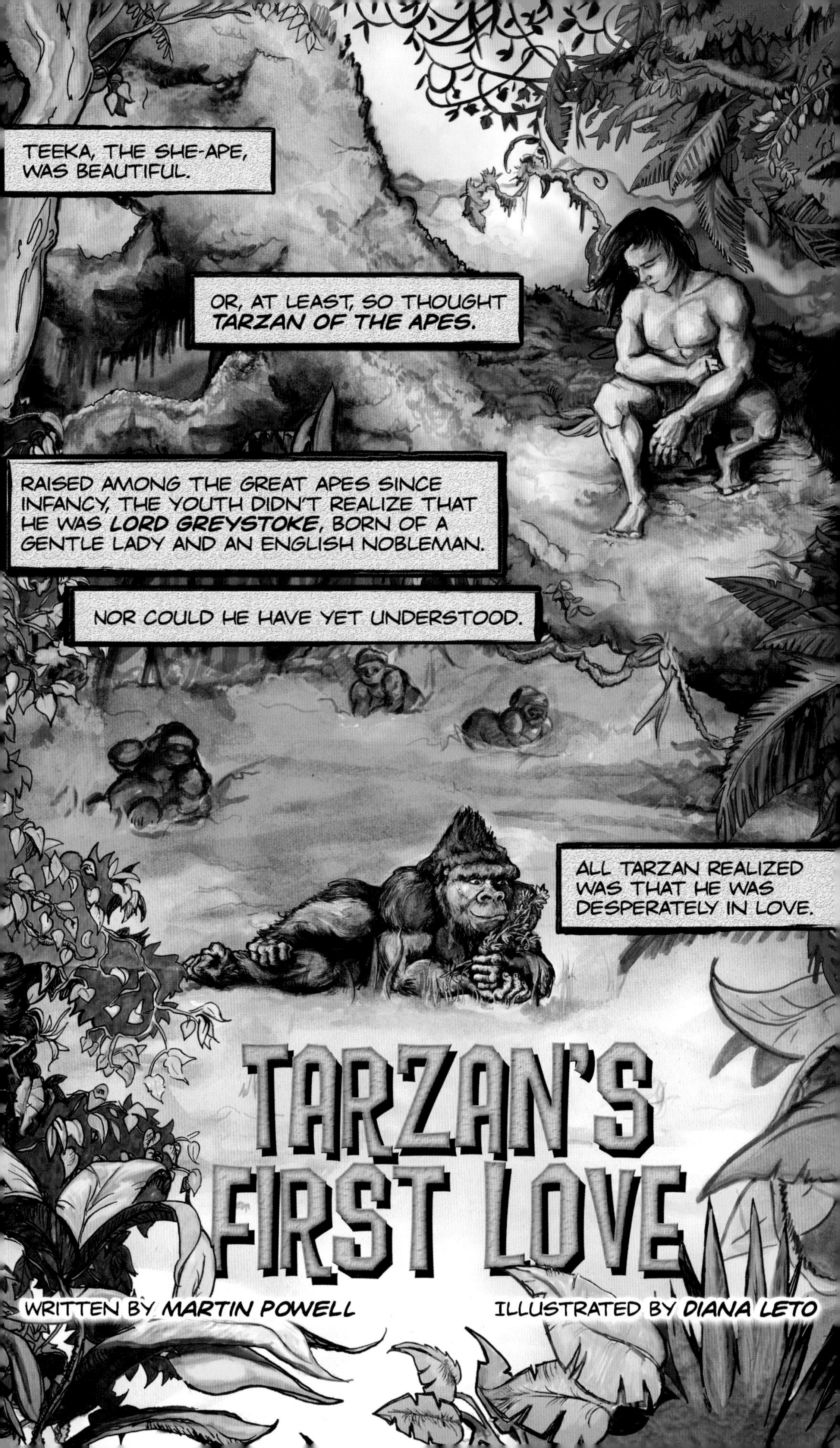
TEEKA, THE SHE-APE, WAS BEAUTIFUL.
OR, AT LEAST, SO THOUGHT TARZAN OF THE APES.
RAISED AMONG THE GREAT APES SINCE INFANCY, THE YOUTH DIDN'T REALIZE THAT HE WAS LORD GREYSTOKE, BORN OF A GENTLE LADY AND AN ENGLISH NOBLEMAN.
NOR COULD HE HAVE YET UNDERSTOOD.
ALL TARZAN REALIZED WAS THAT HE WAS DESPERATELY IN LOVE.
TARZAN'S FIRST LOVE
WRITTEN BY MARTIN POWELL
ILLUSTRATED BY DIANA LETO

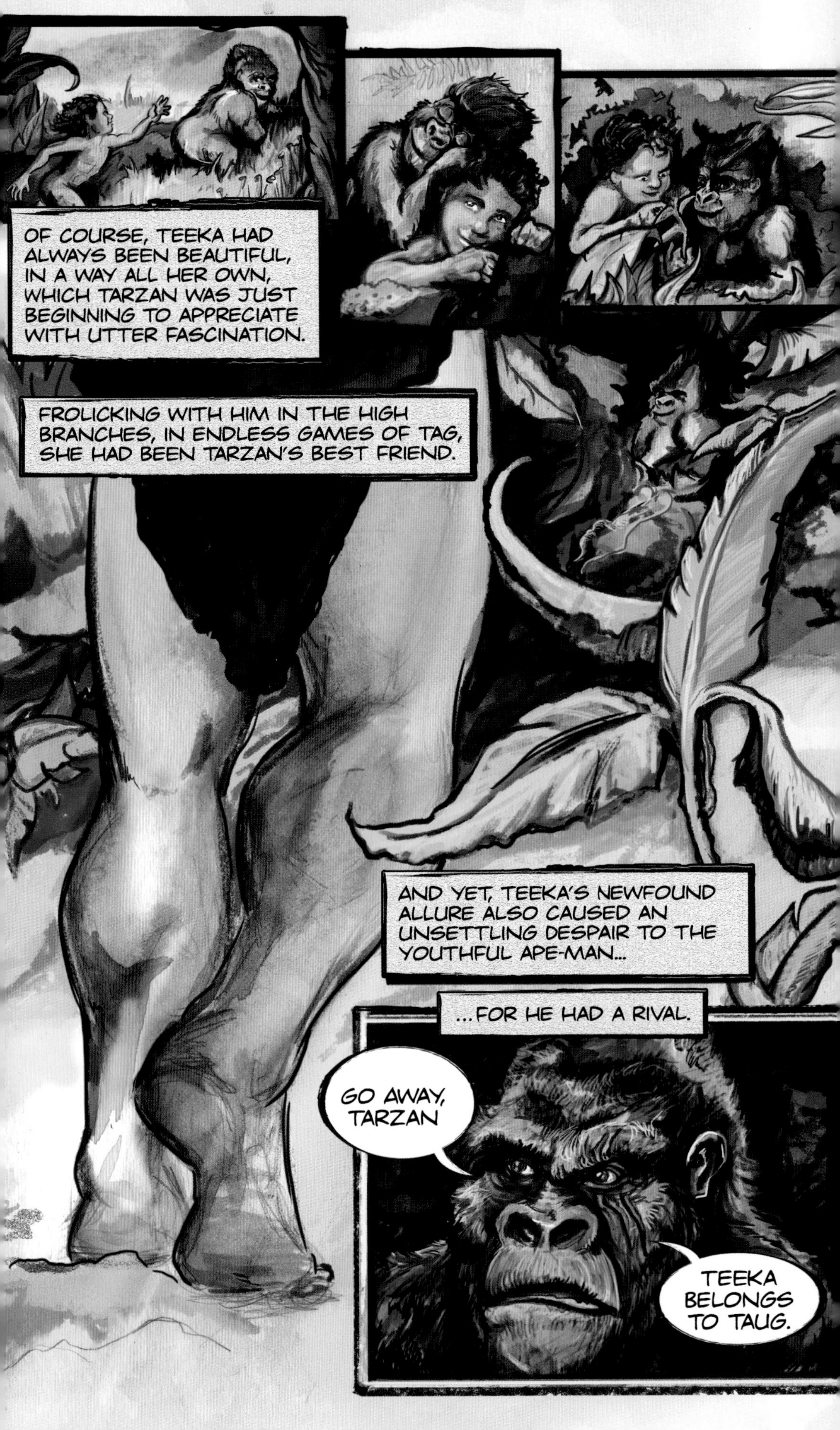
OF COURSE, TEEKA HAD ALWAYS BEEN BEAUTIFUL, IN A WAY ALL HER OWN, WHICH TARZAN WAS JUST BEGINNING TO APPRECIATE WITH UTTER FASCINATION.
FROLICKING WITH HIM IN THE HIGH BRANCHES, IN ENDLESS GAMES OF TAG, SHE HAD BEEN TARZAN'S BEST FRIEND.
AND YET, TEEKA'S NEWFOUND ALLURE ALSO CAUSED AN UNSETTLING DESPAIR TO THE YOUTHFUL APE-MAN...
...FOR HE HAD A RIVAL.
GO AWAY, TARZAN
TEEKA BELONGS TO TAUG.

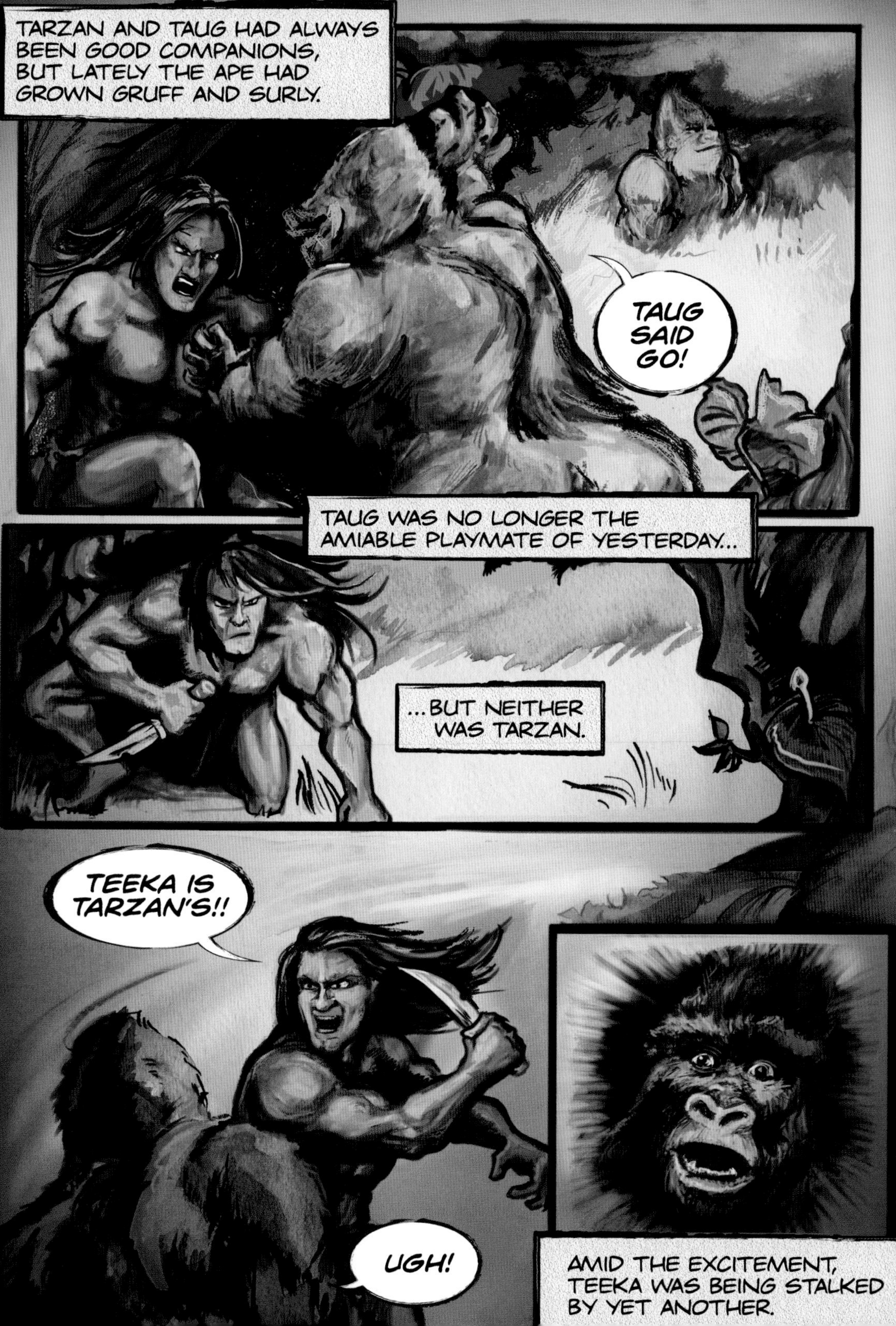
TARZAN AND TAUG HAD ALWAYS BEEN GOOD COMPANIONS, BUT LATELY THE APE HAD GROWN GRUFF AND SURLY.
TAUG SAID GO!
TAUG WAS NO LONGER THE AMIABLE PLAYMATE OF YESTERDAY...
...BUT NEITHER WAS TARZAN.
TEEKA IS TARZAN'S!!
UGH!
AMID THE EXCITEMENT, TEEKA WAS BEING STALKED BY YET ANOTHER.

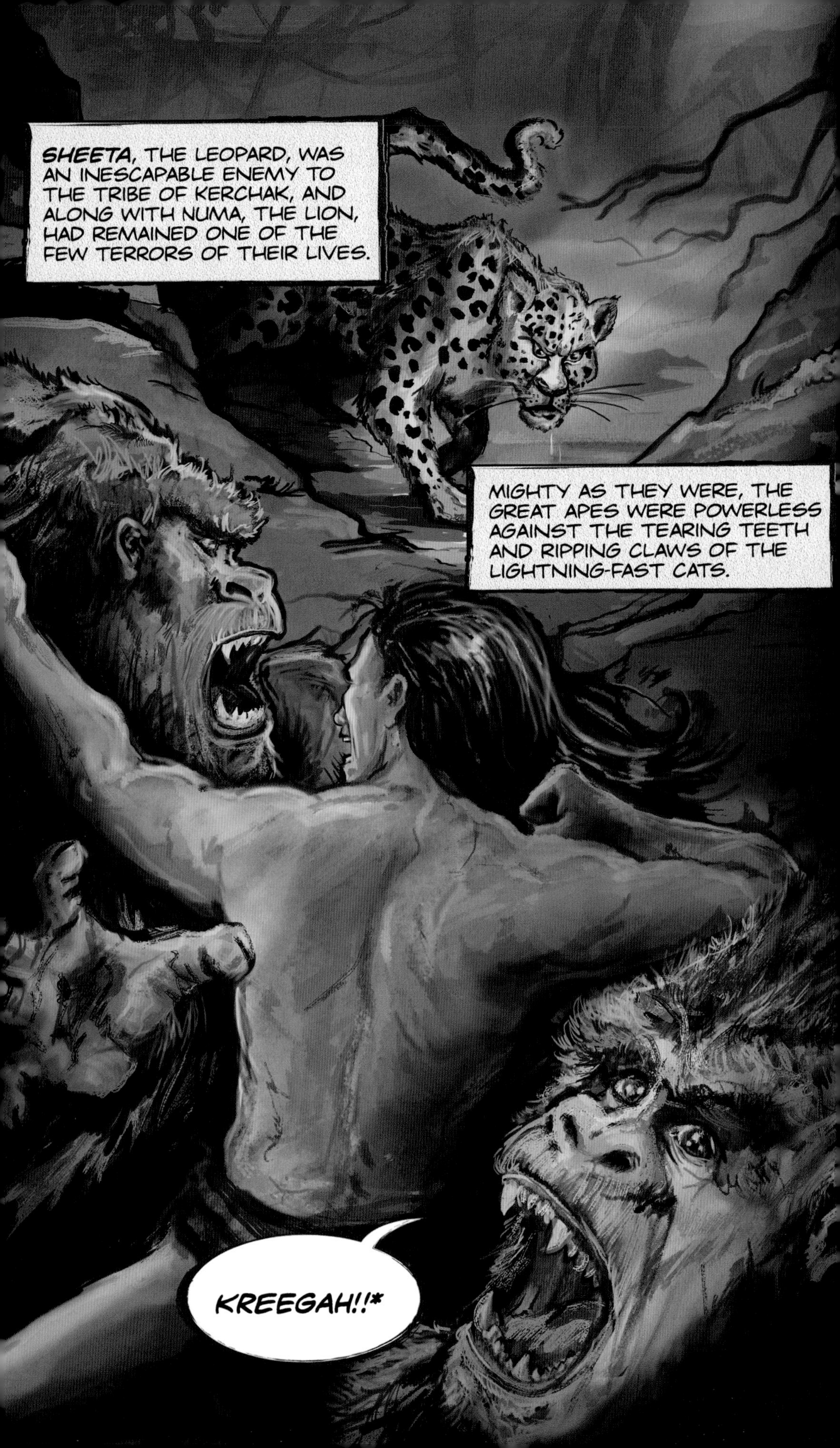
SHEETA, THE LEOPARD, WAS AN INESCAPABLE ENEMY TO THE TRIBE OF KERCHAK, AND ALONG WITH NUMA, THE LION, HAD REMAINED ONE OF THE FEW TERRORS OF THEIR LIVES.
MIGHTY AS THEY WERE, THE GREAT APES WERE POWERLESS AGAINST THE TEARING TEETH AND RIPPING CLAWS OF THE LIGHTNING-FAST CATS.
KREEGAH!!*

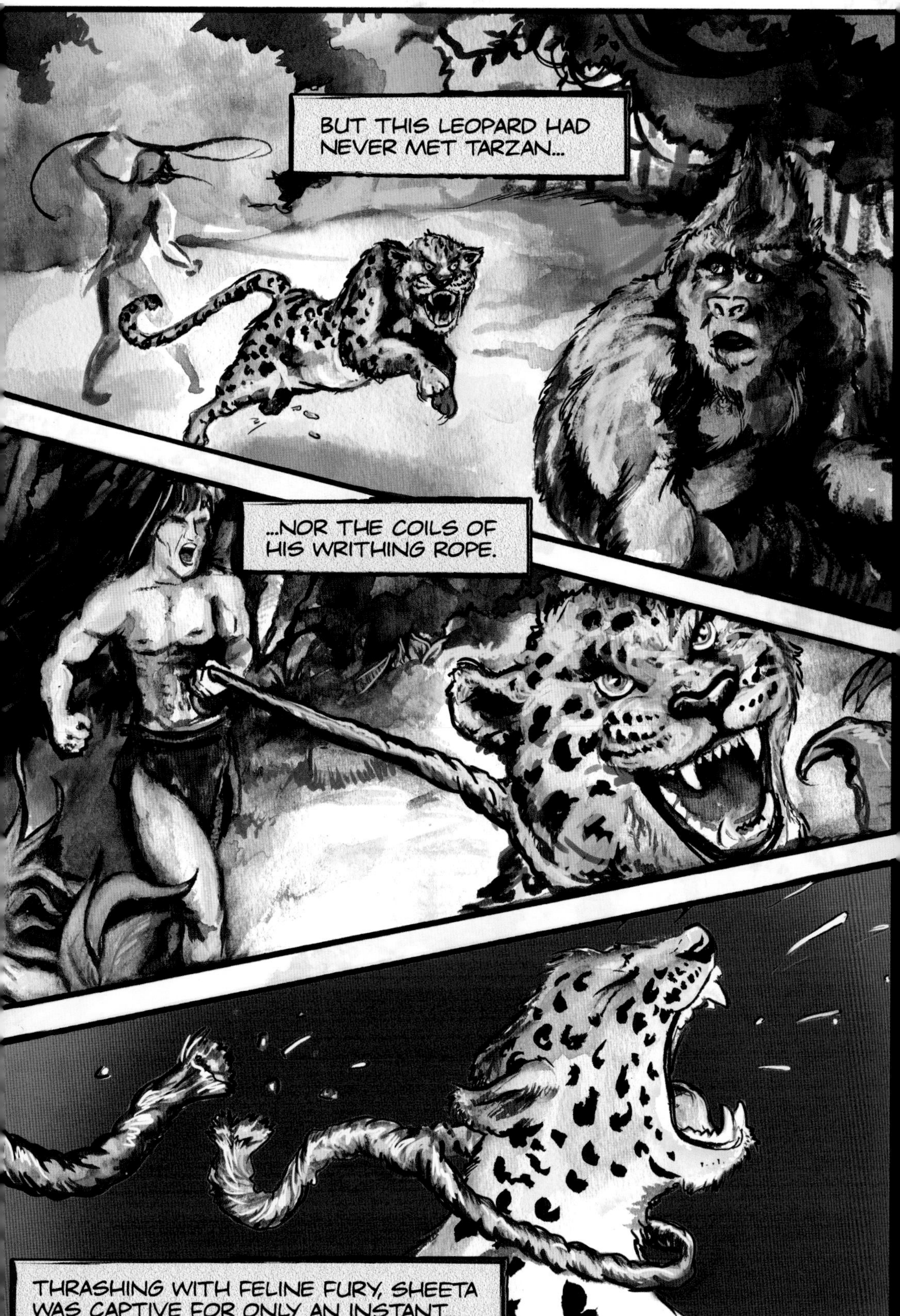
BUT THIS LEOPARD HAD NEVER MET TARZAN...
...NOR THE COILS OF HIS WRITHING ROPE.
THRASHING WITH FELINE FURY, SHEETA WAS CAPTIVE FOR ONLY AN INSTANT...

... BUT IT WAS LONG ENOUGH.

LIMP AWAY AND LICK YOUR WOUNDS, SHEETA.

AND BEWARE... TARZAN'S NEXT ROPE WILL BE STRONGER.

ALTHOUGH TARZAN'S SWIFT ACTION AND INGENUITY HAD SAVED TEEKA FROM A HIDEOUS DEATH, THE MEMORY OF THE GREAT APES WAS FLEETING, AND SHE HAD ALREADY FORGOTTEN THE THREAT OF SHEETA.

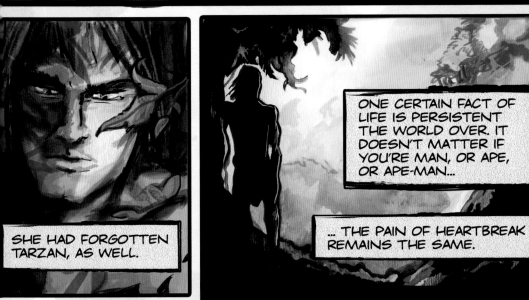

ONE CERTAIN FACT OF LIFE IS PERSISTENT THE WORLD OVER. IT DOESN'T MATTER IF YOU'RE MAN, OR APE, OR APE-MAN...

... THE PAIN OF HEARTBREAK REMAINS THE SAME.

SHE HAD FORGOTTEN TARZAN, AS WELL.

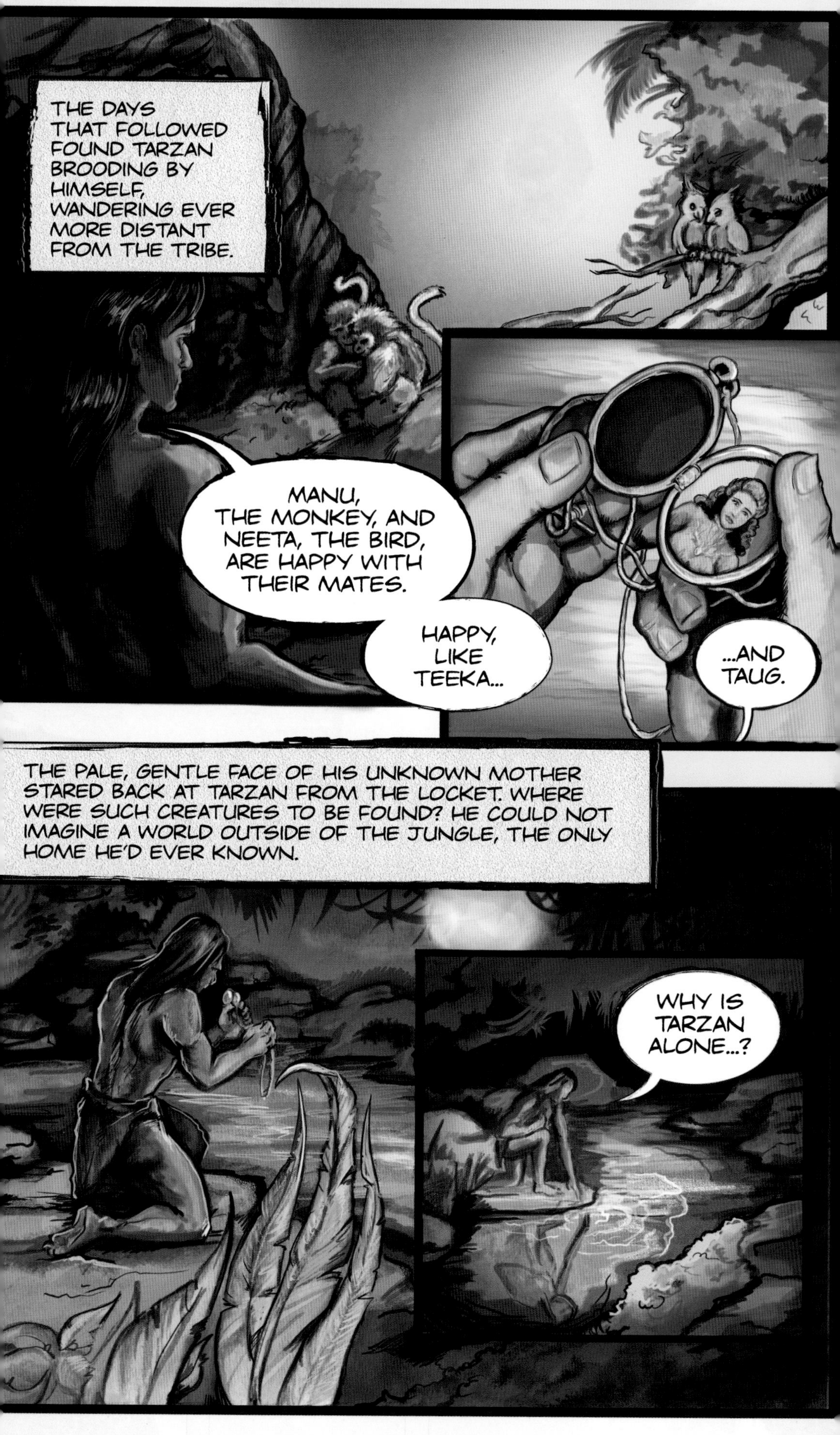

THE DAYS THAT FOLLOWED FOUND TARZAN BROODING BY HIMSELF, WANDERING EVER MORE DISTANT FROM THE TRIBE.
MANU, THE MONKEY, AND NEETA, THE BIRD, ARE HAPPY WITH THEIR MATES.
HAPPY, LIKE TEEKA...
...AND TAUG.
THE PALE, GENTLE FACE OF HIS UNKNOWN MOTHER STARED BACK AT TARZAN FROM THE LOCKET. WHERE WERE SUCH CREATURES TO BE FOUND? HE COULD NOT IMAGINE A WORLD OUTSIDE OF THE JUNGLE, THE ONLY HOME HE'D EVER KNOWN.
WHY IS TARZAN ALONE...?

THE NEXT MORNING, ON HIS MELANCHOLY JOURNEY BACK TO THE TRIBE, THE APE-MAN DISCOVERED AN OCCUPIED NATIVE TRAP...

...AND TARZAN COULD HARDLY BELIEVE HIS LUCK.

TAUG?!

BEFORE TARZAN COULD TAUNT TAUG FOR HIS PRECARIOUS PREDICAMENT, HIS KEEN NOSE CAUGHT THE SCENT OF AN APPROACHING ENEMY.

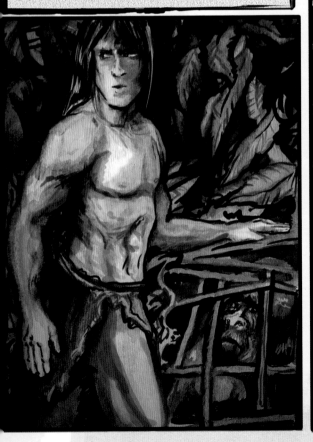

AND SO, TAUG, SULLEN AND HUMILIATED, WAS ABANDONED TO HIS FATE.

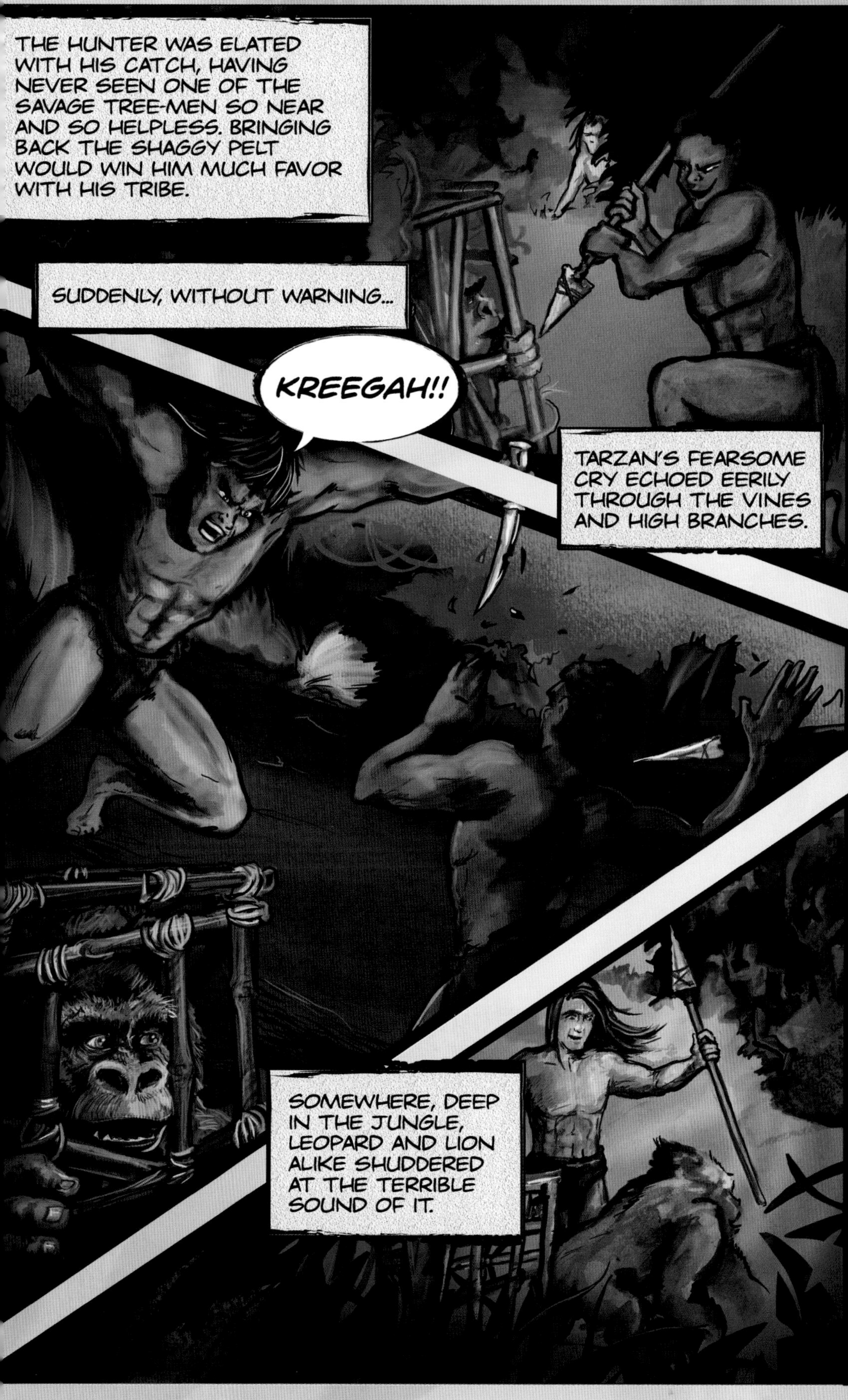
THE HUNTER WAS ELATED WITH HIS CATCH, HAVING NEVER SEEN ONE OF THE SAVAGE TREE-MEN SO NEAR AND SO HELPLESS. BRINGING BACK THE SHAGGY PELT WOULD WIN HIM MUCH FAVOR WITH HIS TRIBE.
SUDDENLY, WITHOUT WARNING...
KREEGAH!!
TARZAN'S FEARSOME CRY ECHOED EERILY THROUGH THE VINES AND HIGH BRANCHES.
SOMEWHERE, DEEP IN THE JUNGLE, LEOPARD AND LION ALIKE SHUDDERED AT THE TERRIBLE SOUND OF IT.

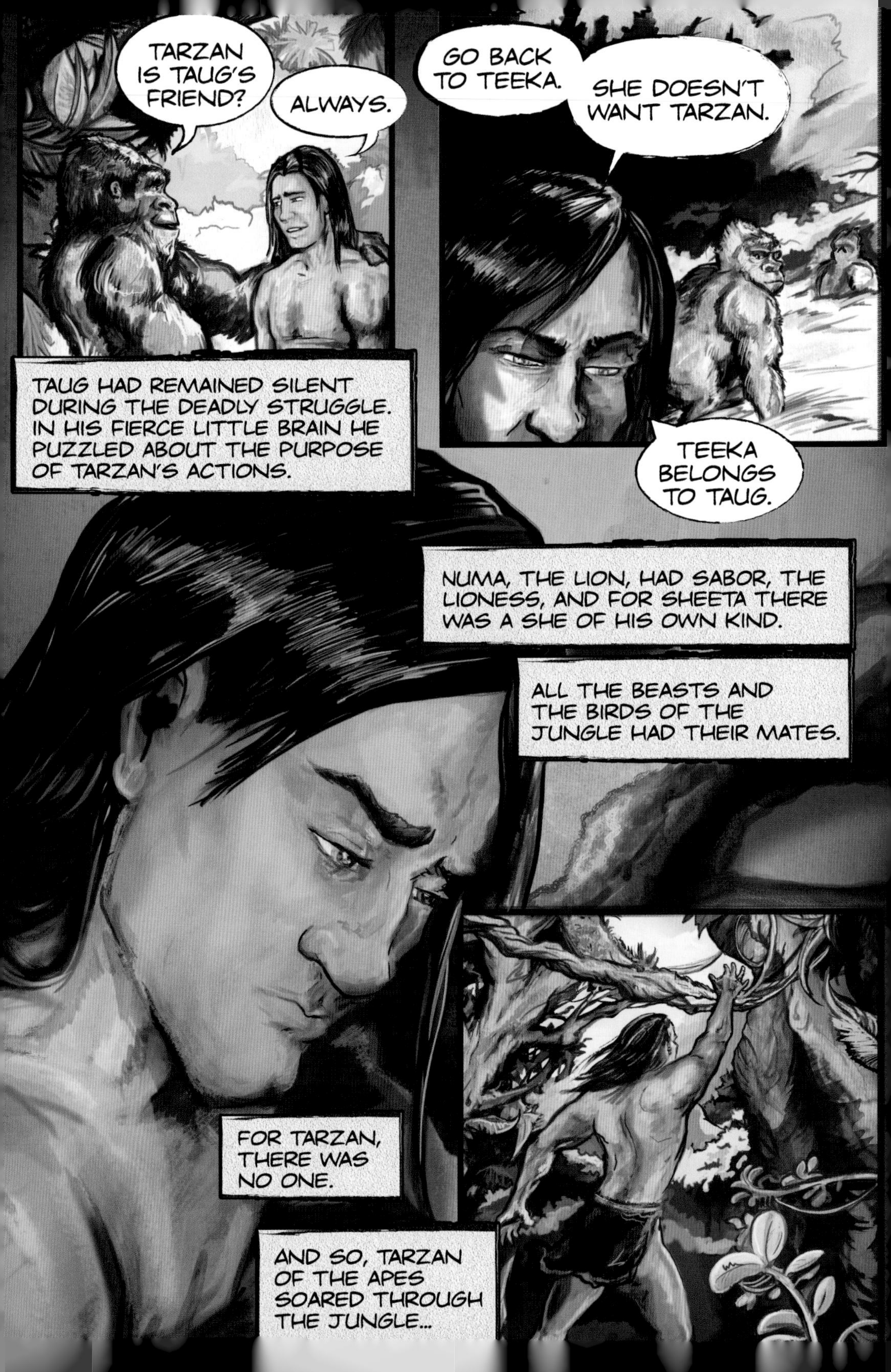

TARZAN IS TAUG'S FRIEND?
ALWAYS.
GO BACK TO TEEKA.
SHE DOESN'T WANT TARZAN.
TAUG HAD REMAINED SILENT DURING THE DEADLY STRUGGLE. IN HIS FIERCE LITTLE BRAIN HE PUZZLED ABOUT THE PURPOSE OF TARZAN'S ACTIONS.
TEEKA BELONGS TO TAUG.
NUMA, THE LION, HAD SABOR, THE LIONESS, AND FOR SHEETA THERE WAS A SHE OF HIS OWN KIND.
ALL THE BEASTS AND THE BIRDS OF THE JUNGLE HAD THEIR MATES.
FOR TARZAN, THERE WAS NO ONE.
AND SO, TARZAN OF THE APES SOARED THROUGH THE JUNGLE...

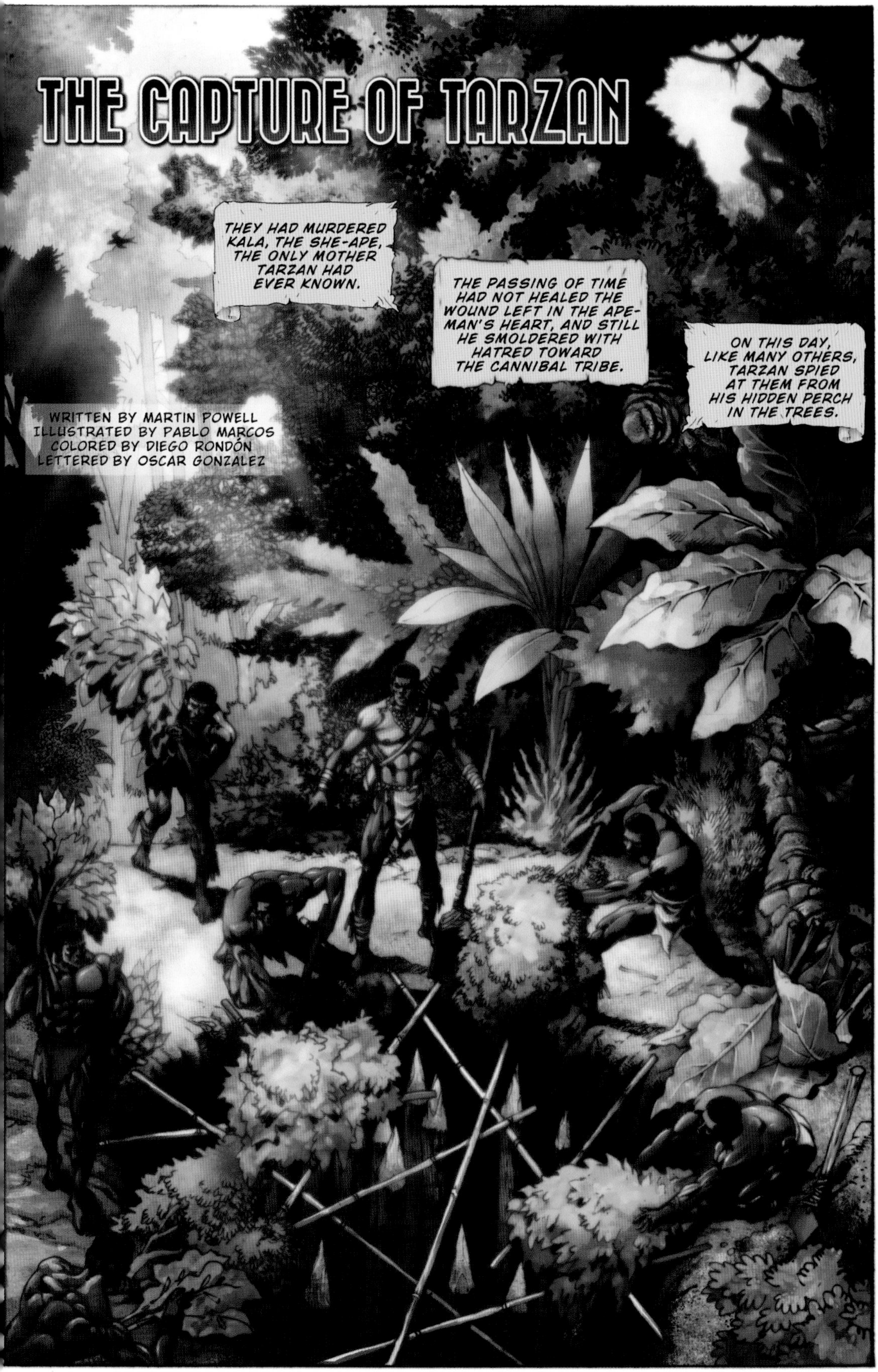
THE CAPTURE OF TARZAN
THEY HAD MURDERED KALA, THE SHE-APE, THE ONLY MOTHER TARZAN HAD EVER KNOWN.
THE PASSING OF TIME HAD NOT HEALED THE WOUND LEFT IN THE APE-MAN'S HEART, AND STILL HE SMOLDERED WITH HATRED TOWARD THE CANNIBAL TRIBE.
ON THIS DAY, LIKE MANY OTHERS, TARZAN SPIED AT THEM FROM HIS HIDDEN PERCH IN THE TREES.
WRITTEN BY MARTIN POWELL
ILLUSTRATED BY PABLO MARCOS
COLORED BY DIEGO RONDÓN
LETTERED BY OSCAR GONZALEZ

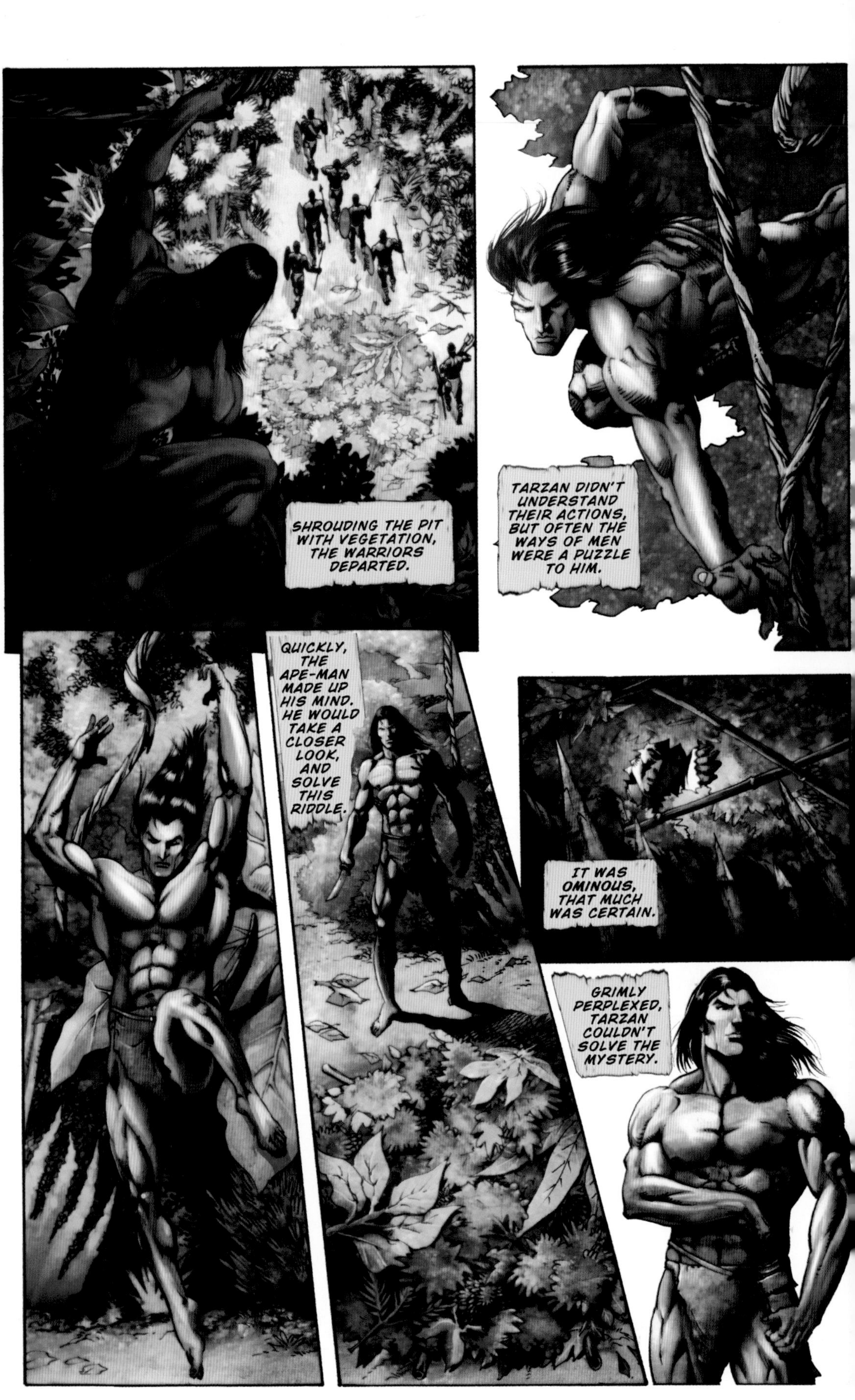
SHROUDING THE PIT WITH VEGETATION, THE WARRIORS DEPARTED.
TARZAN DIDN'T UNDERSTAND THEIR ACTIONS, BUT OFTEN THE WAYS OF MEN WERE A PUZZLE TO HIM.
QUICKLY, THE APE-MAN MADE UP HIS MIND. HE WOULD TAKE A CLOSER LOOK, AND SOLVE THIS RIDDLE.
IT WAS OMINOUS, THAT MUCH WAS CERTAIN.
GRIMLY PERPLEXED, TARZAN COULDN'T SOLVE THE MYSTERY.

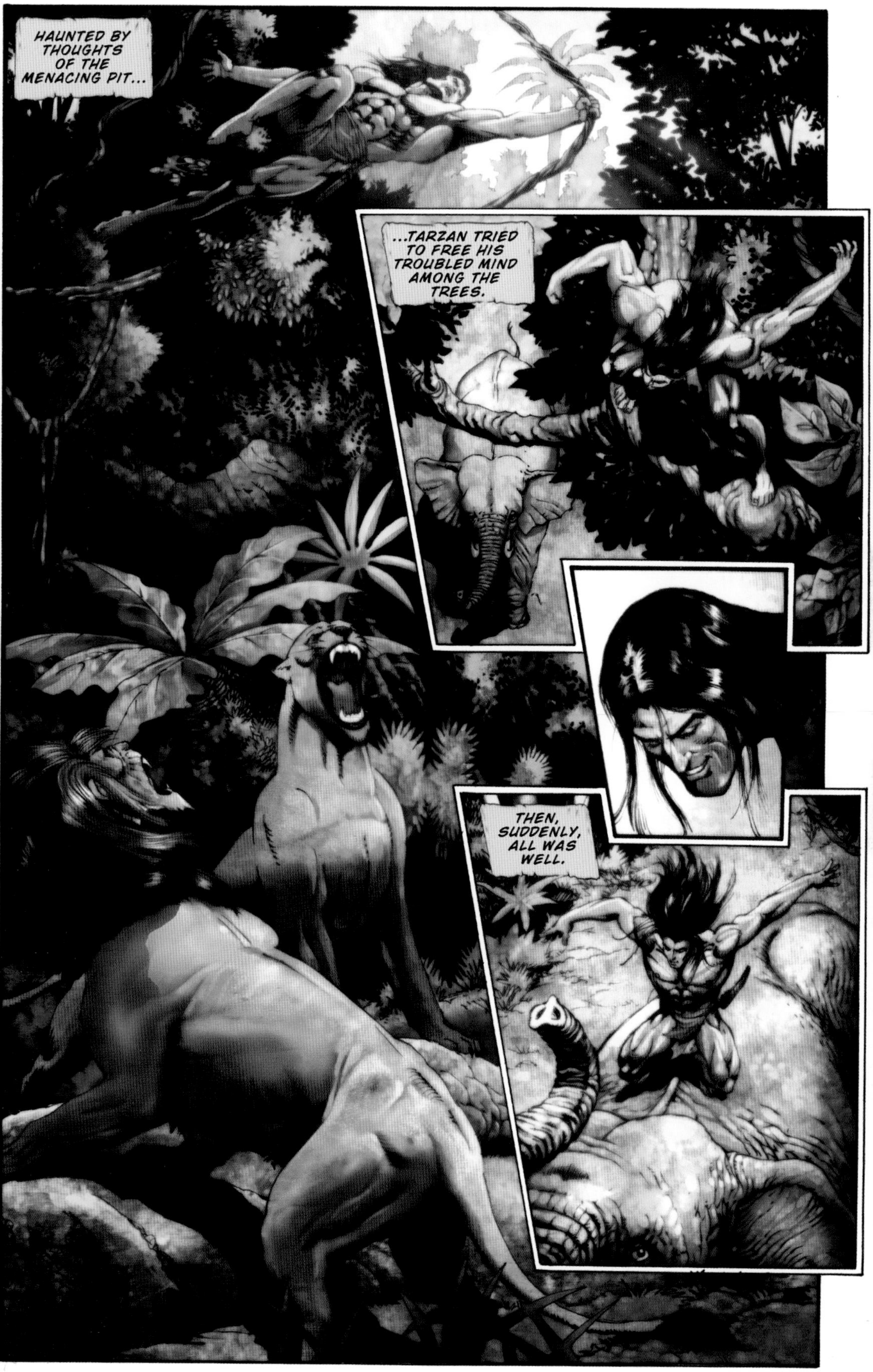
HAUNTED BY THOUGHTS OF THE MENACING PIT...
...TARZAN TRIED TO FREE HIS TROUBLED MIND AMONG THE TREES.
THEN, SUDDENLY, ALL WAS WELL.

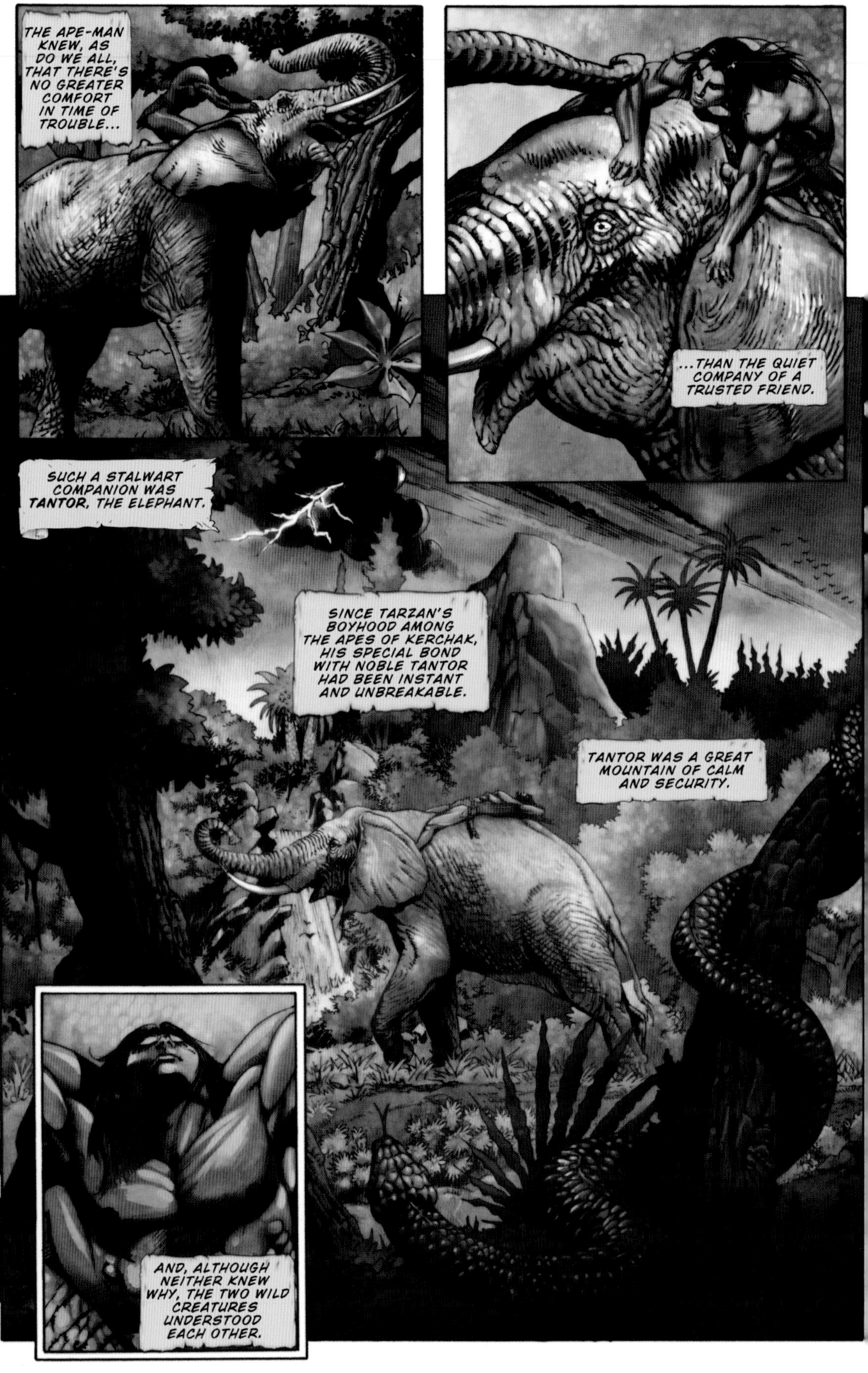
THE APE-MAN KNEW, AS DO WE ALL, THAT THERE'S NO GREATER COMFORT IN TIME OF TROUBLE...
...THAN THE QUIET COMPANY OF A TRUSTED FRIEND.
SUCH A STALWART COMPANION WAS TANTOR, THE ELEPHANT.
SINCE TARZAN'S BOYHOOD AMONG THE APES OF KERCHAK, HIS SPECIAL BOND WITH NOBLE TANTOR HAD BEEN INSTANT AND UNBREAKABLE.
TANTOR WAS A GREAT MOUNTAIN OF CALM AND SECURITY.
AND, ALTHOUGH NEITHER KNEW WHY, THE TWO WILD CREATURES UNDERSTOOD EACH OTHER.

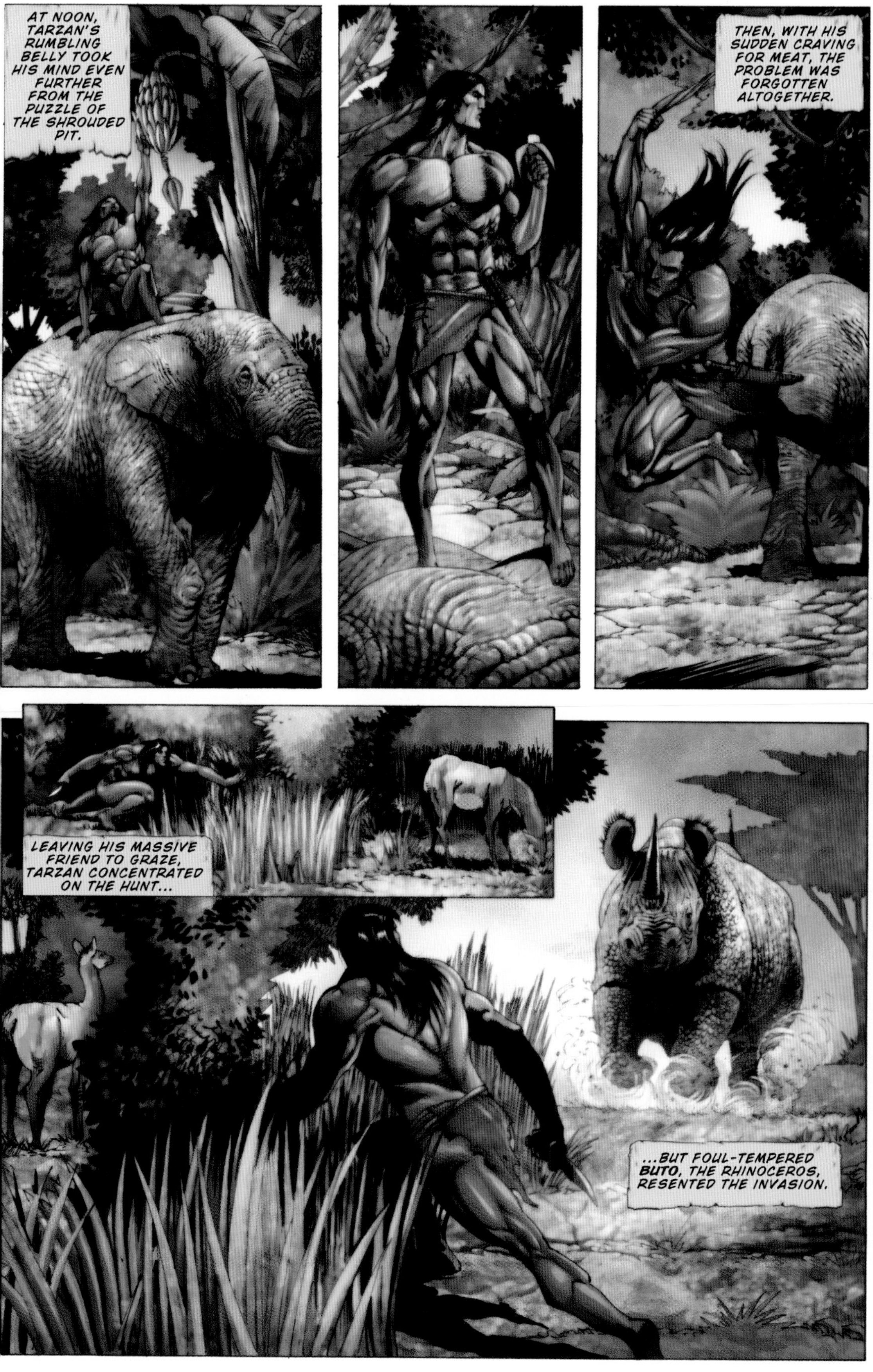
AT NOON, TARZAN'S RUMBLING BELLY TOOK HIS MIND EVEN FURTHER FROM THE PUZZLE OF THE SHROUDED PIT.
THEN, WITH HIS SUDDEN CRAVING FOR MEAT, THE PROBLEM WAS FORGOTTEN ALTOGETHER.
LEAVING HIS MASSIVE FRIEND TO GRAZE, TARZAN CONCENTRATED ON THE HUNT...
...BUT FOUL-TEMPERED BUTO, THE RHINOCEROS, RESENTED THE INVASION.

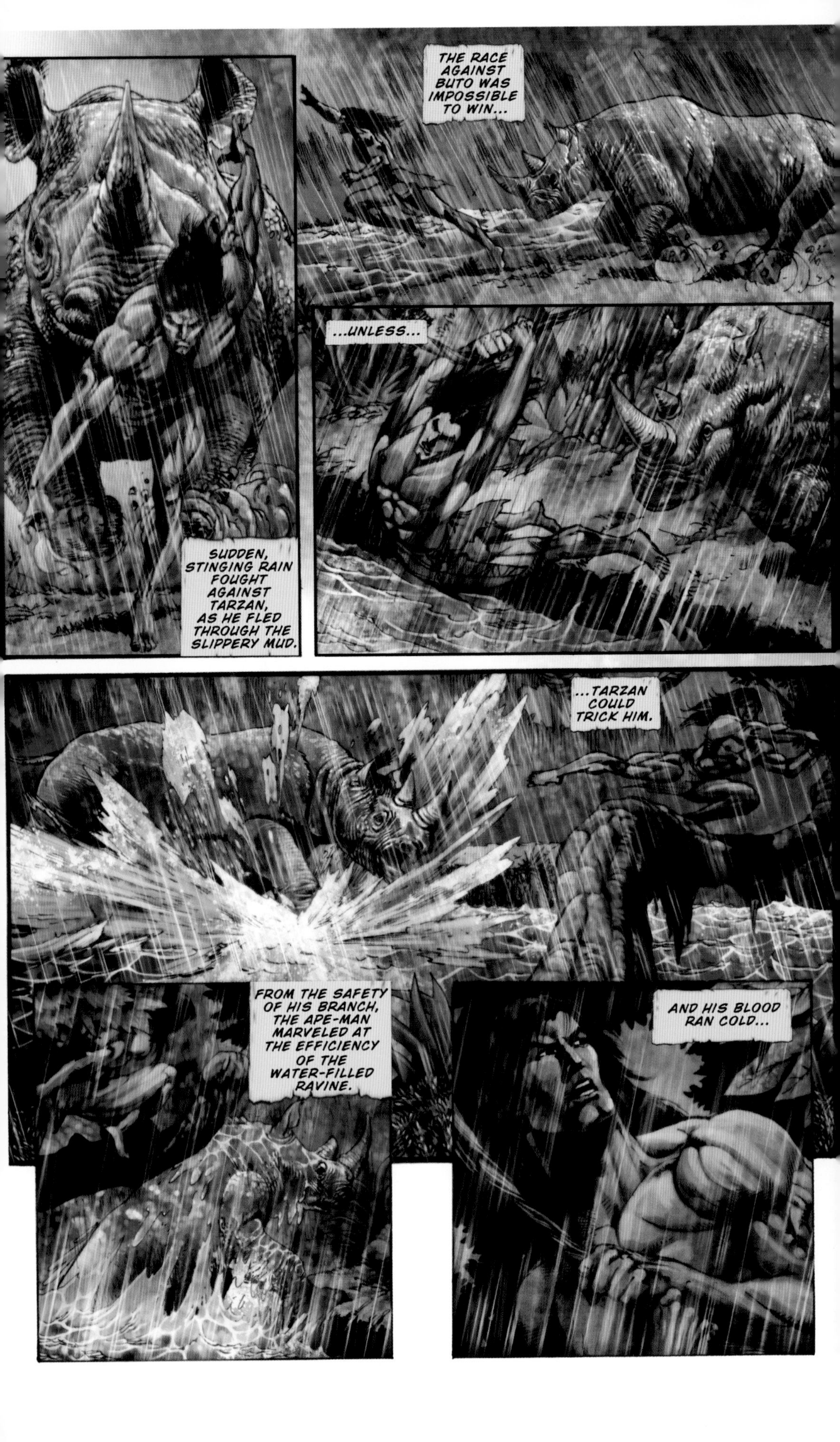
THE RACE AGAINST BUTO WAS IMPOSSIBLE TO WIN...
SUDDEN, STINGING RAIN FOUGHT AGAINST TARZAN, AS HE FLED THROUGH THE SLIPPERY MUD.
...UNLESS...
...TARZAN COULD TRICK HIM.
FROM THE SAFETY OF HIS BRANCH, THE APE-MAN MARVELED AT THE EFFICIENCY OF THE WATER-FILLED RAVINE.
AND HIS BLOOD RAN COLD...

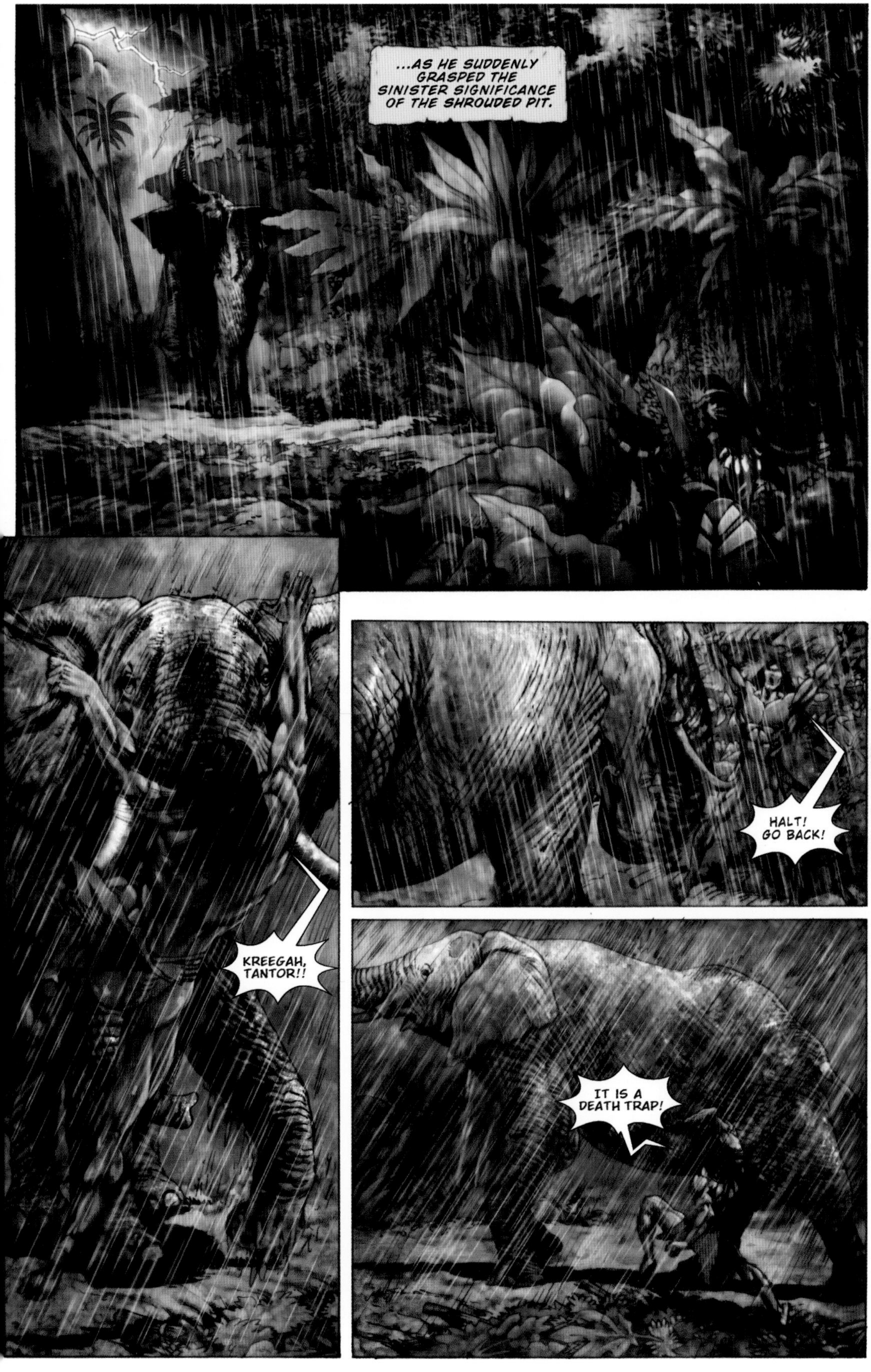
...AS HE SUDDENLY GRASPED THE SINISTER SIGNIFICANCE OF THE SHROUDED PIT.
KREEGAH, TANTOR!!
HALT! GO BACK!
IT IS A DEATH TRAP!

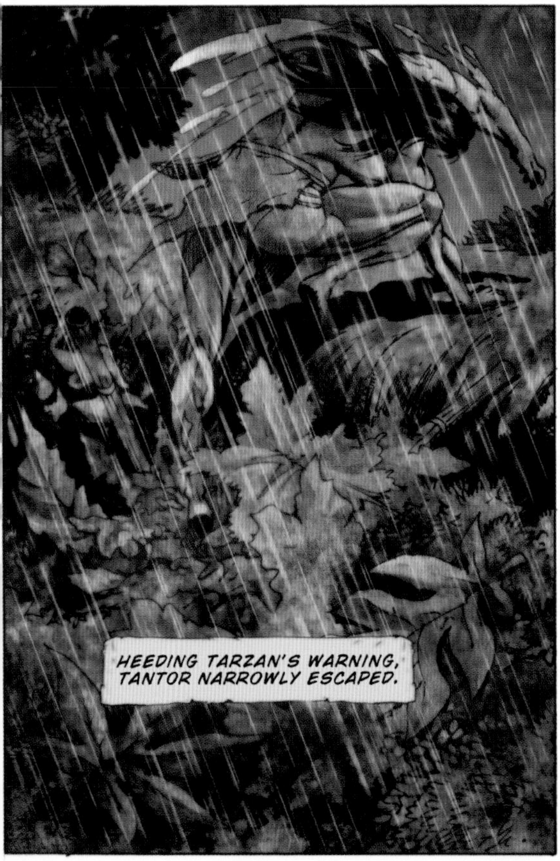
HEEDING TARZAN'S WARNING, TANTOR NARROWLY ESCAPED.

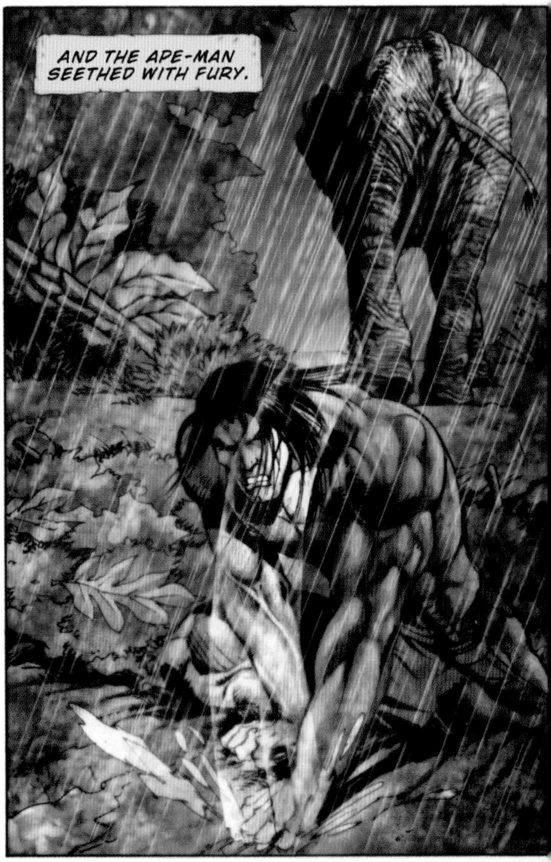
AND THE APE-MAN SEETHED WITH FURY.

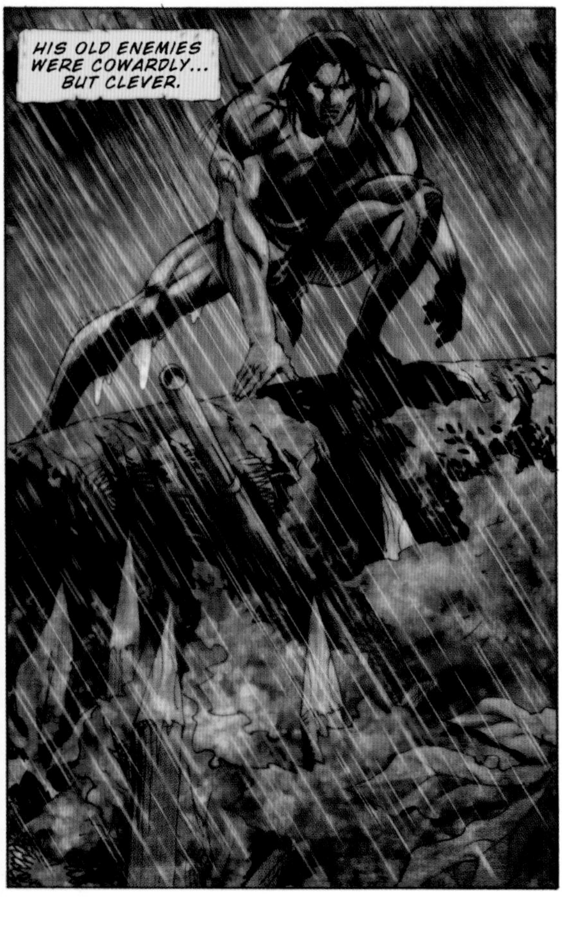
HIS OLD ENEMIES WERE COWARDLY... BUT CLEVER.

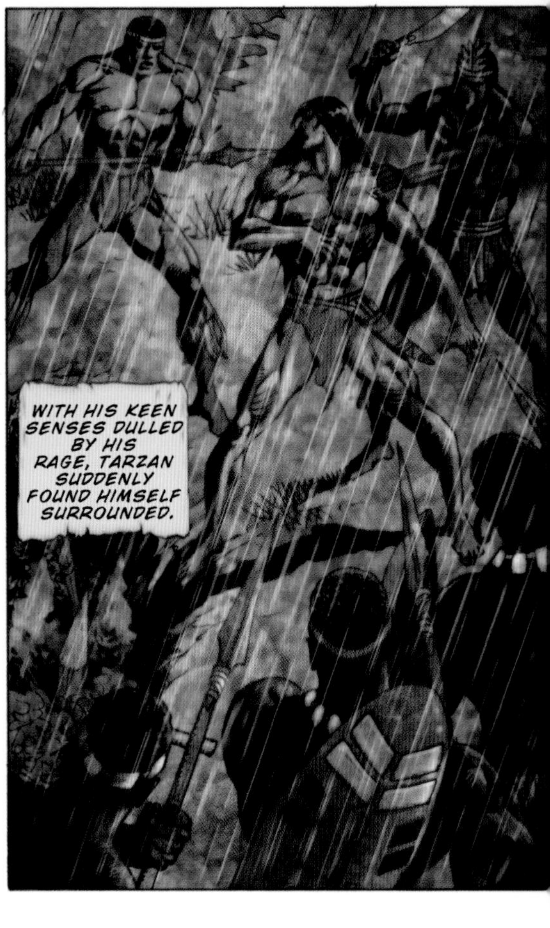
WITH HIS KEEN SENSES DULLED BY HIS RAGE, TARZAN SUDDENLY FOUND HIMSELF SURROUNDED.

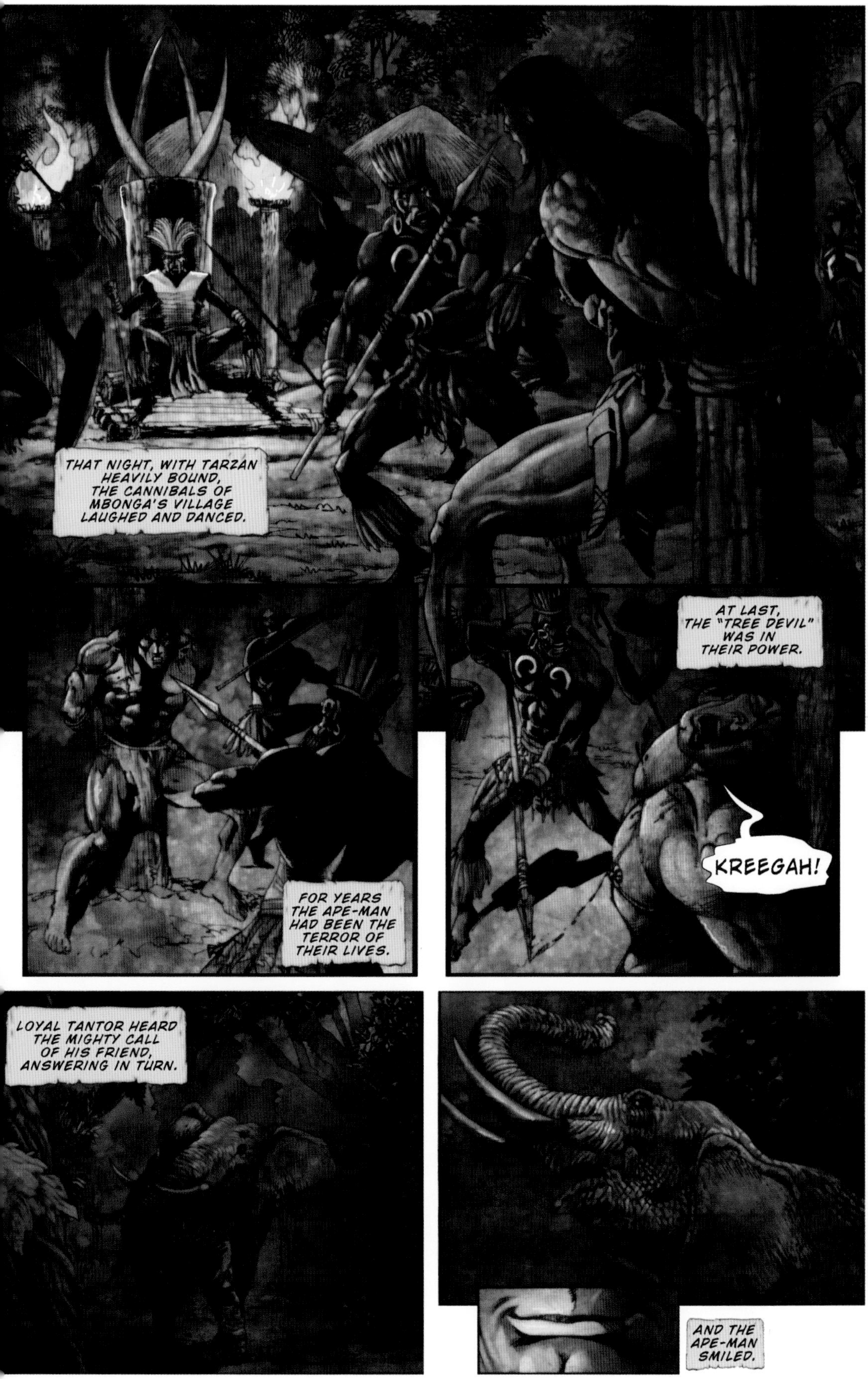
THAT NIGHT, WITH TARZAN HEAVILY BOUND, THE CANNIBALS OF MBONGA'S VILLAGE LAUGHED AND DANCED.
FOR YEARS THE APE-MAN HAD BEEN THE TERROR OF THEIR LIVES.
AT LAST, THE "TREE DEVIL" WAS IN THEIR POWER.
KREEGAH!
LOYAL TANTOR HEARD THE MIGHTY CALL OF HIS FRIEND, ANSWERING IN TURN.
AND THE APE-MAN SMILED.

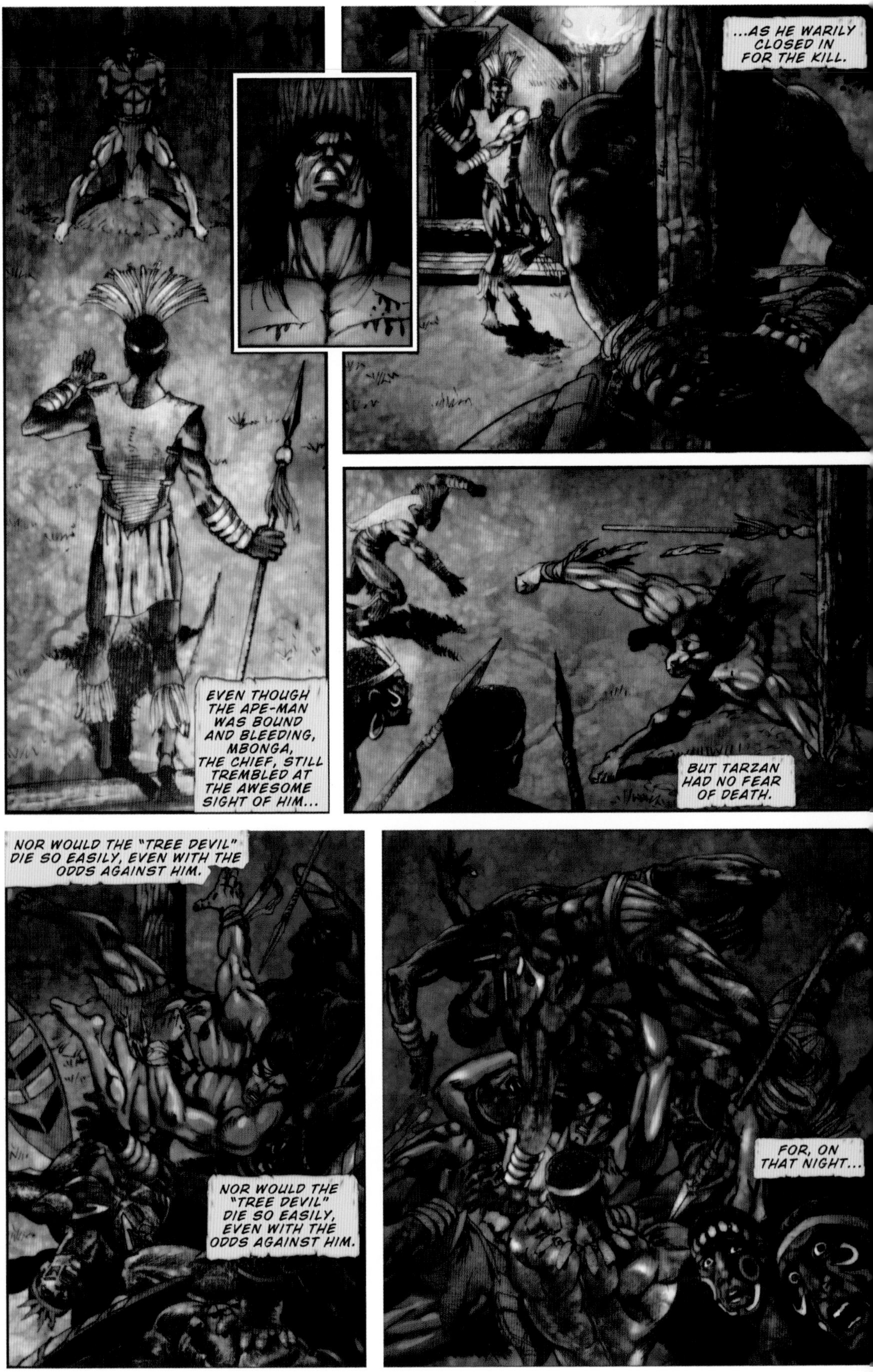
EVEN THOUGH THE APE-MAN WAS BOUND AND BLEEDING, MBONGA, THE CHIEF, STILL TREMBLED AT THE AWESOME SIGHT OF HIM...
...AS HE WARILY CLOSED IN FOR THE KILL.
BUT TARZAN HAD NO FEAR OF DEATH.
NOR WOULD THE "TREE DEVIL" DIE SO EASILY, EVEN WITH THE ODDS AGAINST HIM.
NOR WOULD THE "TREE DEVIL" DIE SO EASILY, EVEN WITH THE ODDS AGAINST HIM.
FOR, ON THAT NIGHT...

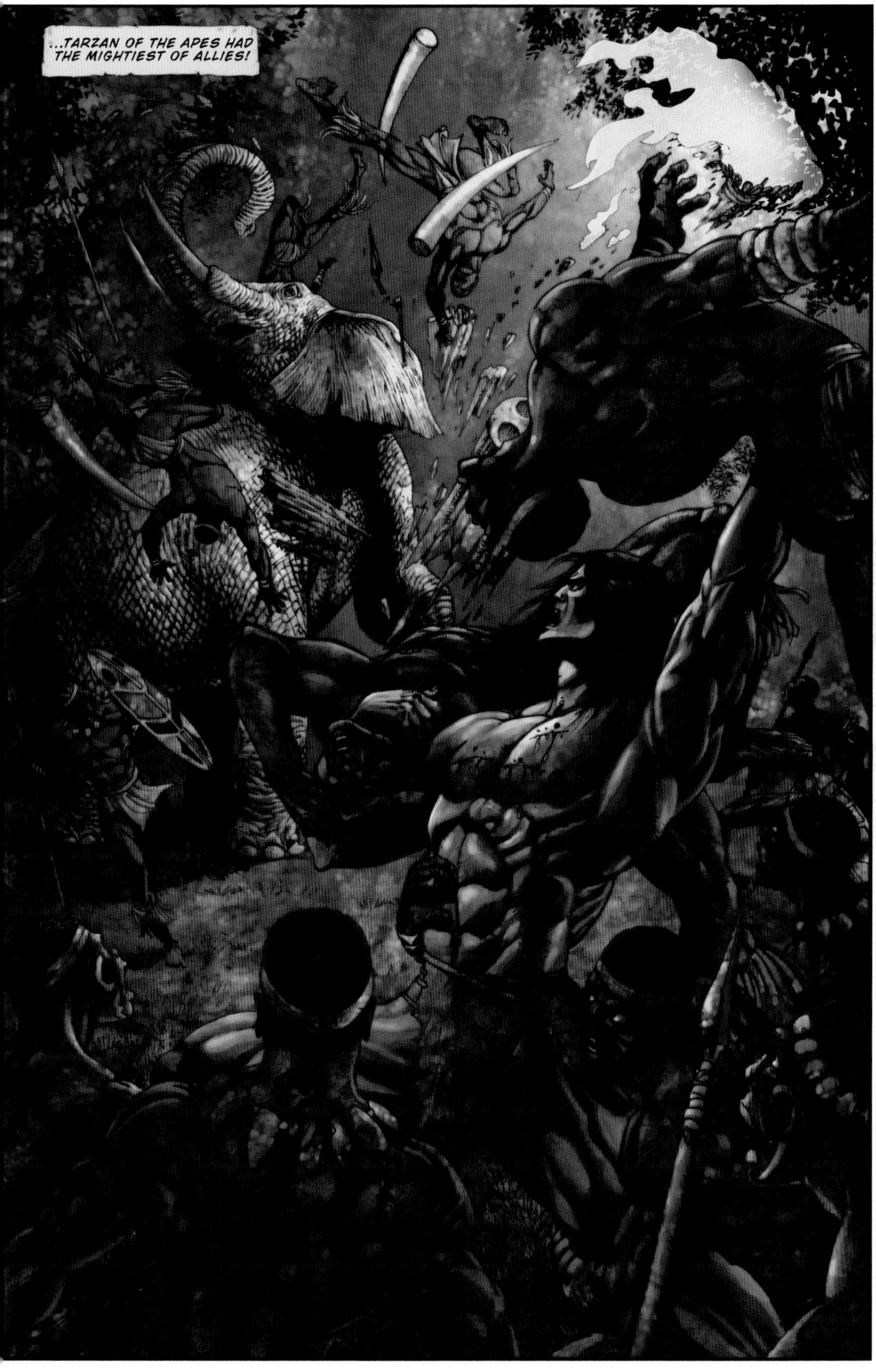
...TARZAN OF THE APES HAD THE MIGHTIEST OF ALLIES!

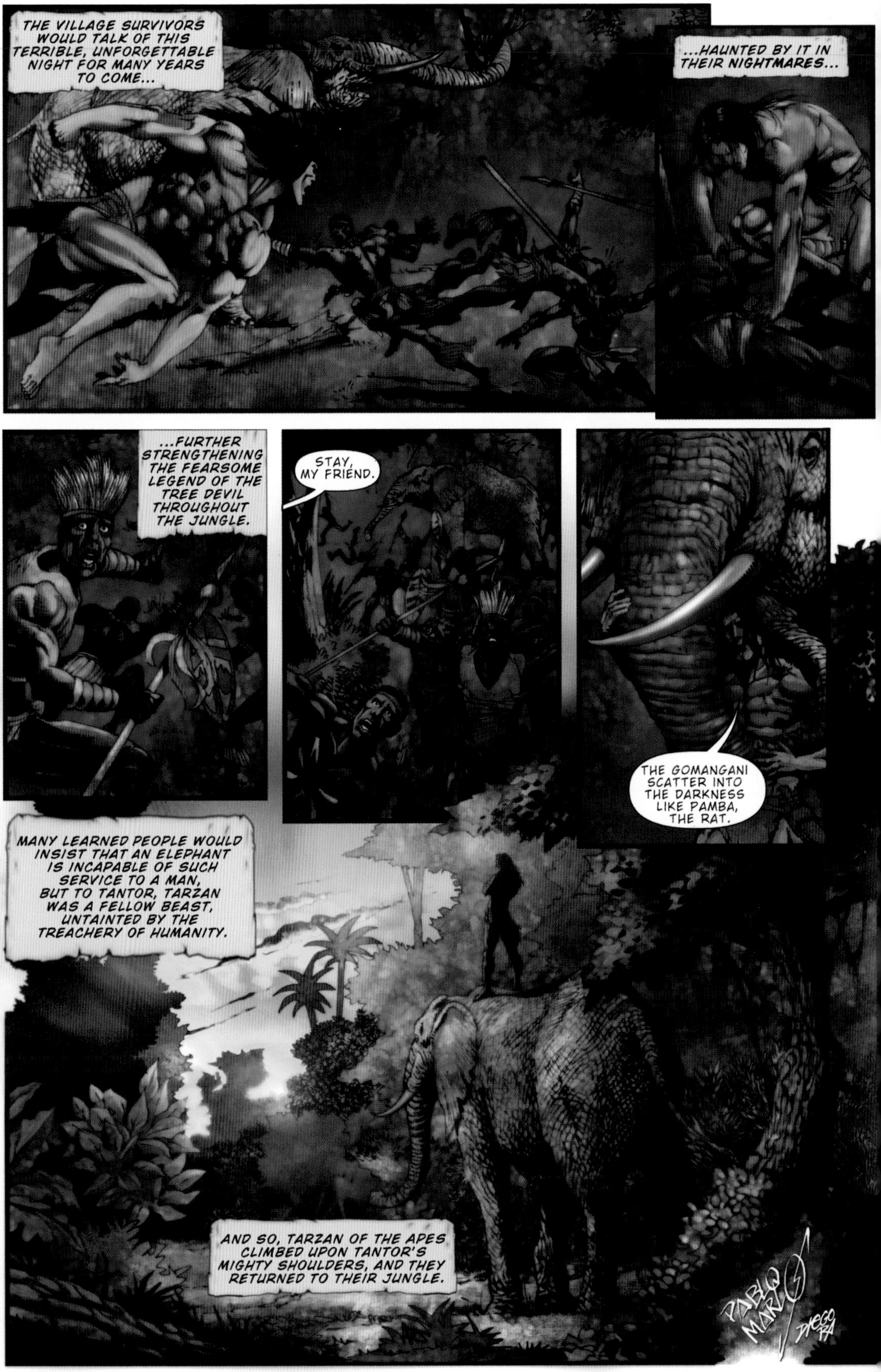
THE VILLAGE SURVIVORS WOULD TALK OF THIS TERRIBLE, UNFORGETTABLE NIGHT FOR MANY YEARS TO COME...
...HAUNTED BY IT IN THEIR NIGHTMARES...
...FURTHER STRENGTHENING THE FEARSOME LEGEND OF THE TREE DEVIL THROUGHOUT THE JUNGLE.
STAY, MY FRIEND.
THE GOMANGANI SCATTER INTO THE DARKNESS LIKE PAMBA, THE RAT.
MANY LEARNED PEOPLE WOULD INSIST THAT AN ELEPHANT IS INCAPABLE OF SUCH SERVICE TO A MAN, BUT TO TANTOR, TARZAN WAS A FELLOW BEAST, UNTAINTED BY THE TREACHERY OF HUMANITY.
AND SO, TARZAN OF THE APES CLIMBED UPON TANTOR'S MIGHTY SHOULDERS, AND THEY RETURNED TO THEIR JUNGLE.
PABLO MARCOS
DIEGO

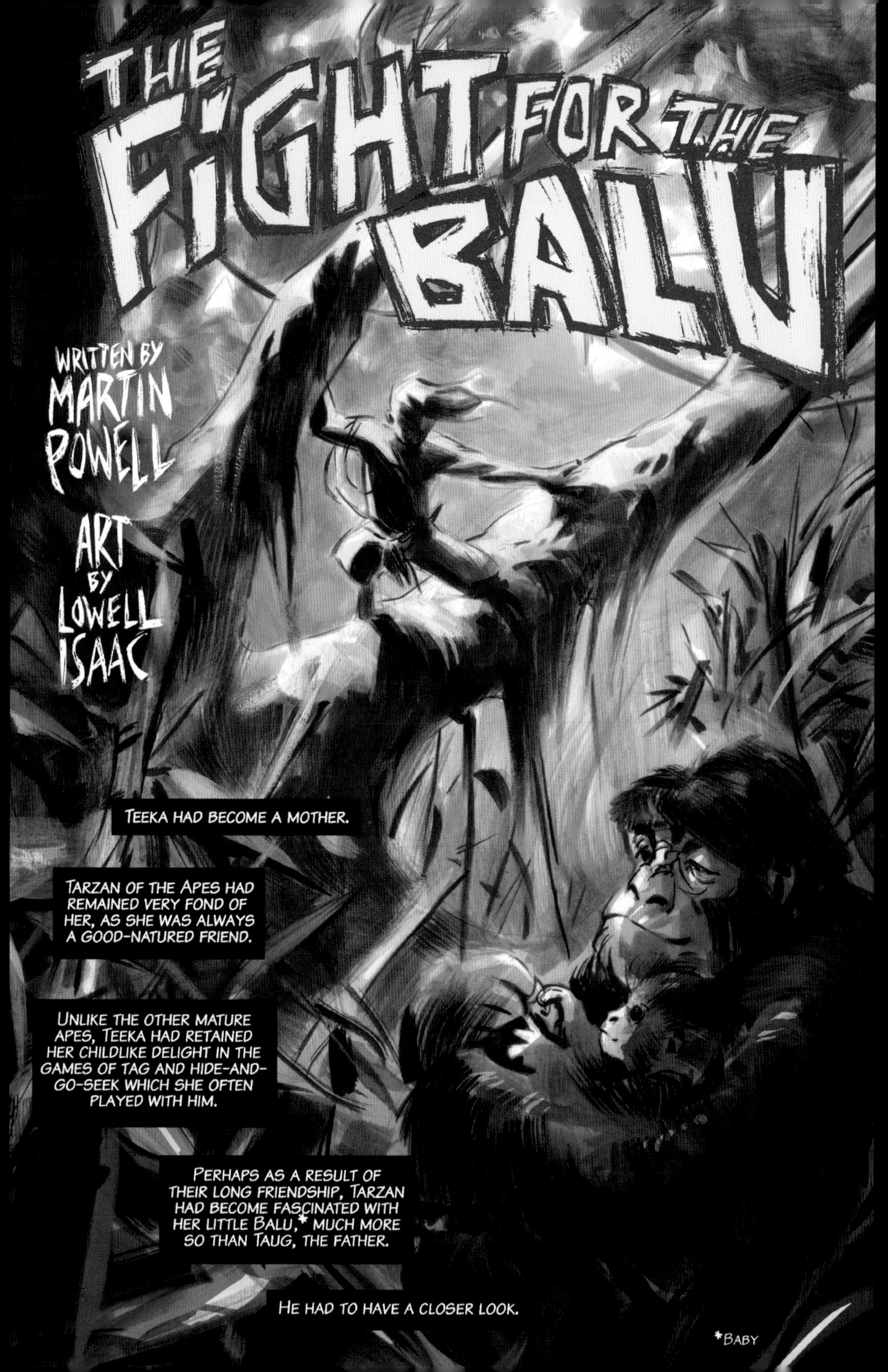
THE FIGHT FOR THE BALU
WRITTEN BY MARTIN POWELL
ART BY LOWELL ISAAC
TEEKA HAD BECOME A MOTHER.
TARZAN OF THE APES HAD REMAINED VERY FOND OF HER, AS SHE WAS ALWAYS A GOOD-NATURED FRIEND.
UNLIKE THE OTHER MATURE APES, TEEKA HAD RETAINED HER CHILDLIKE DELIGHT IN THE GAMES OF TAG AND HIDE-AND-GO-SEEK WHICH SHE OFTEN PLAYED WITH HIM.
PERHAPS AS A RESULT OF THEIR LONG FRIENDSHIP, TARZAN HAD BECOME FASCINATED WITH HER LITTLE BALU,* MUCH MORE SO THAN TAUG, THE FATHER.
HE HAD TO HAVE A CLOSER LOOK.
*BABY

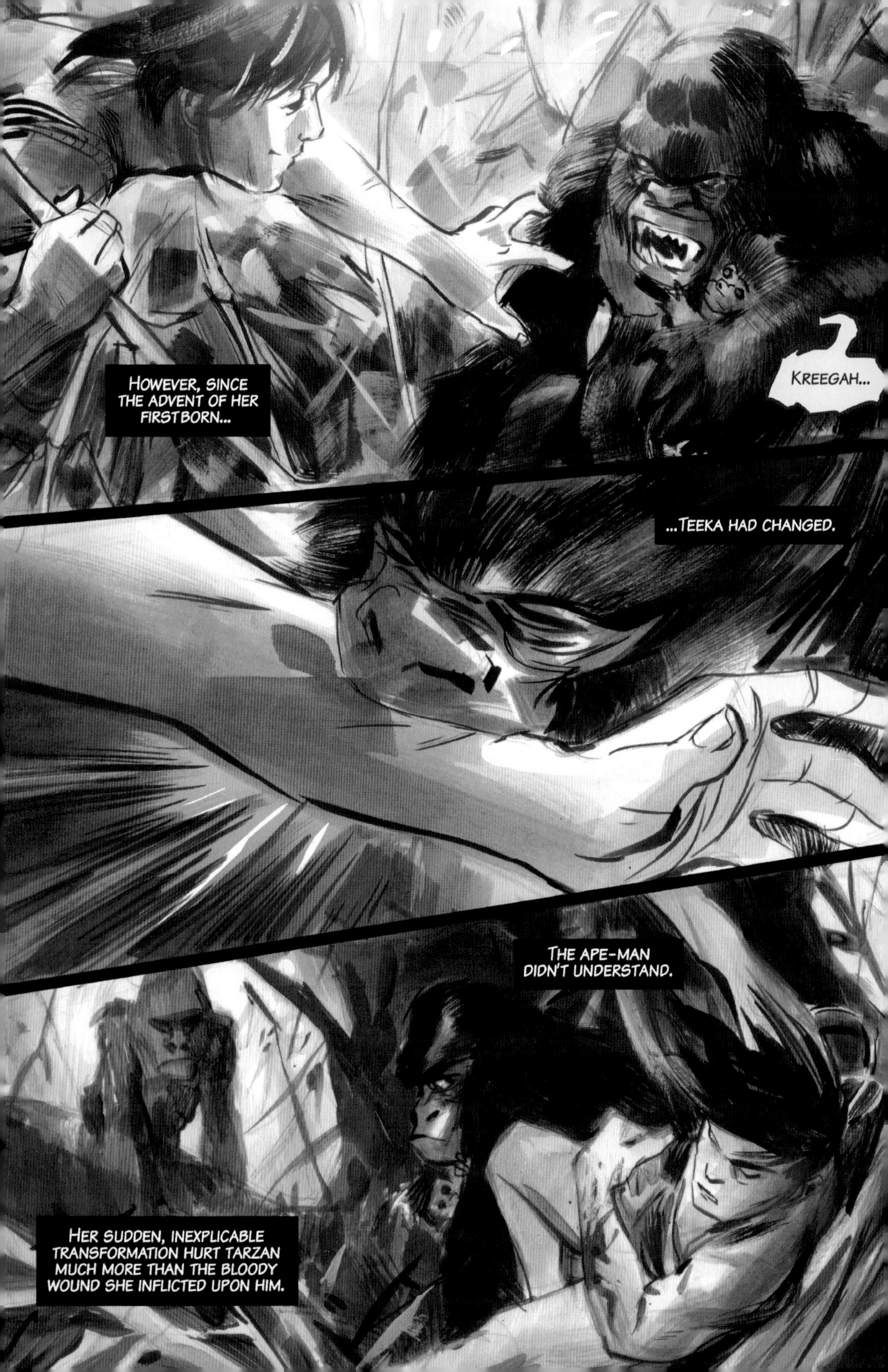
HOWEVER, SINCE THE ADVENT OF HER FIRSTBORN...
KREEGAH...
...TEEKA HAD CHANGED.
THE APE-MAN DIDN'T UNDERSTAND.
HER SUDDEN, INEXPLICABLE TRANSFORMATION HURT TARZAN MUCH MORE THAN THE BLOODY WOUND SHE INFLICTED UPON HIM.

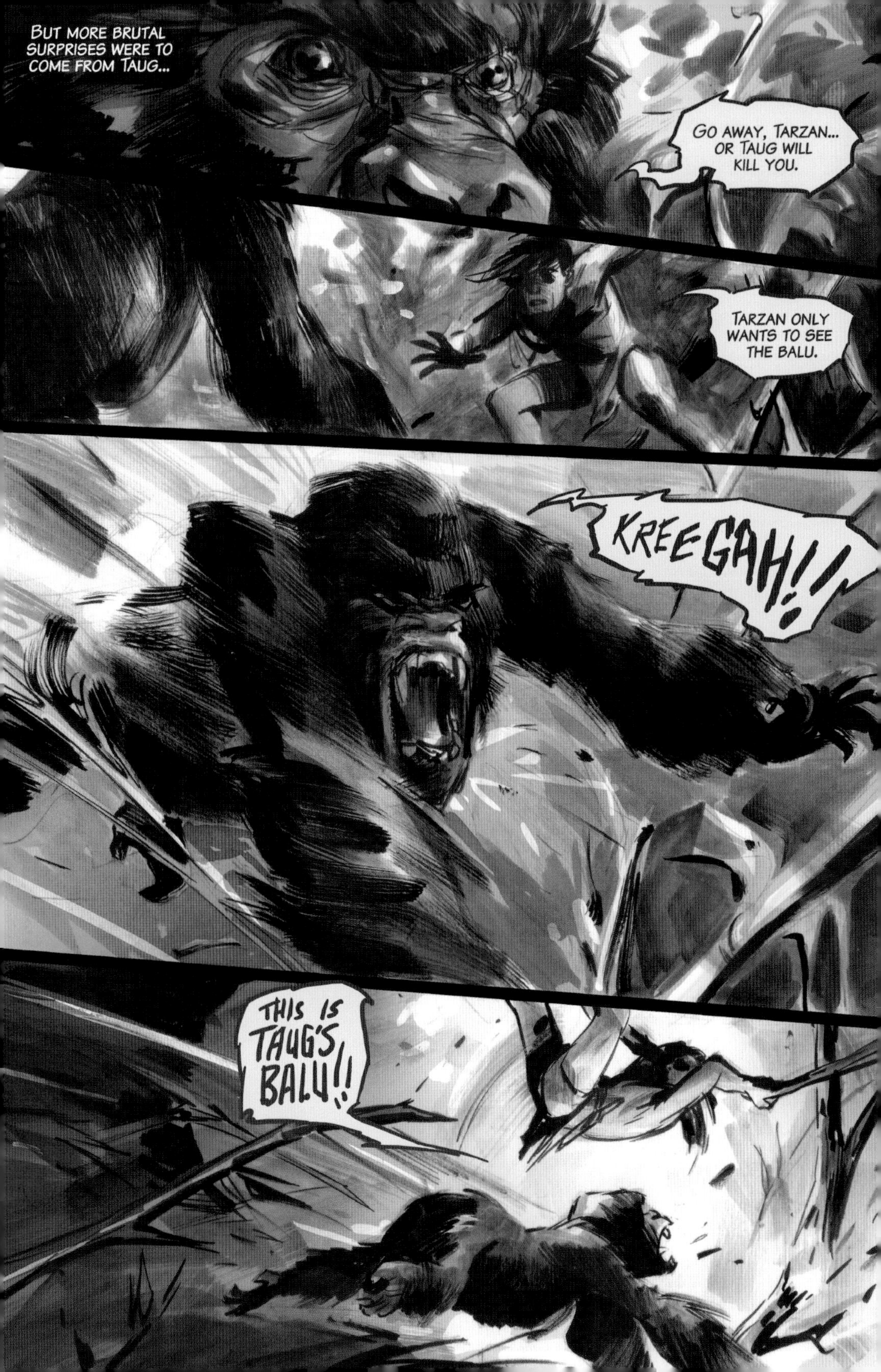
BUT MORE BRUTAL SURPRISES WERE TO COME FROM TAUG...
GO AWAY, TARZAN... OR TAUG WILL KILL YOU.
TARZAN ONLY WANTS TO SEE THE BALU.
KREEGAH!!
THIS IS TAUG'S BALU!!

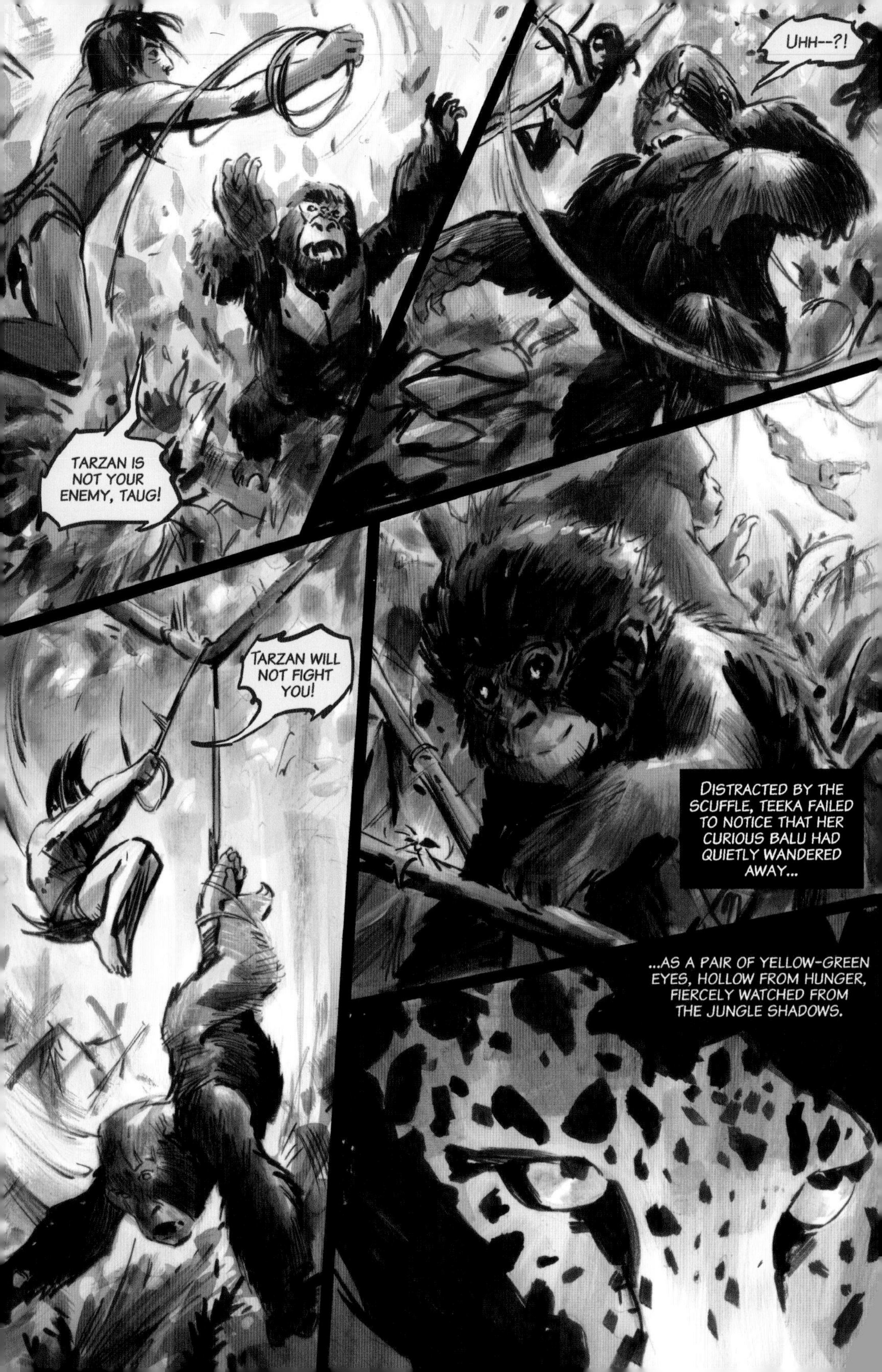
TARZAN IS NOT YOUR ENEMY, TAUG!
UHH--?!
TARZAN WILL NOT FIGHT YOU!
DISTRACTED BY THE SCUFFLE, TEEKA FAILED TO NOTICE THAT HER CURIOUS BALU HAD QUIETLY WANDERED AWAY...
...AS A PAIR OF YELLOW-GREEN EYES, HOLLOW FROM HUNGER, FIERCELY WATCHED FROM THE JUNGLE SHADOWS.

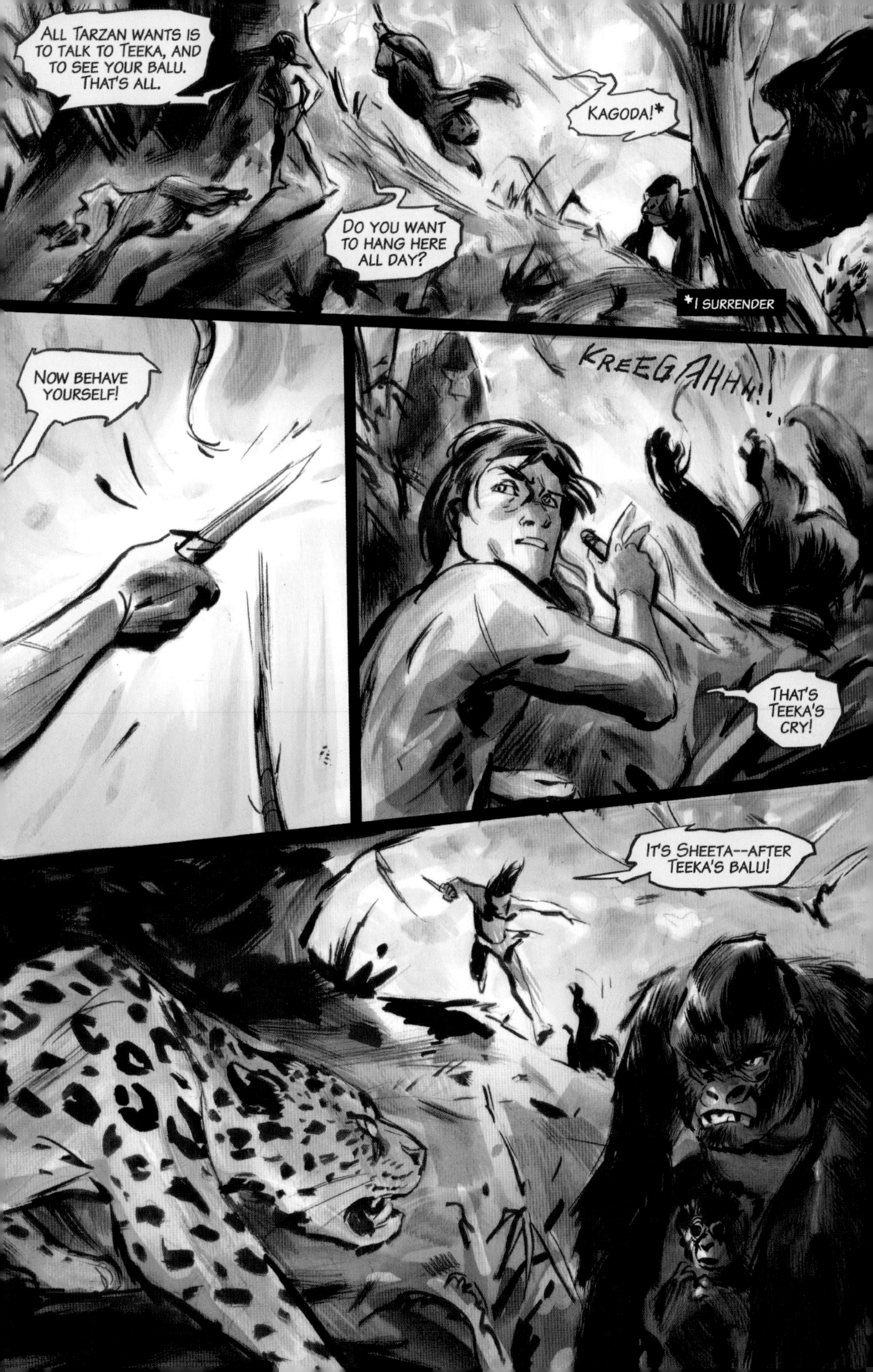
All Tarzan wants is to talk to Teeka, and to see your balu. That's all.
Kagoda!*
Do you want to hang here all day?
*I surrender
Now behave yourself!
KREEGAHHHH!!
That's Teeka's cry!
It's Sheeta--after Teeka's balu!

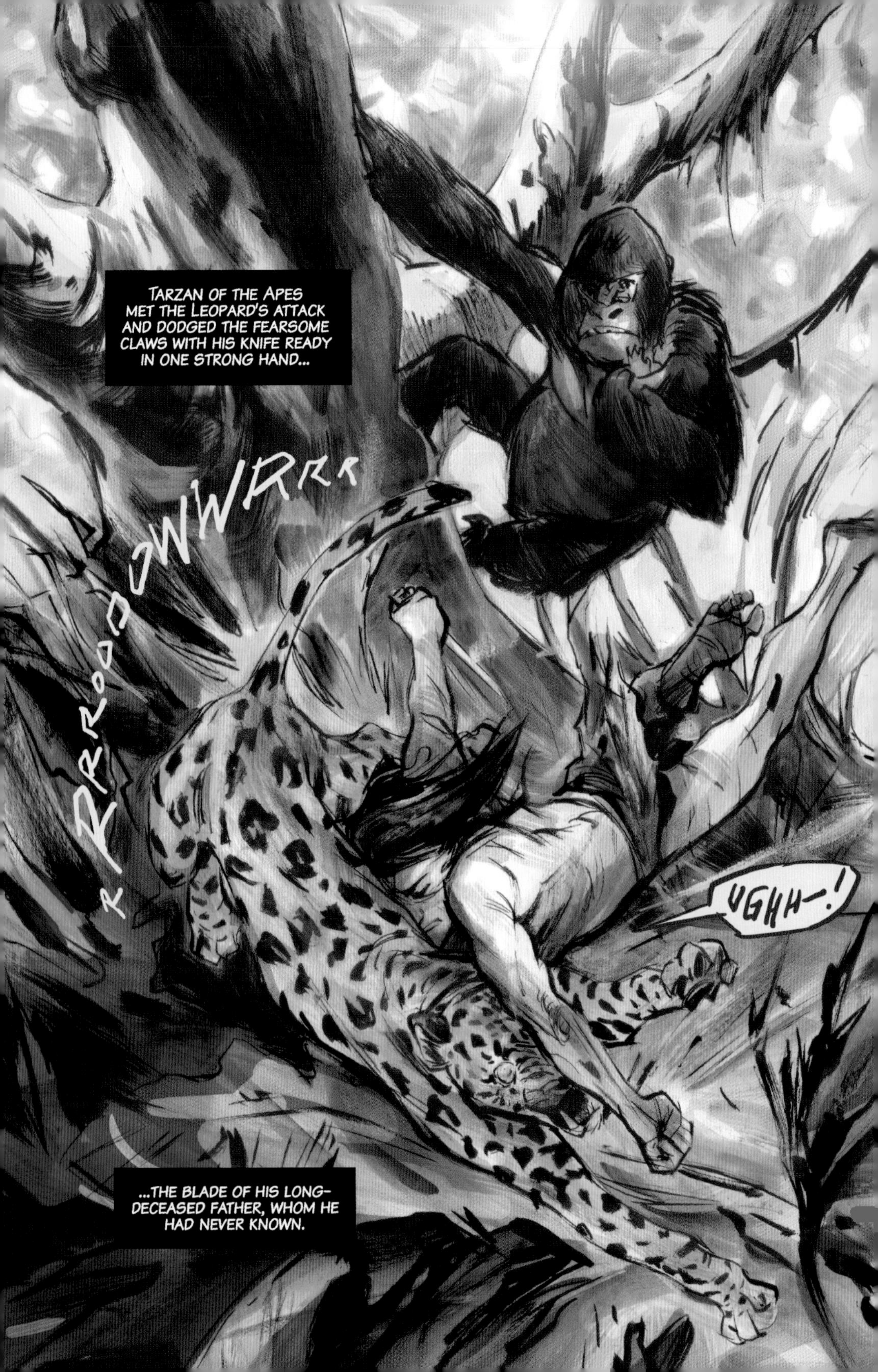
TARZAN OF THE APES MET THE LEOPARD'S ATTACK AND DODGED THE FEARSOME CLAWS WITH HIS KNIFE READY IN ONE STRONG HAND...
RRRROOOOWWRRRR
UGHH—!
...THE BLADE OF HIS LONG-DECEASED FATHER, WHOM HE HAD NEVER KNOWN.

OVER AND OVER UPON THE GRASS THEY ROLLED, GROWLING, SCREAMING, CLAWING, AND BITING...

...UNTIL...

...FREEING HIS LEGS FROM THE TANGLES OF THE HUMILIATING ROPE, TAUG PONDERED THE FEROCIOUS FIGHT WITH HIS RED-RIMMED, SAVAGE LITTLE EYES.

WITH THE SUDDEN SPILLING OF TARZAN'S BLOOD CAME TAUG'S ANSWER.

WHAT WAS PASSING IN HIS BESTIAL BRAIN? DID AUG LONG TO SEE SHEETA'S FANGS SINK INTO THE THROAT OF THE APE-MAN?

OR DID THE APE DIMLY REALIZE THE SELFLESS COURAGE THAT HAD PROMPTED TARZAN TO RUSH TO THE LITTLE BALU'S RESCUE?

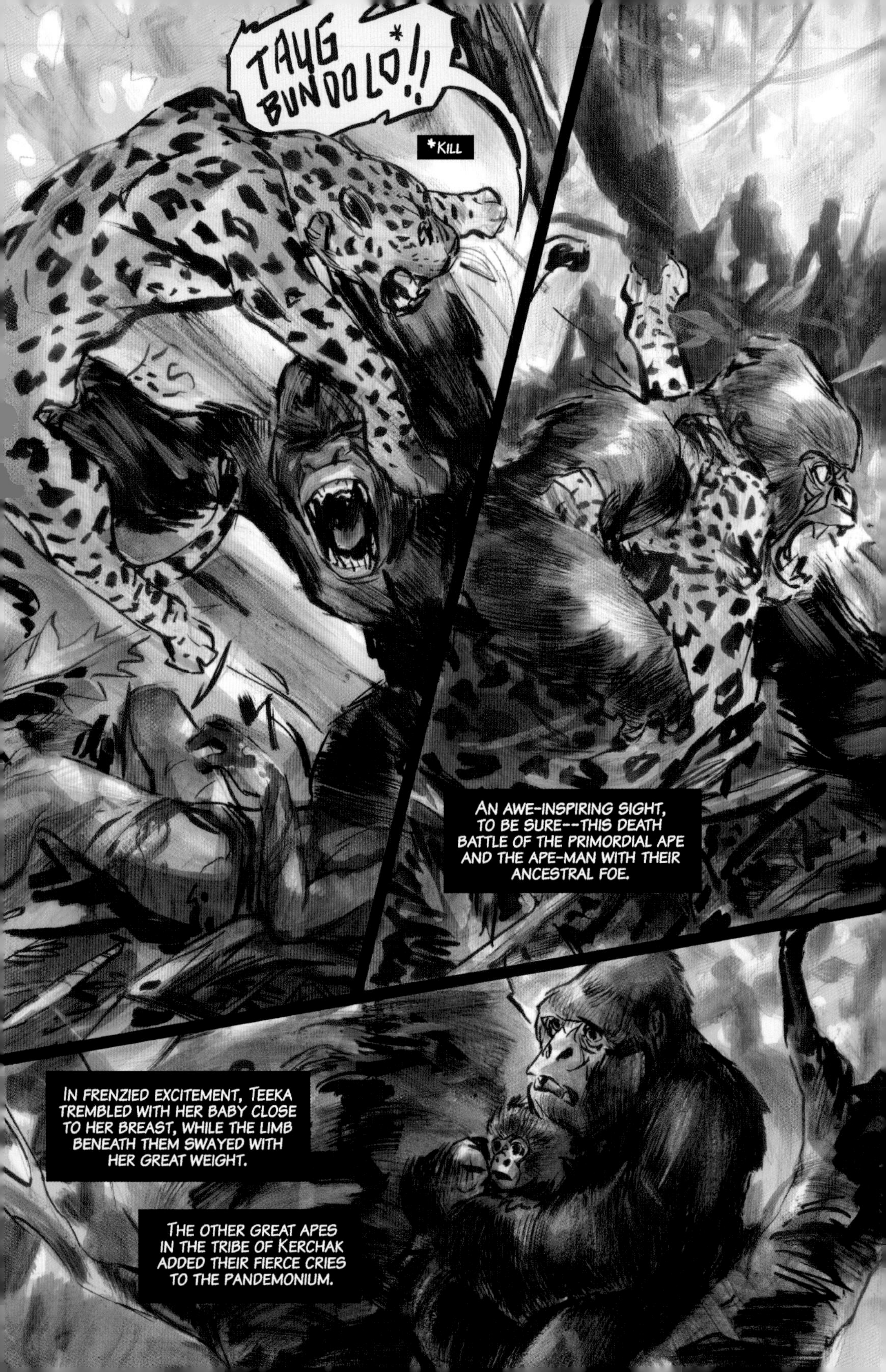

TAUG* BUNDOLO!!
*KILL
AN AWE-INSPIRING SIGHT, TO BE SURE--THIS DEATH BATTLE OF THE PRIMORDIAL APE AND THE APE-MAN WITH THEIR ANCESTRAL FOE.
IN FRENZIED EXCITEMENT, TEEKA TREMBLED WITH HER BABY CLOSE TO HER BREAST, WHILE THE LIMB BENEATH THEM SWAYED WITH HER GREAT WEIGHT.
THE OTHER GREAT APES IN THE TRIBE OF KERCHAK ADDED THEIR FIERCE CRIES TO THE PANDEMONIUM.

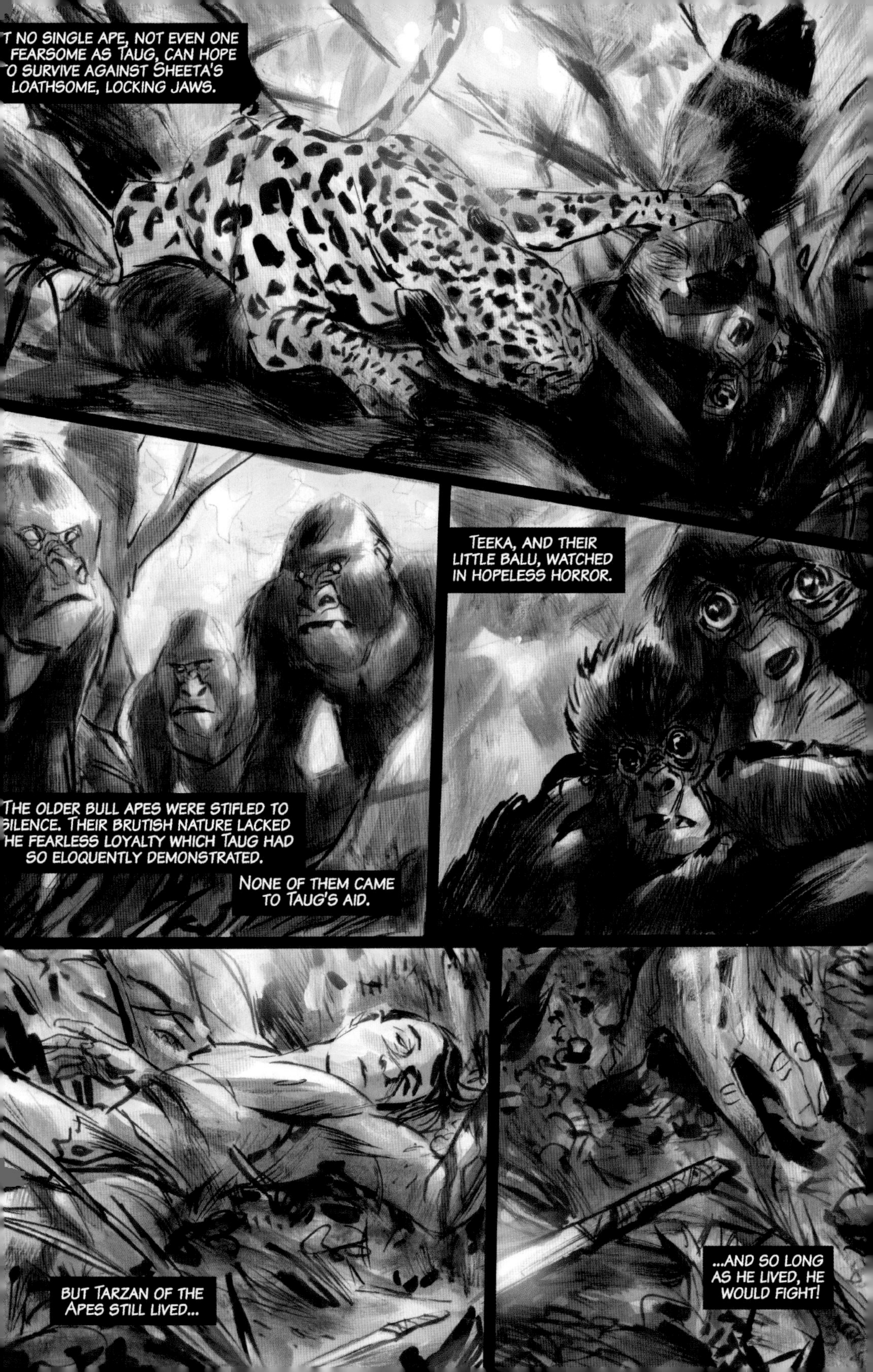
T NO SINGLE APE, NOT EVEN ONE FEARSOME AS TAUG, CAN HOPE O SURVIVE AGAINST SHEETA'S LOATHSOME, LOCKING JAWS.
TEEKA, AND THEIR LITTLE BALU, WATCHED IN HOPELESS HORROR.
THE OLDER BULL APES WERE STIFLED TO SILENCE. THEIR BRUTISH NATURE LACKED HE FEARLESS LOYALTY WHICH TAUG HAD SO ELOQUENTLY DEMONSTRATED.
NONE OF THEM CAME TO TAUG'S AID.
BUT TARZAN OF THE APES STILL LIVED...
...AND SO LONG AS HE LIVED, HE WOULD FIGHT!

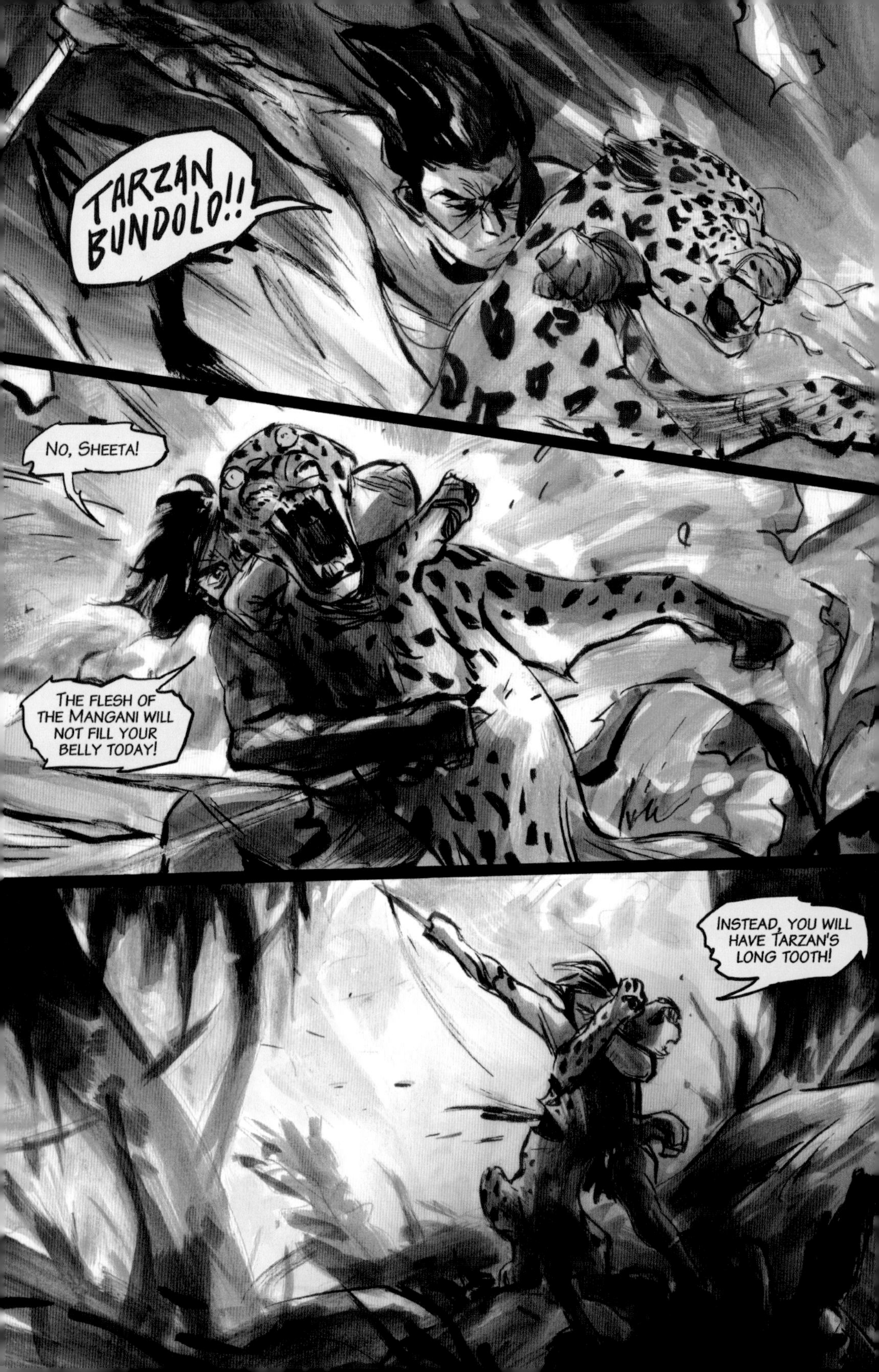
TARZAN BUNDOLO!!
NO, SHEETA!
THE FLESH OF THE MANGANI WILL NOT FILL YOUR BELLY TODAY!
INSTEAD, YOU WILL HAVE TARZAN'S LONG TOOTH!

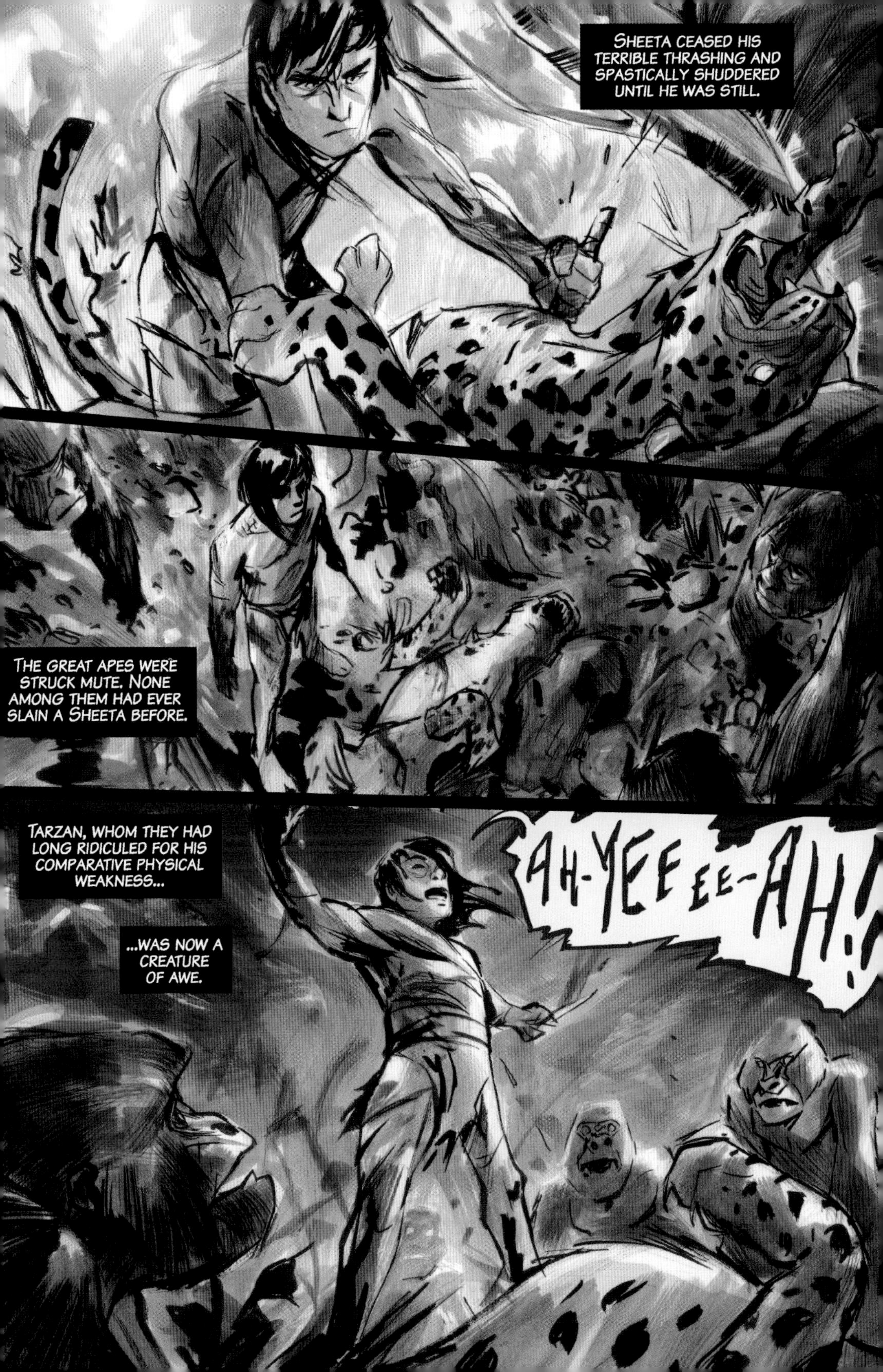
SHEETA CEASED HIS TERRIBLE THRASHING AND SPASTICALLY SHUDDERED UNTIL HE WAS STILL.
THE GREAT APES WERE STRUCK MUTE. NONE AMONG THEM HAD EVER SLAIN A SHEETA BEFORE.
TARZAN, WHOM THEY HAD LONG RIDICULED FOR HIS COMPARATIVE PHYSICAL WEAKNESS...
...WAS NOW A CREATURE OF AWE.
AH-YEEEEE-AH!

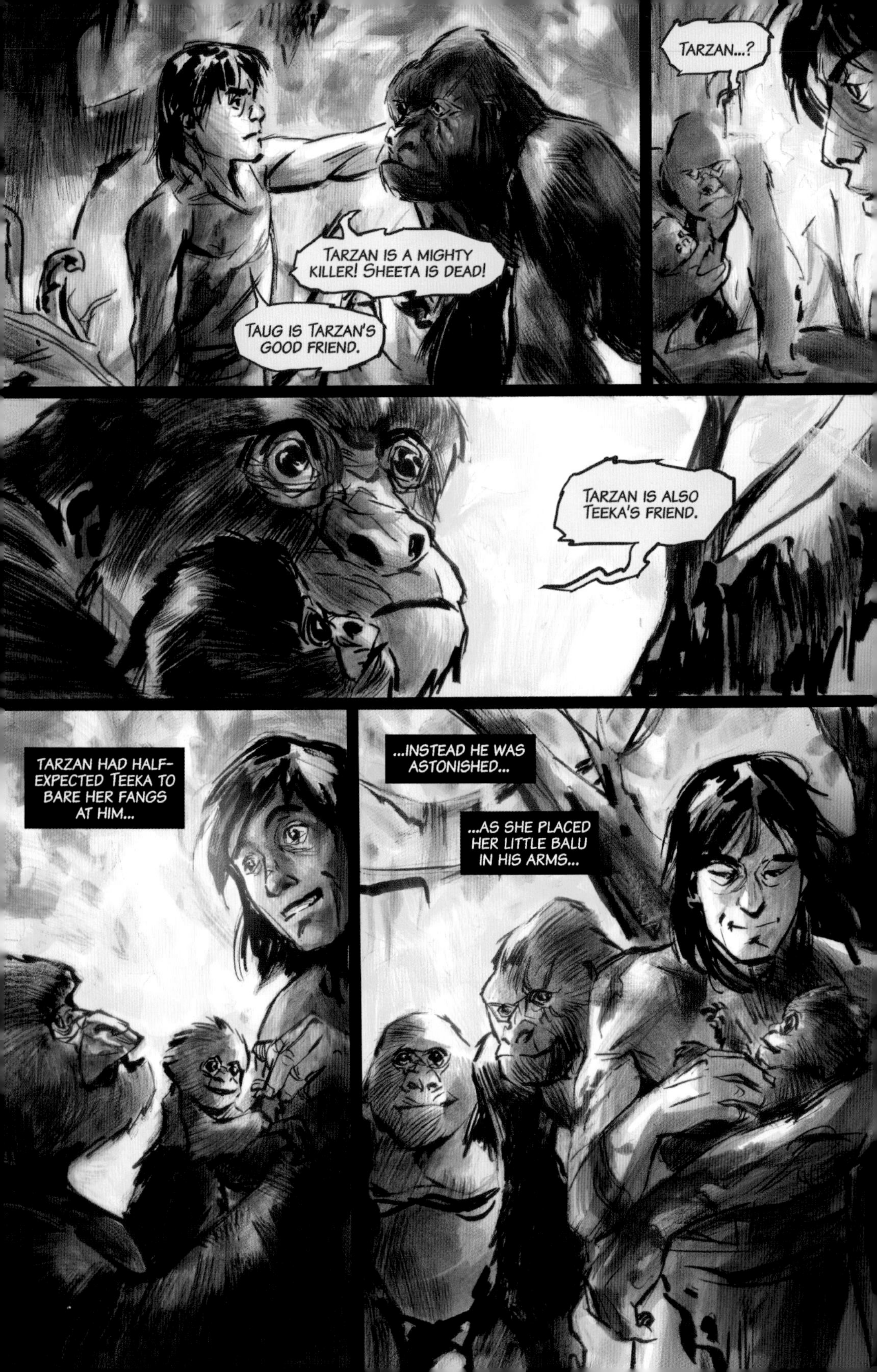
TARZAN IS A MIGHTY KILLER! SHEETA IS DEAD!
TAUG IS TARZAN'S GOOD FRIEND.
TARZAN...?
TARZAN IS ALSO TEEKA'S FRIEND.
TARZAN HAD HALF-EXPECTED TEEKA TO BARE HER FANGS AT HIM...
...INSTEAD HE WAS ASTONISHED...
...AS SHE PLACED HER LITTLE BALU IN HIS ARMS...

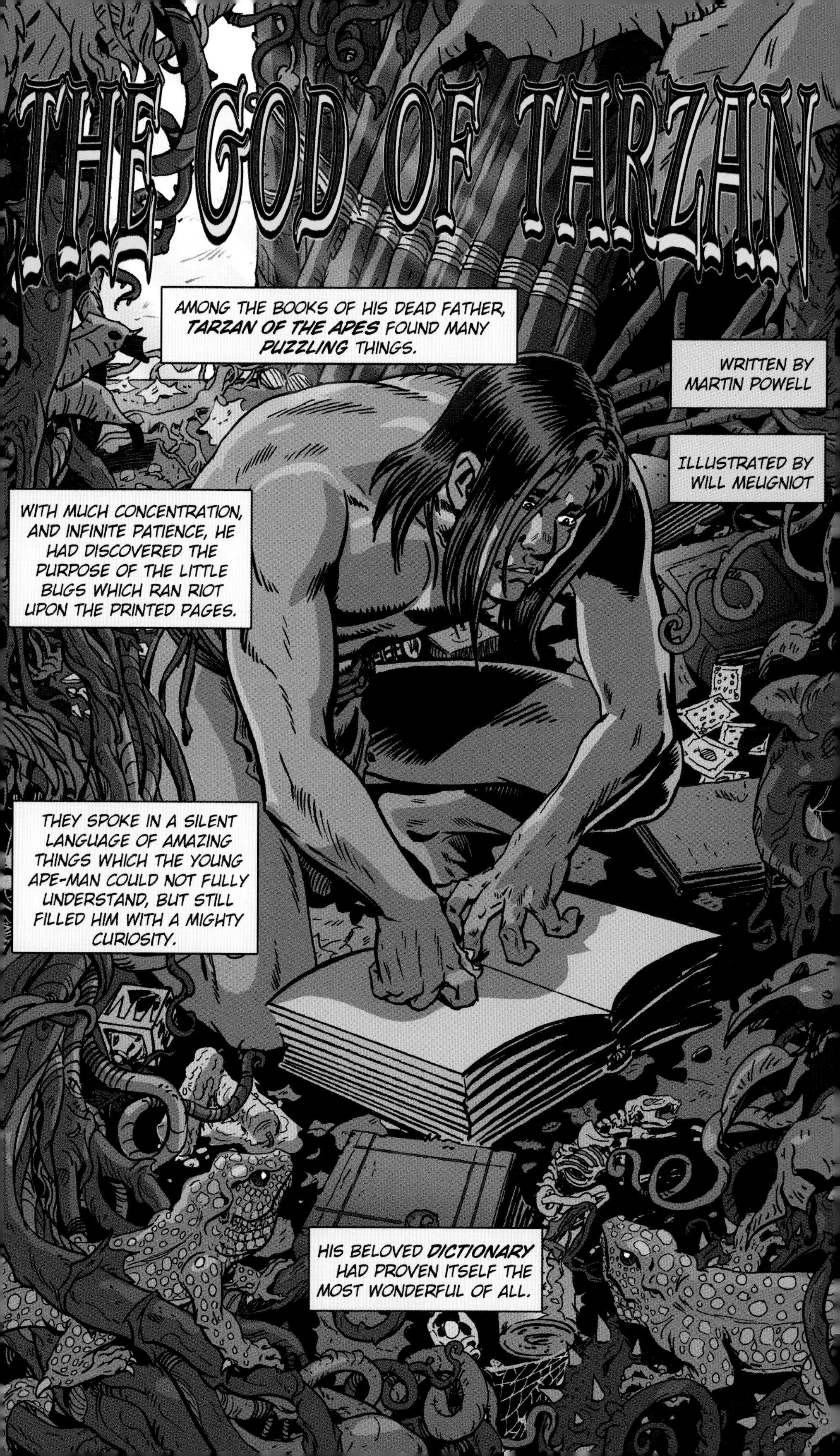
THE GOD OF TARZAN
AMONG THE BOOKS OF HIS DEAD FATHER, TARZAN OF THE APES FOUND MANY PUZZLING THINGS.
WRITTEN BY MARTIN POWELL
ILLUSTRATED BY WILL MEUGNIOT
WITH MUCH CONCENTRATION, AND INFINITE PATIENCE, HE HAD DISCOVERED THE PURPOSE OF THE LITTLE BUGS WHICH RAN RIOT UPON THE PRINTED PAGES.
THEY SPOKE IN A SILENT LANGUAGE OF AMAZING THINGS WHICH THE YOUNG APE-MAN COULD NOT FULLY UNDERSTAND, BUT STILL FILLED HIM WITH A MIGHTY CURIOSITY.
HIS BELOVED DICTIONARY HAD PROVEN ITSELF THE MOST WONDERFUL OF ALL.

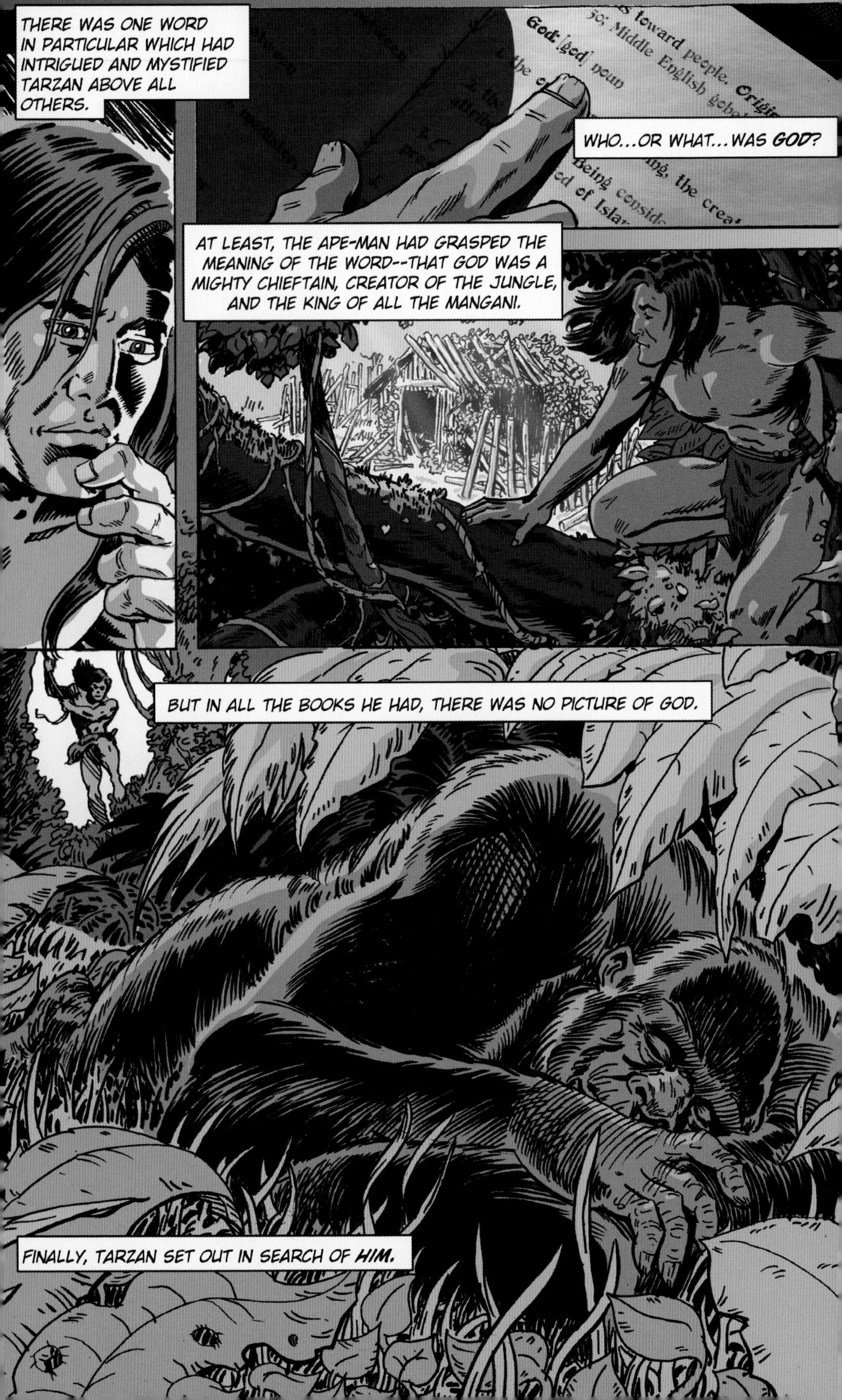
THERE WAS ONE WORD IN PARTICULAR WHICH HAD INTRIGUED AND MYSTIFIED TARZAN ABOVE ALL OTHERS.
WHO...OR WHAT...WAS *GOD*?
AT LEAST, THE APE-MAN HAD GRASPED THE MEANING OF THE WORD--THAT GOD WAS A MIGHTY CHIEFTAIN, CREATOR OF THE JUNGLE, AND THE KING OF ALL THE MANGANI.
BUT IN ALL THE BOOKS HE HAD, THERE WAS NO PICTURE OF GOD.
FINALLY, TARZAN SET OUT IN SEARCH OF *HIM.*

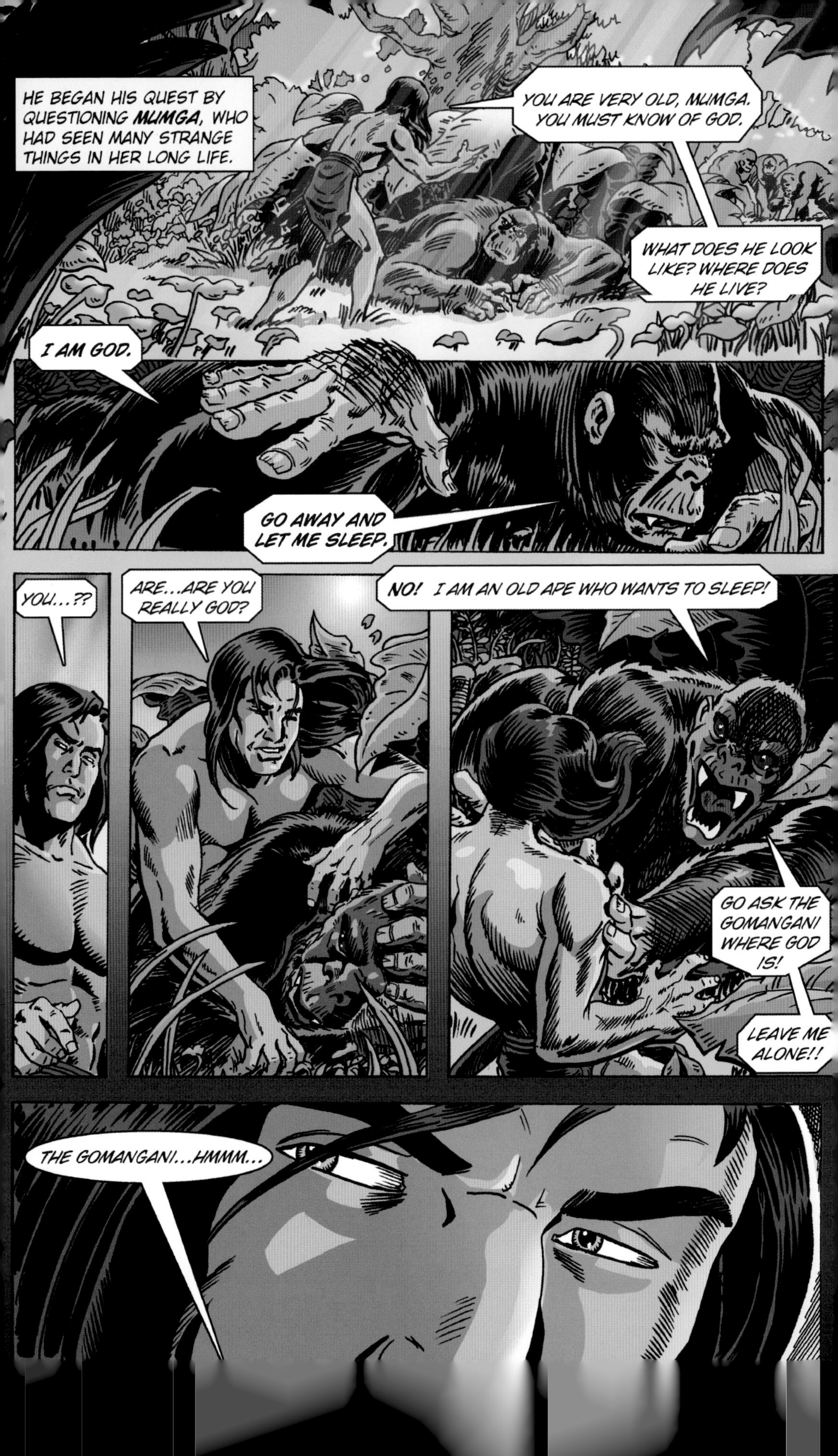

HE BEGAN HIS QUEST BY QUESTIONING MUMGA, WHO HAD SEEN MANY STRANGE THINGS IN HER LONG LIFE.
YOU ARE VERY OLD, MUMGA. YOU MUST KNOW OF GOD.
WHAT DOES HE LOOK LIKE? WHERE DOES HE LIVE?
I AM GOD.
GO AWAY AND LET ME SLEEP.
YOU...??
ARE...ARE YOU REALLY GOD?
NO! I AM AN OLD APE WHO WANTS TO SLEEP!
GO ASK THE GOMANGANI WHERE GOD IS!
LEAVE ME ALONE!!
THE GOMANGANI...HMMM...

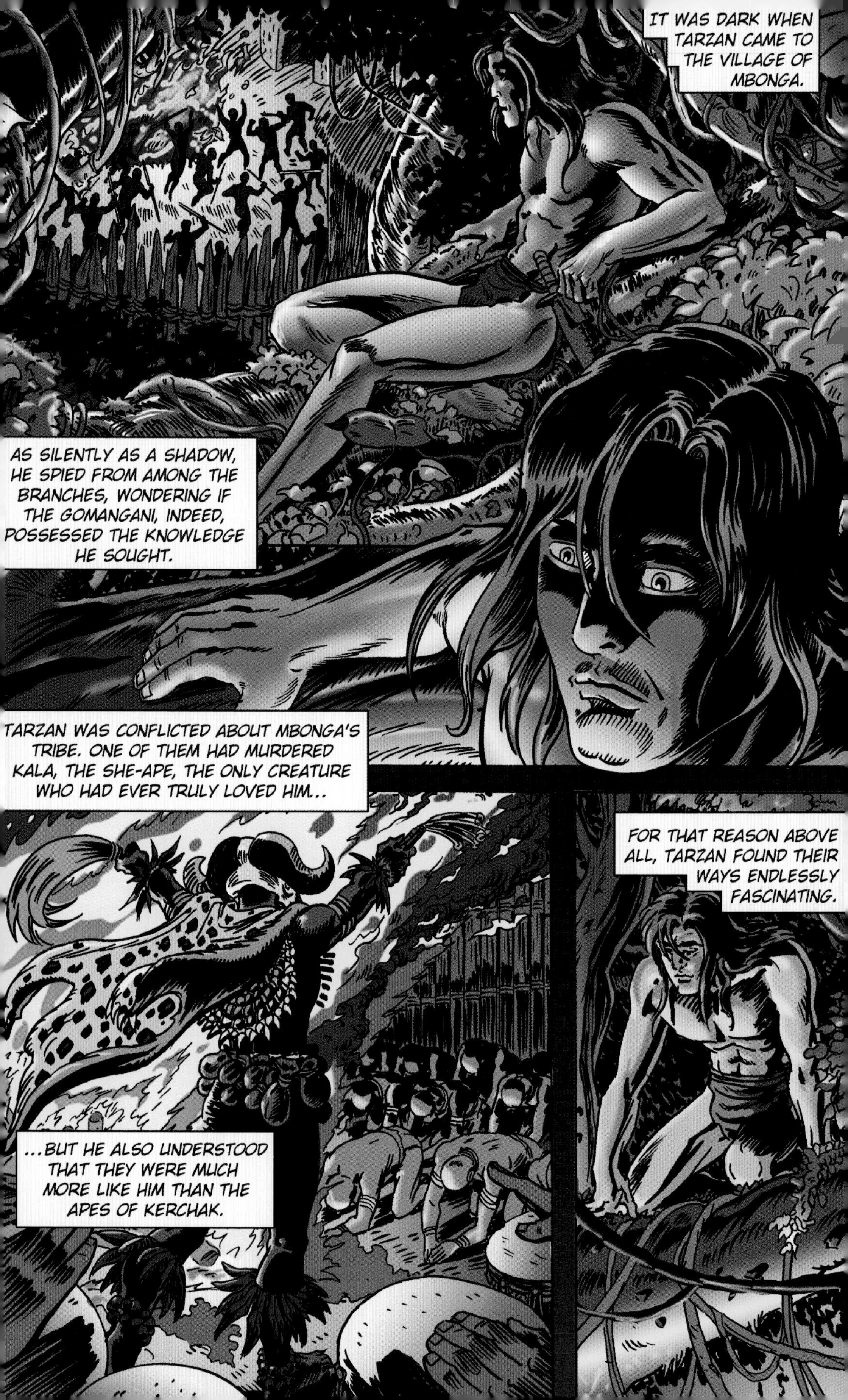
IT WAS DARK WHEN TARZAN CAME TO THE VILLAGE OF MBONGA.
AS SILENTLY AS A SHADOW, HE SPIED FROM AMONG THE BRANCHES, WONDERING IF THE GOMANGANI, INDEED, POSSESSED THE KNOWLEDGE HE SOUGHT.
TARZAN WAS CONFLICTED ABOUT MBONGA'S TRIBE. ONE OF THEM HAD MURDERED KALA, THE SHE-APE, THE ONLY CREATURE WHO HAD EVER TRULY LOVED HIM...
...BUT HE ALSO UNDERSTOOD THAT THEY WERE MUCH MORE LIKE HIM THAN THE APES OF KERCHAK.
FOR THAT REASON ABOVE ALL, TARZAN FOUND THEIR WAYS ENDLESSLY FASCINATING.

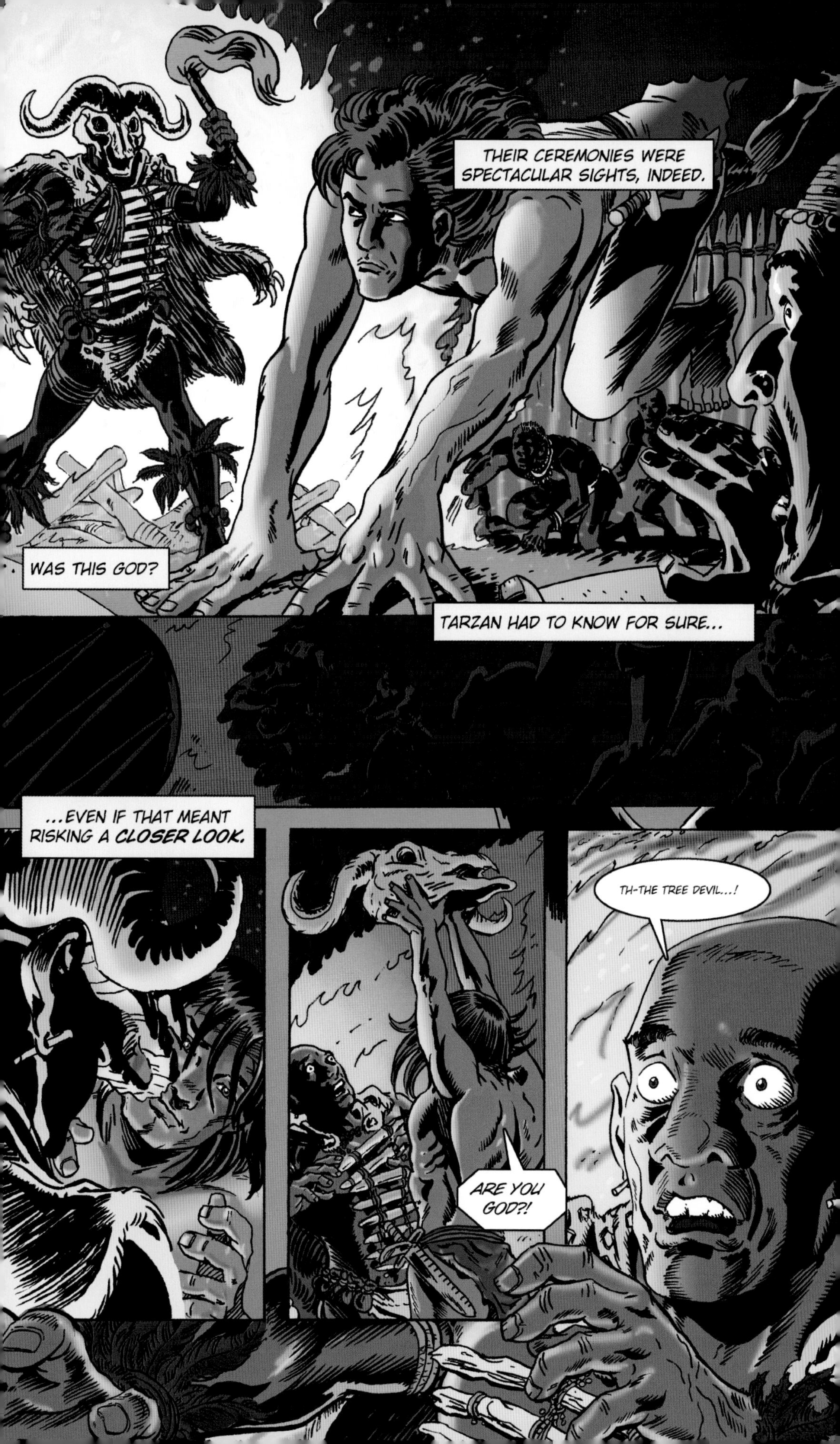
THEIR CEREMONIES WERE SPECTACULAR SIGHTS, INDEED.
WAS THIS GOD?
TARZAN HAD TO KNOW FOR SURE...
...EVEN IF THAT MEANT RISKING A CLOSER LOOK.
ARE YOU GOD?!
TH-THE TREE DEVIL...!

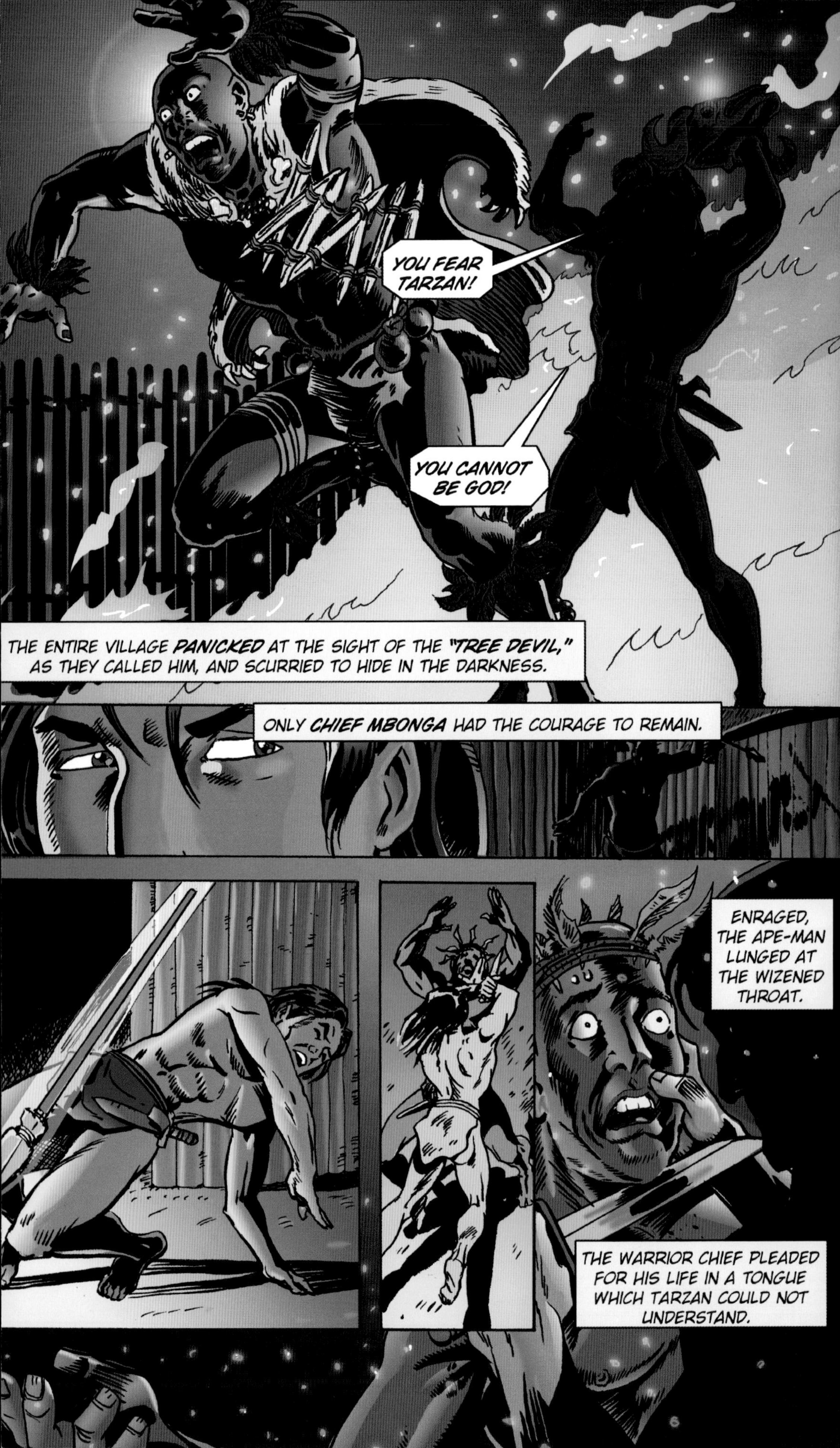
YOU FEAR TARZAN!
YOU CANNOT BE GOD!
THE ENTIRE VILLAGE PANICKED AT THE SIGHT OF THE "TREE DEVIL," AS THEY CALLED HIM, AND SCURRIED TO HIDE IN THE DARKNESS.
ONLY CHIEF MBONGA HAD THE COURAGE TO REMAIN.
ENRAGED, THE APE-MAN LUNGED AT THE WIZENED THROAT.
THE WARRIOR CHIEF PLEADED FOR HIS LIFE IN A TONGUE WHICH TARZAN COULD NOT UNDERSTAND.

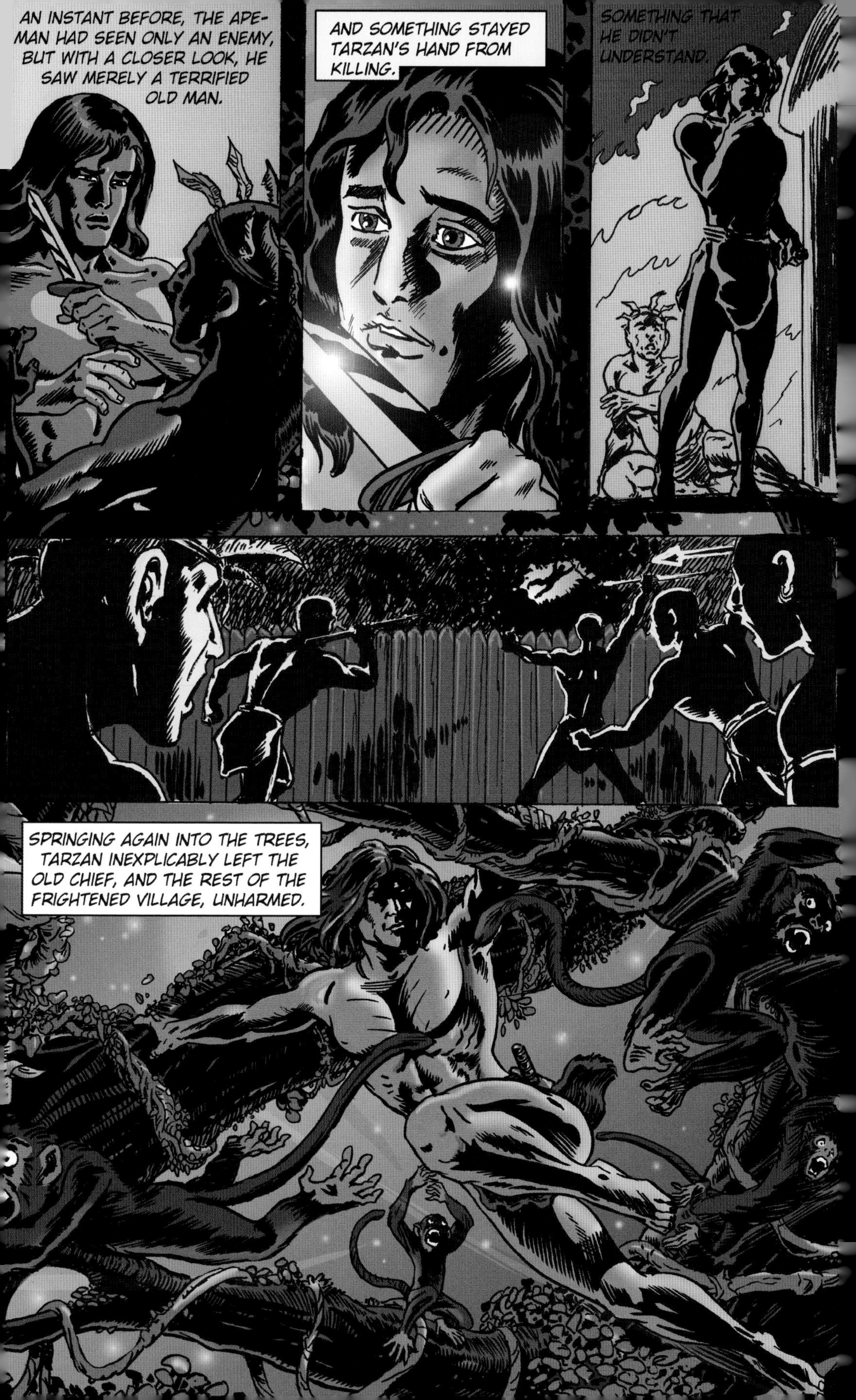
AN INSTANT BEFORE, THE APE-MAN HAD SEEN ONLY AN ENEMY, BUT WITH A CLOSER LOOK, HE SAW MERELY A TERRIFIED OLD MAN.
AND SOMETHING STAYED TARZAN'S HAND FROM KILLING.
SOMETHING THAT HE DIDN'T UNDERSTAND.
SPRINGING AGAIN INTO THE TREES, TARZAN INEXPLICABLY LEFT THE OLD CHIEF, AND THE REST OF THE FRIGHTENED VILLAGE, UNHARMED.

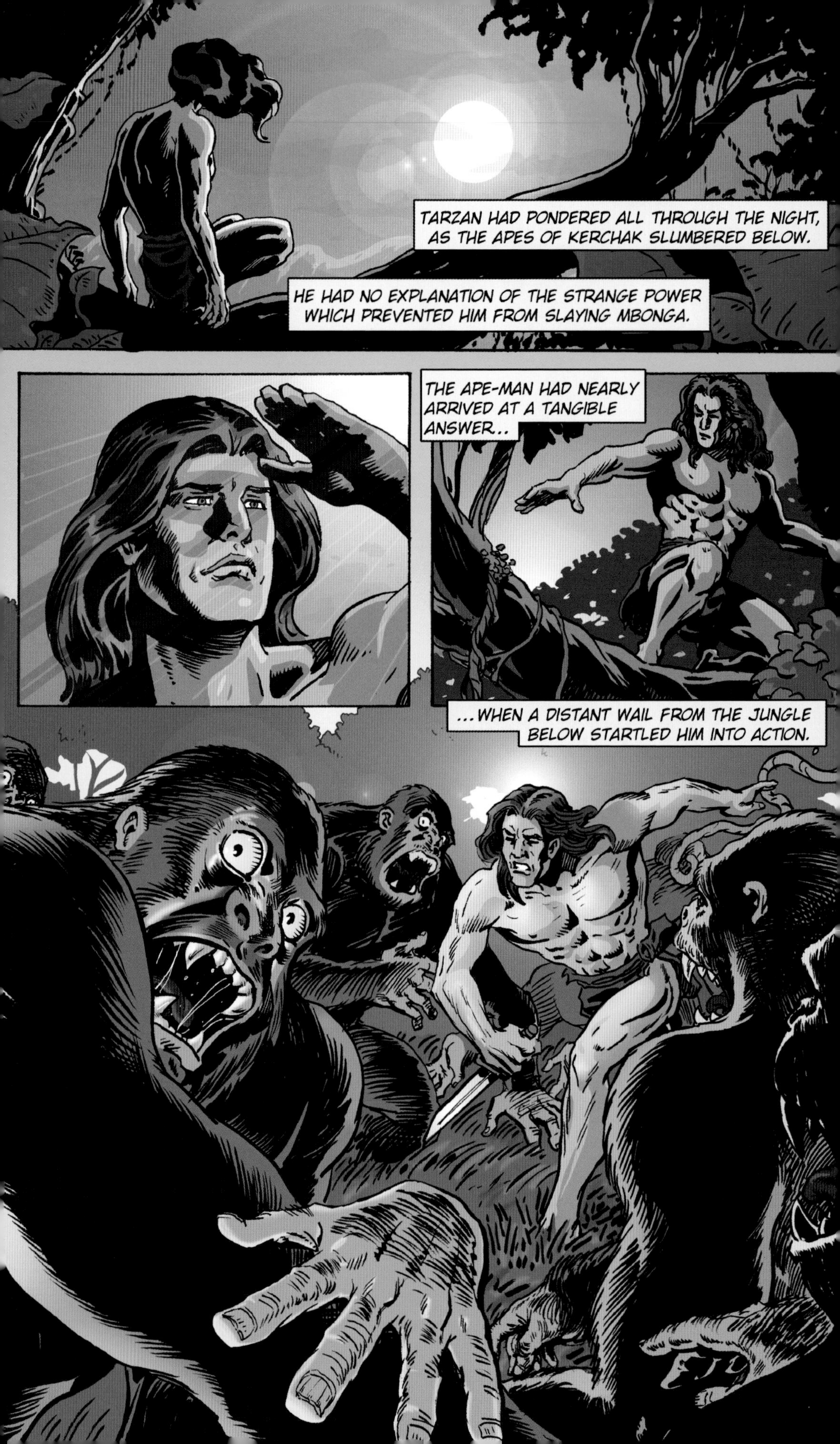
TARZAN HAD PONDERED ALL THROUGH THE NIGHT, AS THE APES OF KERCHAK SLUMBERED BELOW.
HE HAD NO EXPLANATION OF THE STRANGE POWER WHICH PREVENTED HIM FROM SLAYING MBONGA.
THE APE-MAN HAD NEARLY ARRIVED AT A TANGIBLE ANSWER...
...WHEN A DISTANT WAIL FROM THE JUNGLE BELOW STARTLED HIM INTO ACTION.

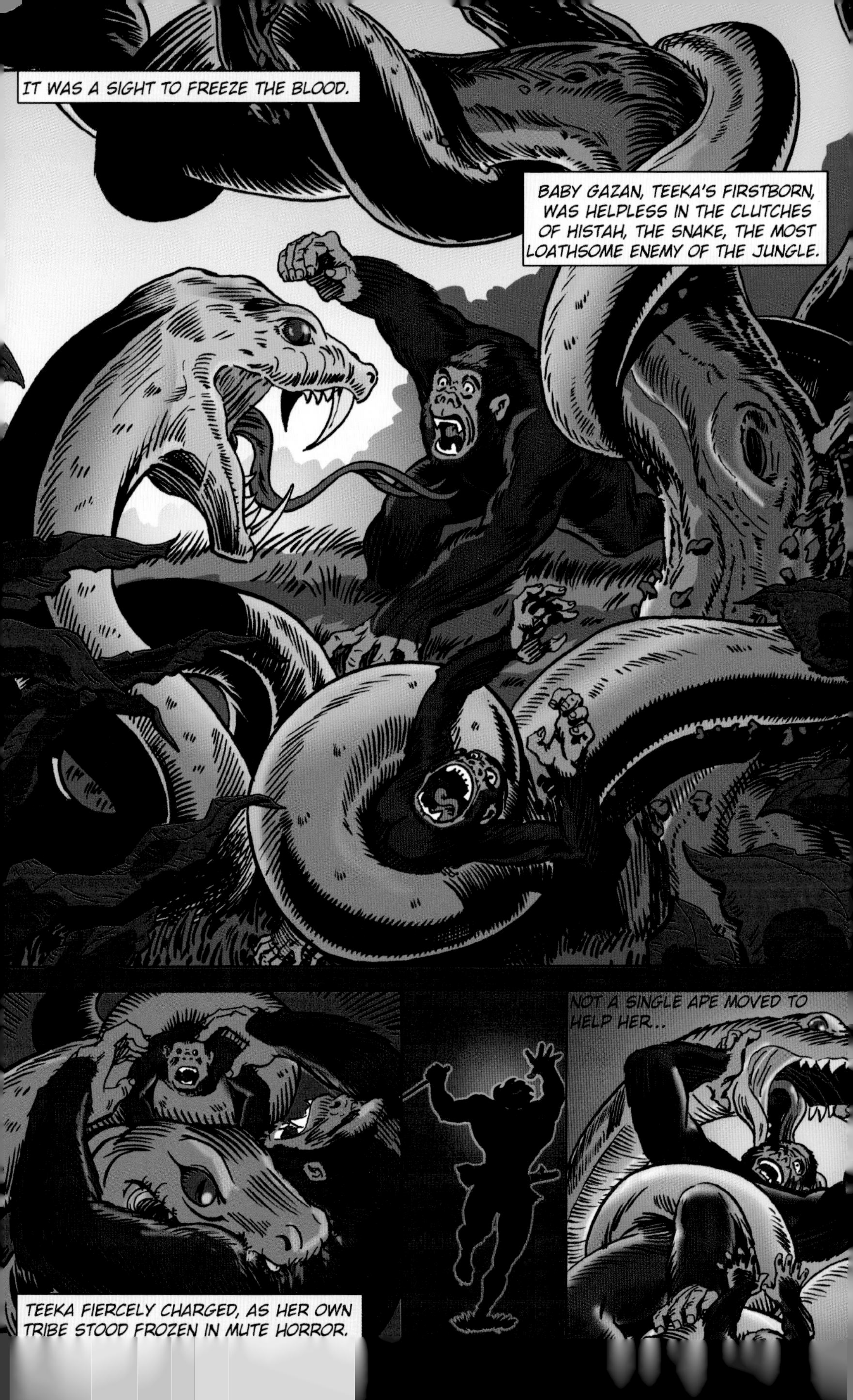
IT WAS A SIGHT TO FREEZE THE BLOOD.
BABY GAZAN, TEEKA'S FIRSTBORN, WAS HELPLESS IN THE CLUTCHES OF HISTAH, THE SNAKE, THE MOST LOATHSOME ENEMY OF THE JUNGLE.
TEEKA FIERCELY CHARGED, AS HER OWN TRIBE STOOD FROZEN IN MUTE HORROR.
NOT A SINGLE APE MOVED TO HELP HER...

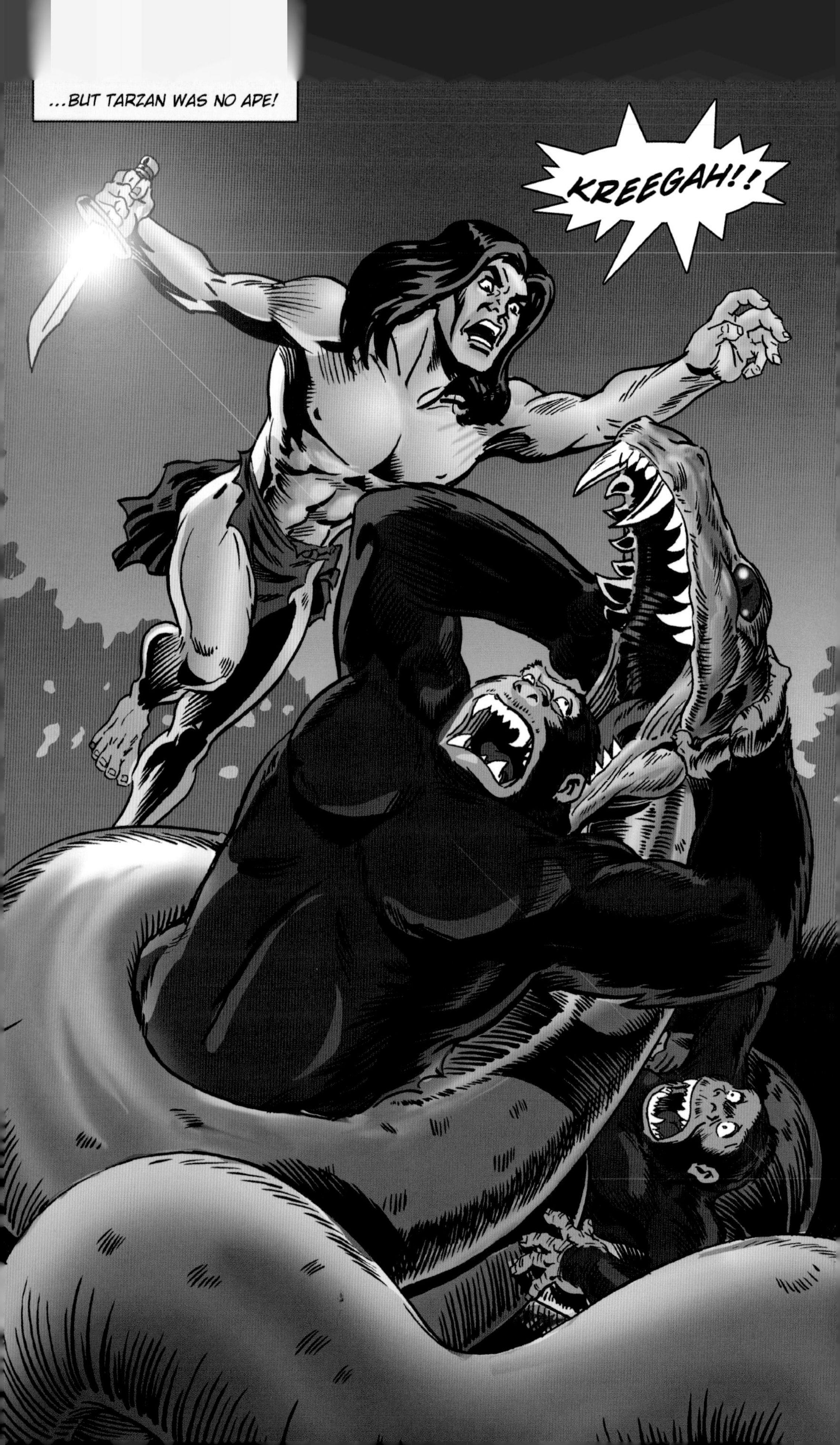
...BUT TARZAN WAS NO APE!
KREEGAH!!

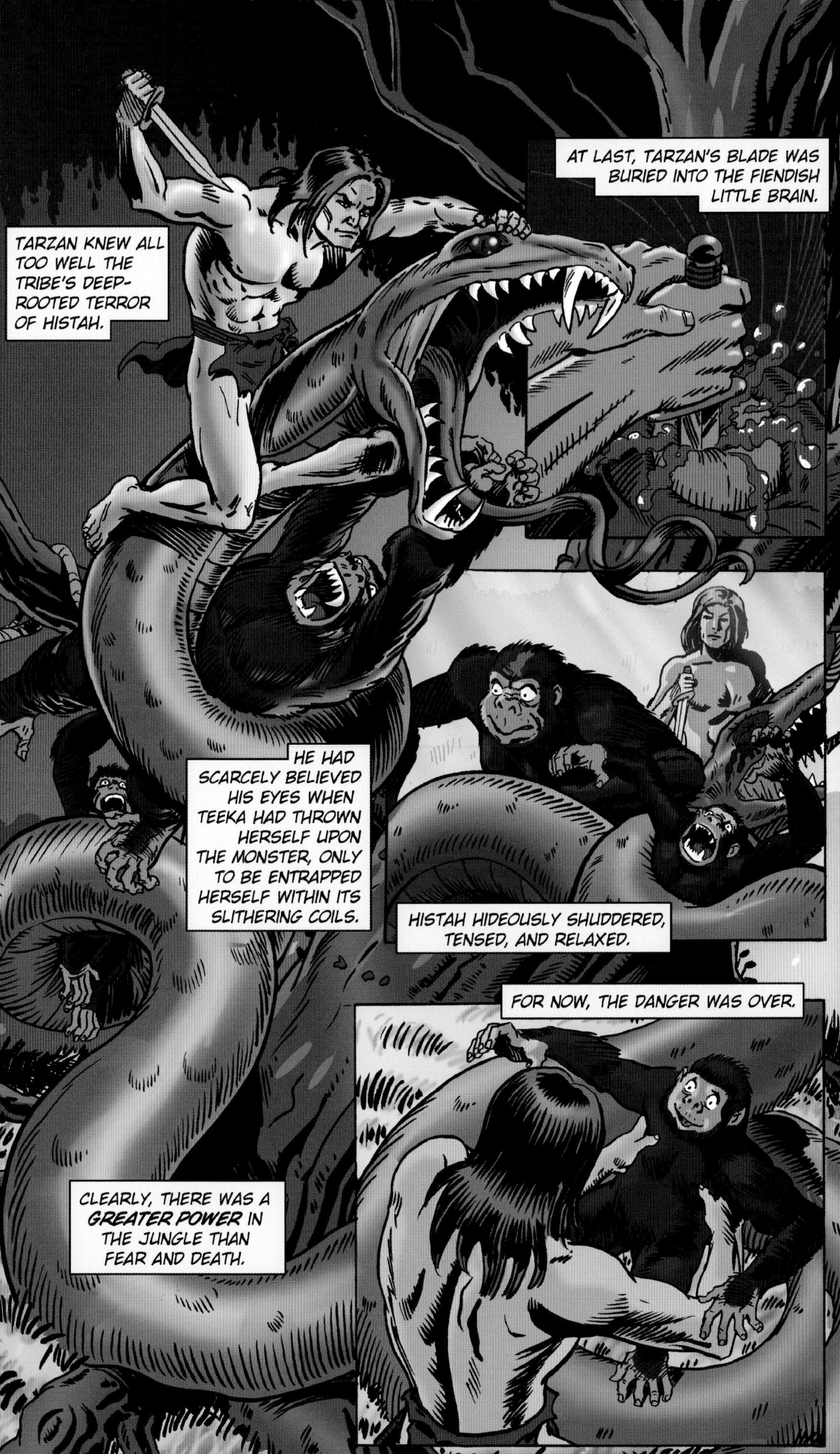
TARZAN KNEW ALL TOO WELL THE TRIBE'S DEEP-ROOTED TERROR OF HISTAH.
AT LAST, TARZAN'S BLADE WAS BURIED INTO THE FIENDISH LITTLE BRAIN.
HE HAD SCARCELY BELIEVED HIS EYES WHEN TEEKA HAD THROWN HERSELF UPON THE MONSTER, ONLY TO BE ENTRAPPED HERSELF WITHIN ITS SLITHERING COILS.
HISTAH HIDEOUSLY SHUDDERED, TENSED, AND RELAXED.
FOR NOW, THE DANGER WAS OVER.
CLEARLY, THERE WAS A **GREATER POWER** IN THE JUNGLE THAN FEAR AND DEATH.

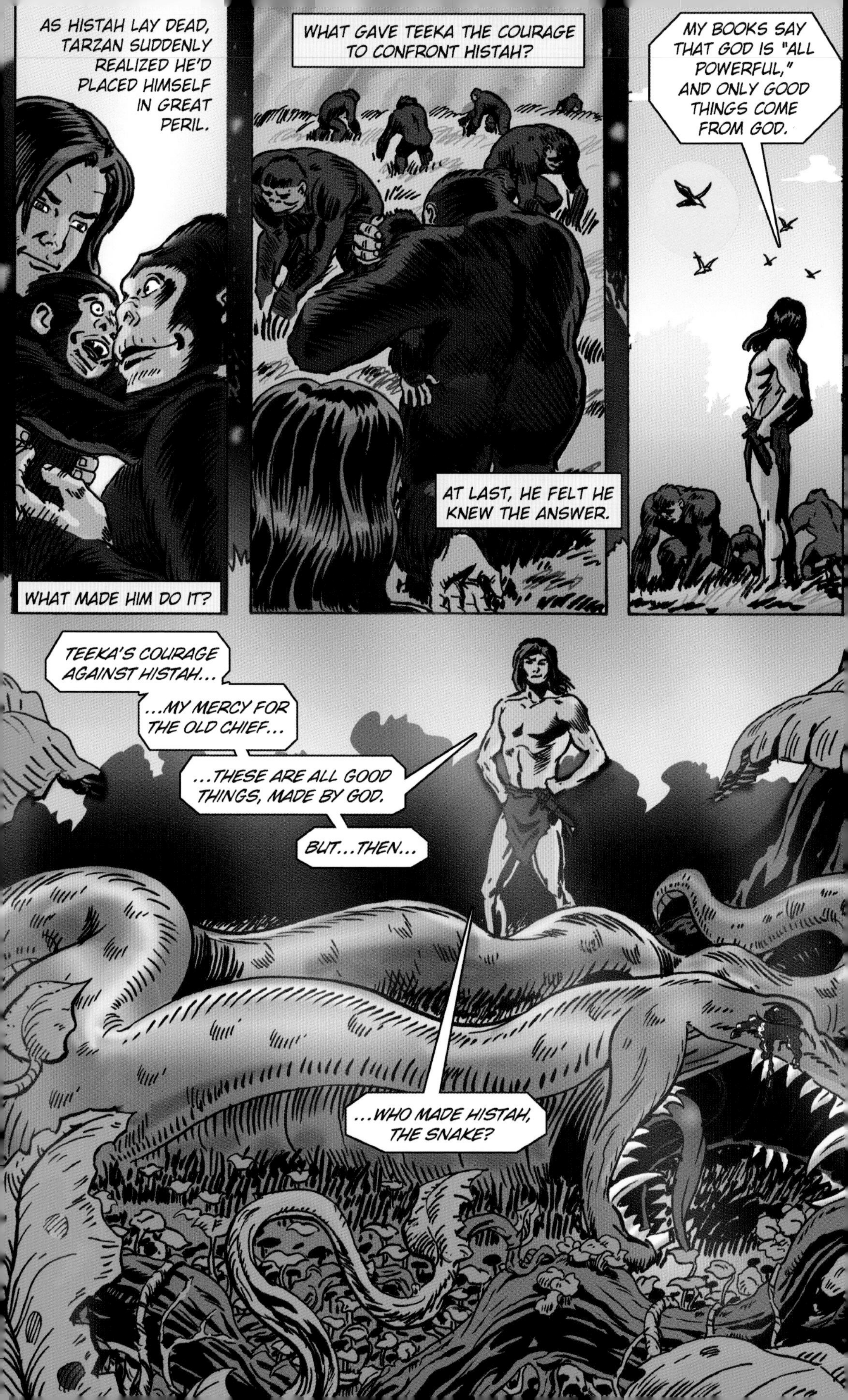

AS HISTAH LAY DEAD, TARZAN SUDDENLY REALIZED HE'D PLACED HIMSELF IN GREAT PERIL.
WHAT MADE HIM DO IT?
WHAT GAVE TEEKA THE COURAGE TO CONFRONT HISTAH?
AT LAST, HE FELT HE KNEW THE ANSWER.
MY BOOKS SAY THAT GOD IS "ALL POWERFUL," AND ONLY GOOD THINGS COME FROM GOD.
TEEKA'S COURAGE AGAINST HISTAH...
...MY MERCY FOR THE OLD CHIEF...
...THESE ARE ALL GOOD THINGS, MADE BY GOD.
BUT...THEN...
...WHO MADE HISTAH, THE SNAKE?

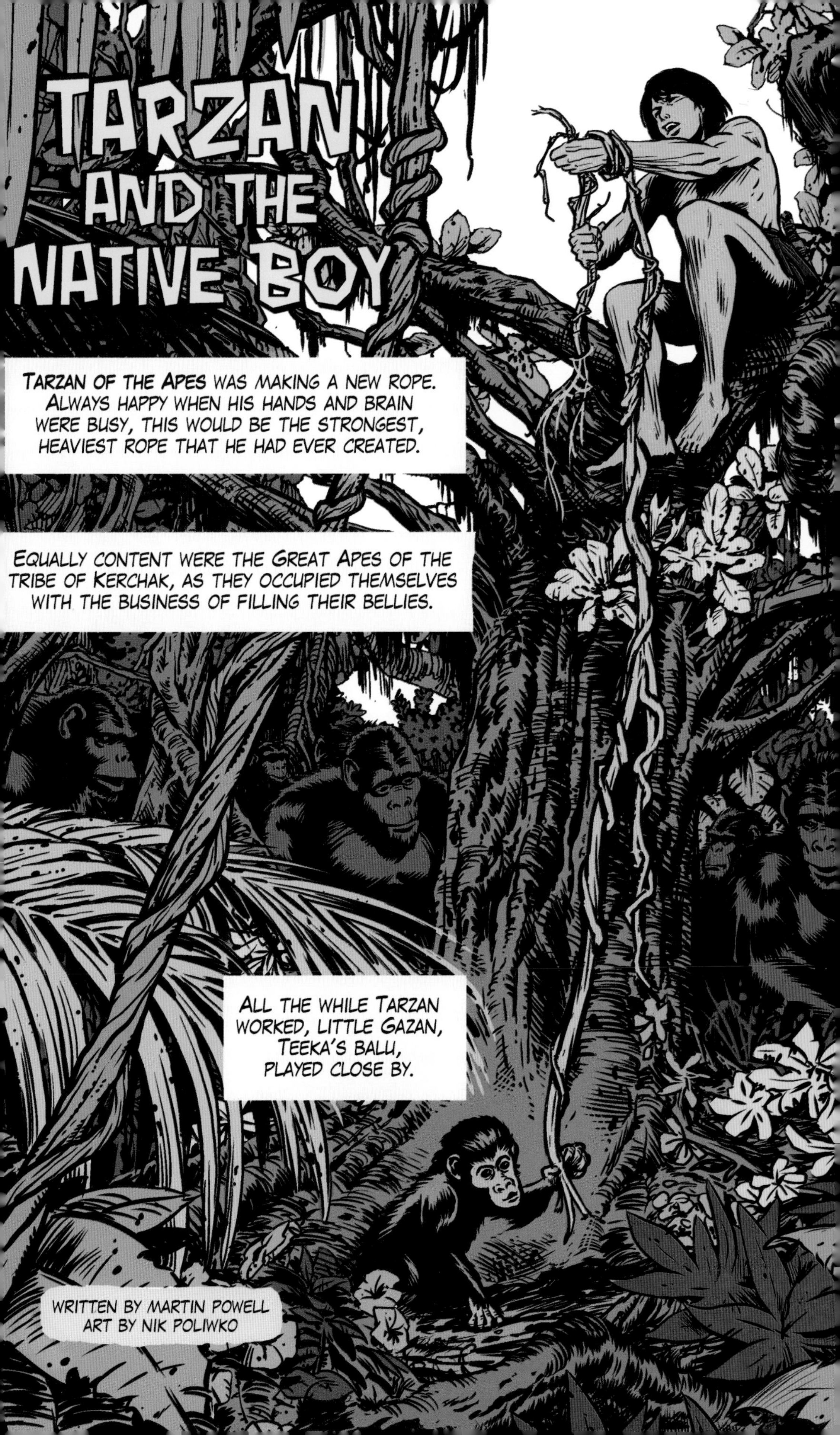
TARZAN AND THE NATIVE BOY
TARZAN OF THE APES WAS MAKING A NEW ROPE. ALWAYS HAPPY WHEN HIS HANDS AND BRAIN WERE BUSY, THIS WOULD BE THE STRONGEST, HEAVIEST ROPE THAT HE HAD EVER CREATED.
EQUALLY CONTENT WERE THE GREAT APES OF THE TRIBE OF KERCHAK, AS THEY OCCUPIED THEMSELVES WITH THE BUSINESS OF FILLING THEIR BELLIES.
ALL THE WHILE TARZAN WORKED, LITTLE GAZAN, TEEKA'S BALU, PLAYED CLOSE BY.
WRITTEN BY MARTIN POWELL
ART BY NIK POLIWKO

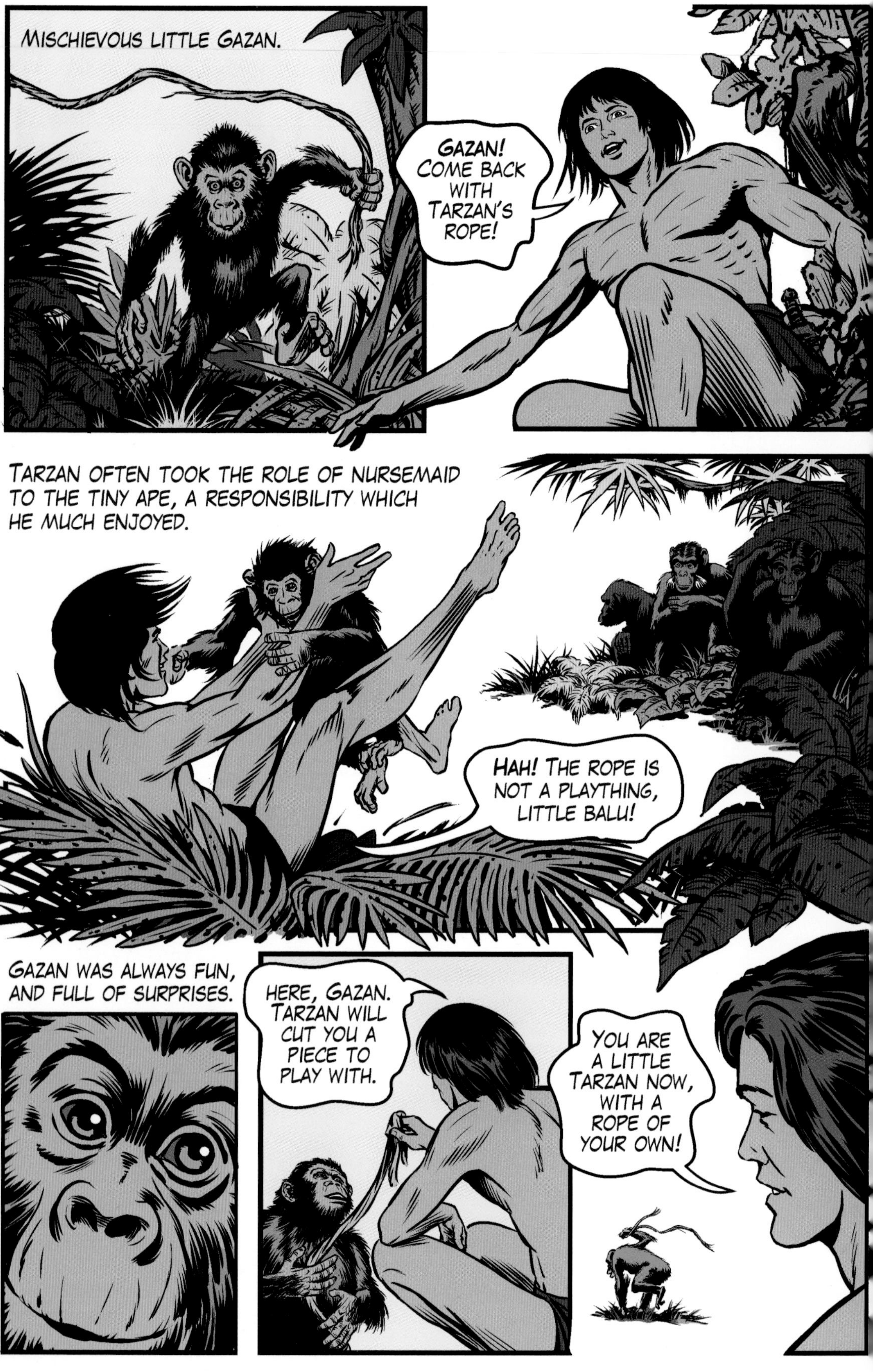
MISCHIEVOUS LITTLE GAZAN.
GAZAN! COME BACK WITH TARZAN'S ROPE!
TARZAN OFTEN TOOK THE ROLE OF NURSEMAID TO THE TINY APE, A RESPONSIBILITY WHICH HE MUCH ENJOYED.
HAH! THE ROPE IS NOT A PLAYTHING, LITTLE BALU!
GAZAN WAS ALWAYS FUN, AND FULL OF SURPRISES.
HERE, GAZAN. TARZAN WILL CUT YOU A PIECE TO PLAY WITH.
YOU ARE A LITTLE TARZAN NOW, WITH A ROPE OF YOUR OWN!

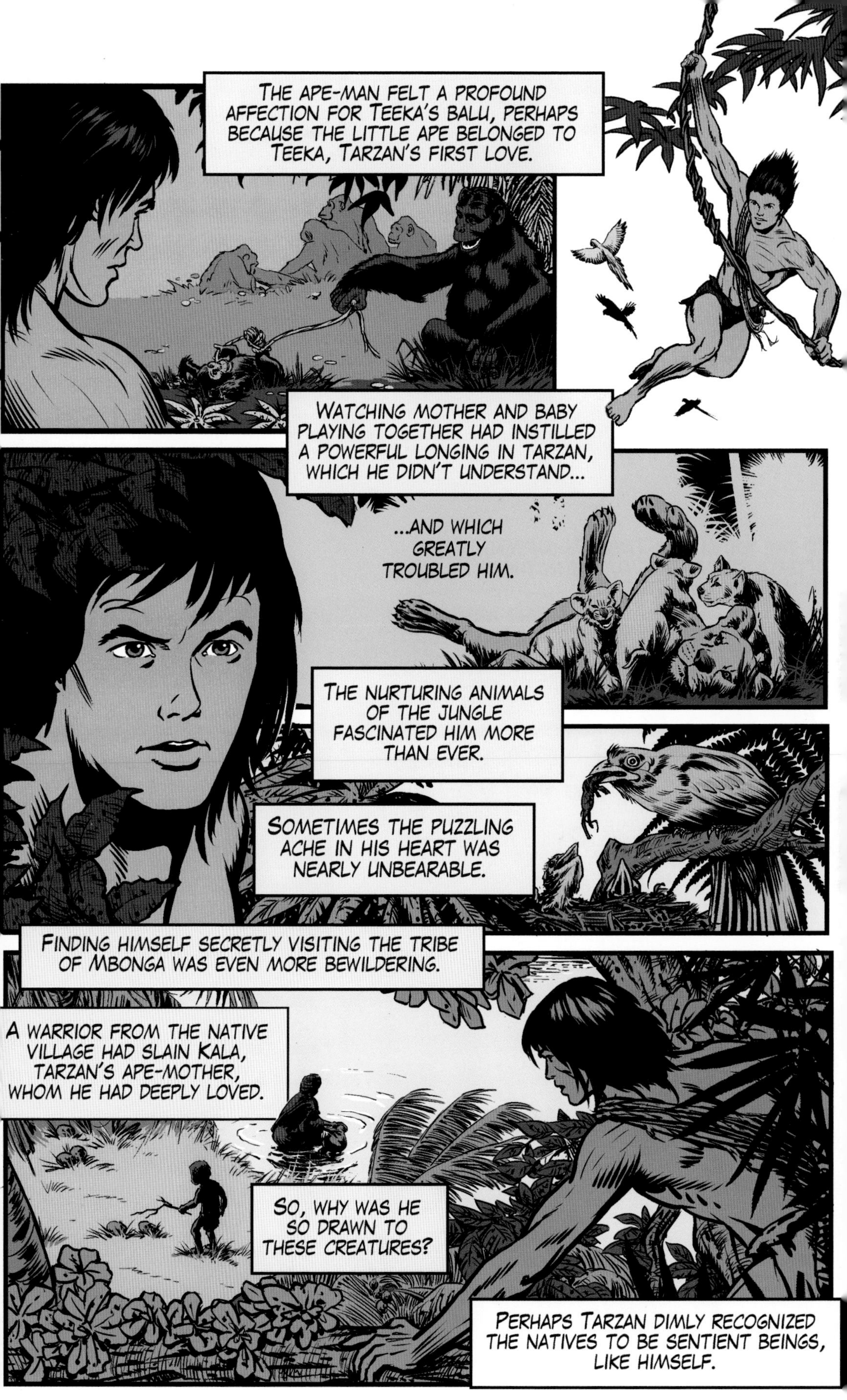

THE APE-MAN FELT A PROFOUND AFFECTION FOR TEEKA'S BALU, PERHAPS BECAUSE THE LITTLE APE BELONGED TO TEEKA, TARZAN'S FIRST LOVE.
WATCHING MOTHER AND BABY PLAYING TOGETHER HAD INSTILLED A POWERFUL LONGING IN TARZAN, WHICH HE DIDN'T UNDERSTAND...
...AND WHICH GREATLY TROUBLED HIM.
THE NURTURING ANIMALS OF THE JUNGLE FASCINATED HIM MORE THAN EVER.
SOMETIMES THE PUZZLING ACHE IN HIS HEART WAS NEARLY UNBEARABLE.
FINDING HIMSELF SECRETLY VISITING THE TRIBE OF MBONGA WAS EVEN MORE BEWILDERING.
A WARRIOR FROM THE NATIVE VILLAGE HAD SLAIN KALA, TARZAN'S APE-MOTHER, WHOM HE HAD DEEPLY LOVED.
SO, WHY WAS HE SO DRAWN TO THESE CREATURES?
PERHAPS TARZAN DIMLY RECOGNIZED THE NATIVES TO BE SENTIENT BEINGS, LIKE HIMSELF.

AND, FOR THE FIRST TIME IN HIS YOUTHFUL LIFE, TARZAN WAS LONELY.

I'M GOING TO PICK SOME BERRIES, TIBO. DON'T GET TOO CLOSE TO THE WATER.

I WON'T, MOTHER.

TO THE YOUNG BOY, TARZAN'S SUDDEN, UTTERLY SILENT ARRIVAL WAS NOTHING SHORT OF SUPERNATURAL.

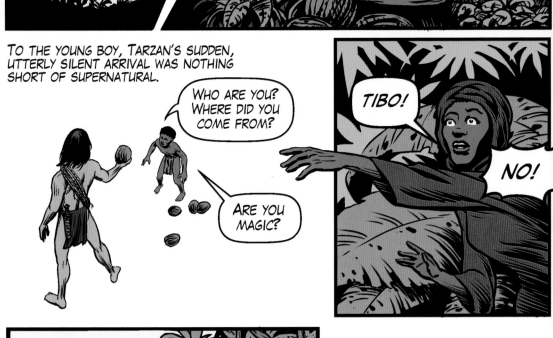

WHO ARE YOU? WHERE DID YOU COME FROM?

ARE YOU MAGIC?

TIBO!

NO!

STARTLED, TARZAN PROTECTIVELY SNATCHED UP THE BOY, INSTINCTIVELY ESCAPING INTO THE TREES.

IT-IT'S THE TREE DEVIL!

HE'S STOLE MY BABY!!

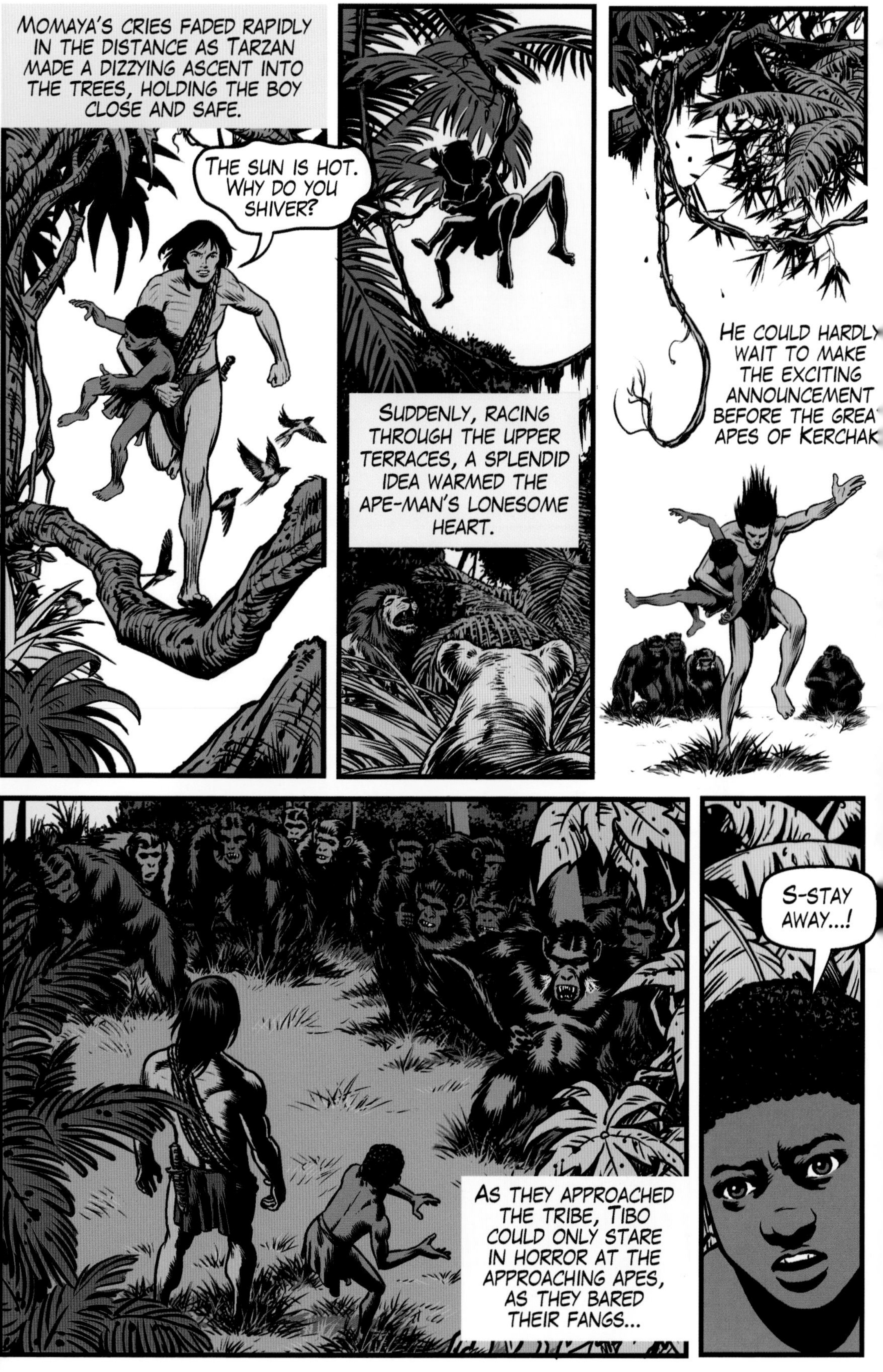
MOMAYA'S CRIES FADED RAPIDLY IN THE DISTANCE AS TARZAN MADE A DIZZYING ASCENT INTO THE TREES, HOLDING THE BOY CLOSE AND SAFE.
THE SUN IS HOT. WHY DO YOU SHIVER?
SUDDENLY, RACING THROUGH THE UPPER TERRACES, A SPLENDID IDEA WARMED THE APE-MAN'S LONESOME HEART.
HE COULD HARDLY WAIT TO MAKE THE EXCITING ANNOUNCEMENT BEFORE THE GREAT APES OF KERCHAK
AS THEY APPROACHED THE TRIBE, TIBO COULD ONLY STARE IN HORROR AT THE APPROACHING APES, AS THEY BARED THEIR FANGS...
S-STAY AWAY...!

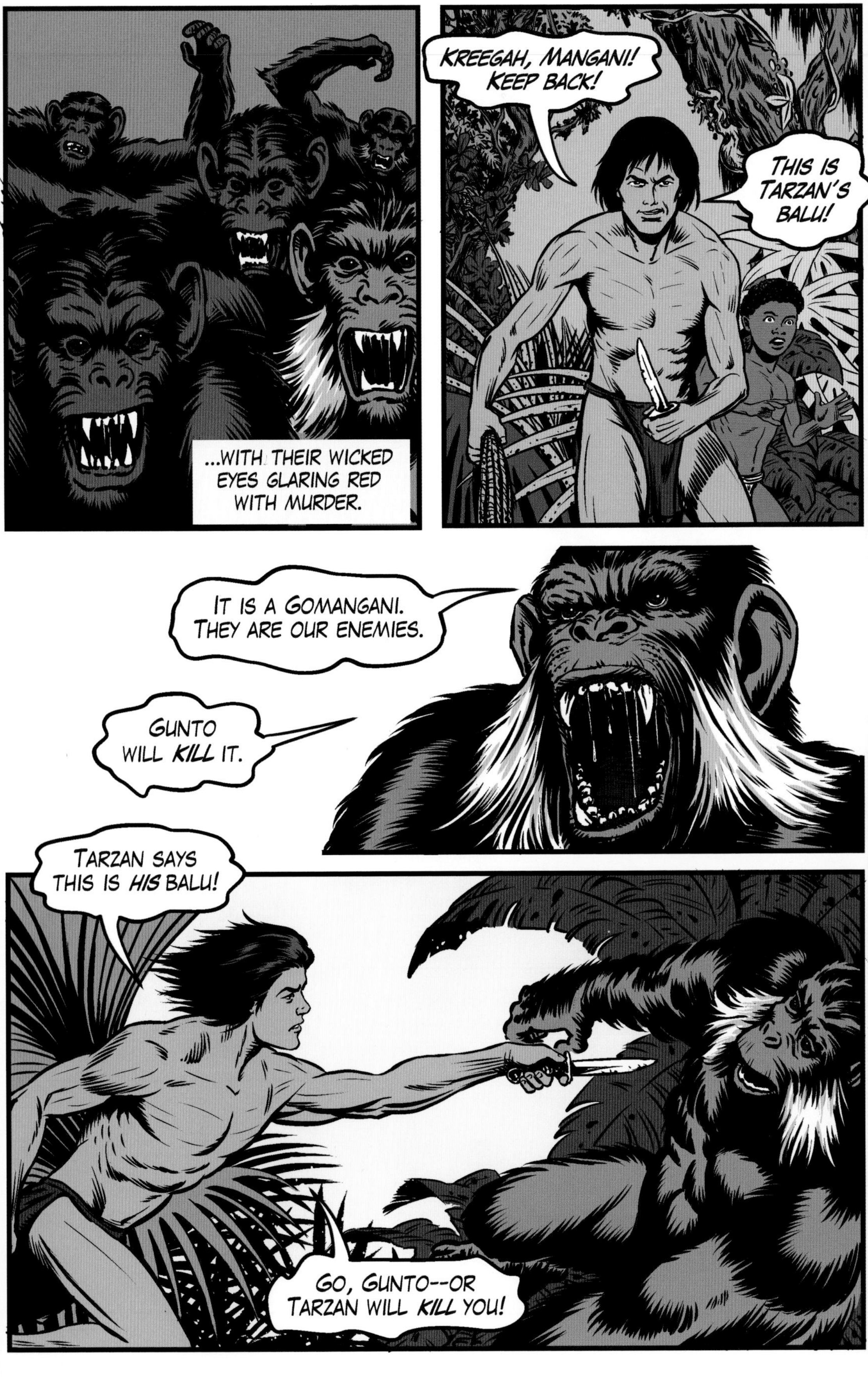
...WITH THEIR WICKED EYES GLARING RED WITH MURDER.
KREEGAH, MANGANI! KEEP BACK!
THIS IS TARZAN'S BALU!
IT IS A GOMANGANI. THEY ARE OUR ENEMIES.
GUNTO WILL KILL IT.
TARZAN SAYS THIS IS HIS BALU!
GO, GUNTO--OR TARZAN WILL KILL YOU!

IT'S ALL RIGHT, LITTLE BALU. YOU'RE SAFE NOW.

TARZAN WILL PROTECT YOU.

TIME HAD PASSED PAINFULLY FOR MOMAYA. FINALLY, IN BLEAK DESPERATION, SHE HAD NO OTHER CHOICE THAN TO SEEK OUT THE EVIL OLD WITCH DOCTOR.

ENTER, WOMAN.

COME CLOSER...

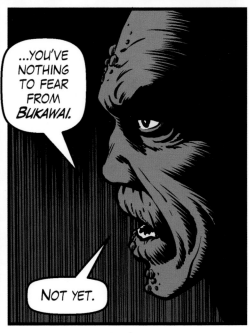

...YOU'VE NOTHING TO FEAR FROM *BUKAWAI.*

NOT YET.

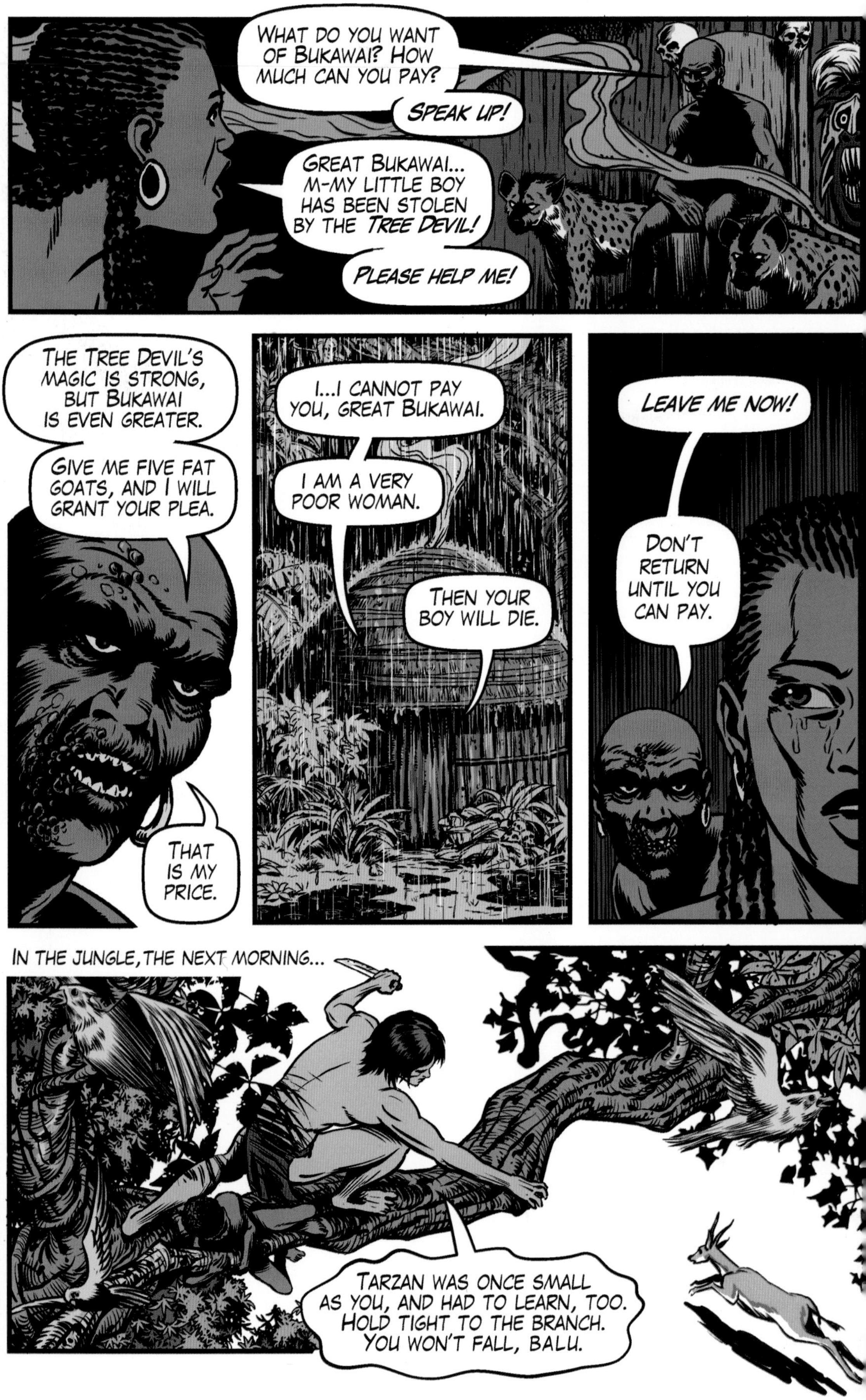

WHAT DO YOU WANT OF BUKAWAI? HOW MUCH CAN YOU PAY?
SPEAK UP!
GREAT BUKAWAI... M-MY LITTLE BOY HAS BEEN STOLEN BY THE TREE DEVIL!
PLEASE HELP ME!
THE TREE DEVIL'S MAGIC IS STRONG, BUT BUKAWAI IS EVEN GREATER.
GIVE ME FIVE FAT GOATS, AND I WILL GRANT YOUR PLEA.
THAT IS MY PRICE.
I...I CANNOT PAY YOU, GREAT BUKAWAI.
I AM A VERY POOR WOMAN.
THEN YOUR BOY WILL DIE.
LEAVE ME NOW!
DON'T RETURN UNTIL YOU CAN PAY.
IN THE JUNGLE, THE NEXT MORNING...
TARZAN WAS ONCE SMALL AS YOU, AND HAD TO LEARN, TOO. HOLD TIGHT TO THE BRANCH. YOU WON'T FALL, BALU.

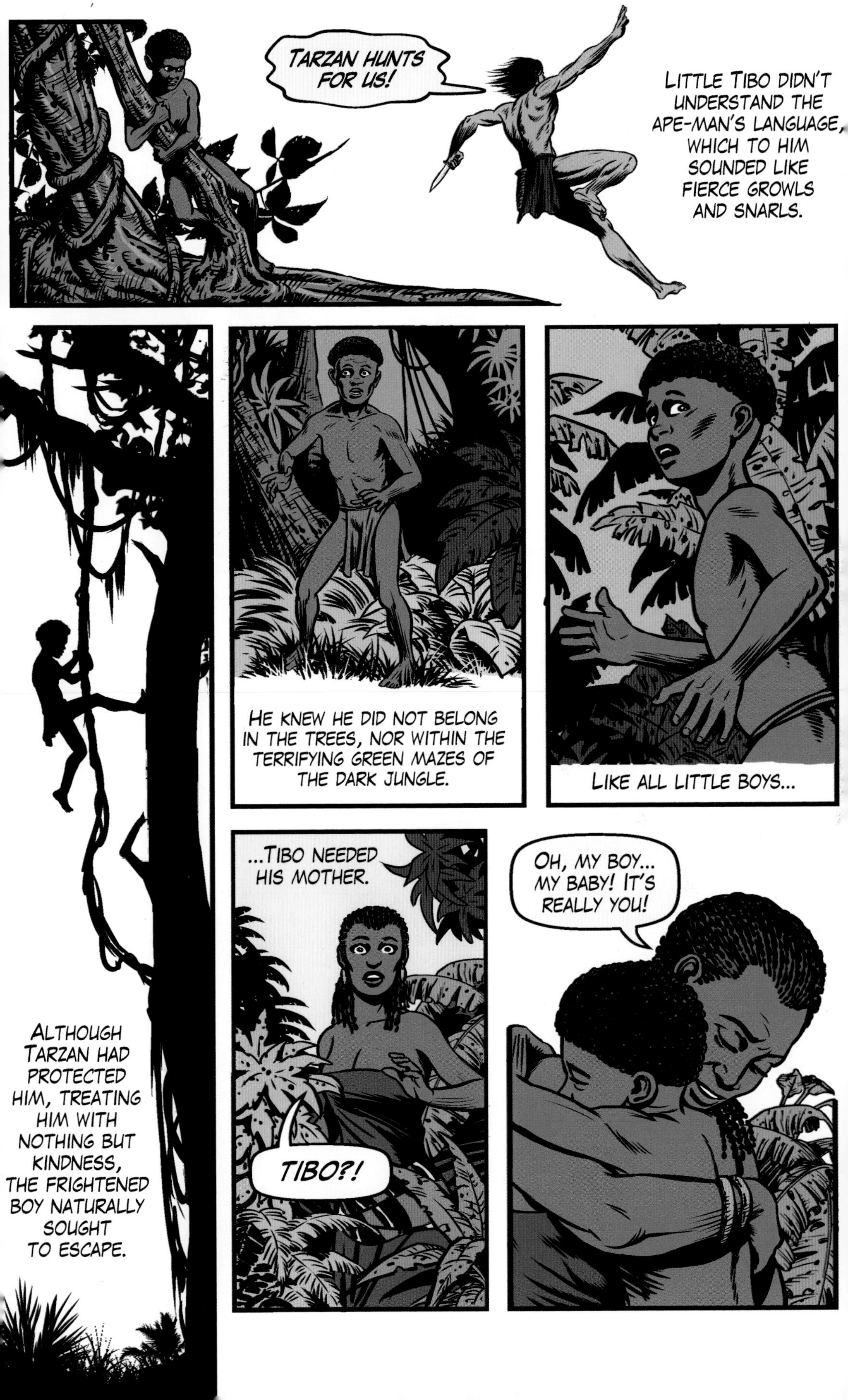
TARZAN HUNTS FOR US!
LITTLE TIBO DIDN'T UNDERSTAND THE APE-MAN'S LANGUAGE, WHICH TO HIM SOUNDED LIKE FIERCE GROWLS AND SNARLS.
ALTHOUGH TARZAN HAD PROTECTED HIM, TREATING HIM WITH NOTHING BUT KINDNESS, THE FRIGHTENED BOY NATURALLY SOUGHT TO ESCAPE.
HE KNEW HE DID NOT BELONG IN THE TREES, NOR WITHIN THE TERRIFYING GREEN MAZES OF THE DARK JUNGLE.
LIKE ALL LITTLE BOYS...
...TIBO NEEDED HIS MOTHER.
TIBO?!
OH, MY BOY... MY BABY! IT'S REALLY YOU!

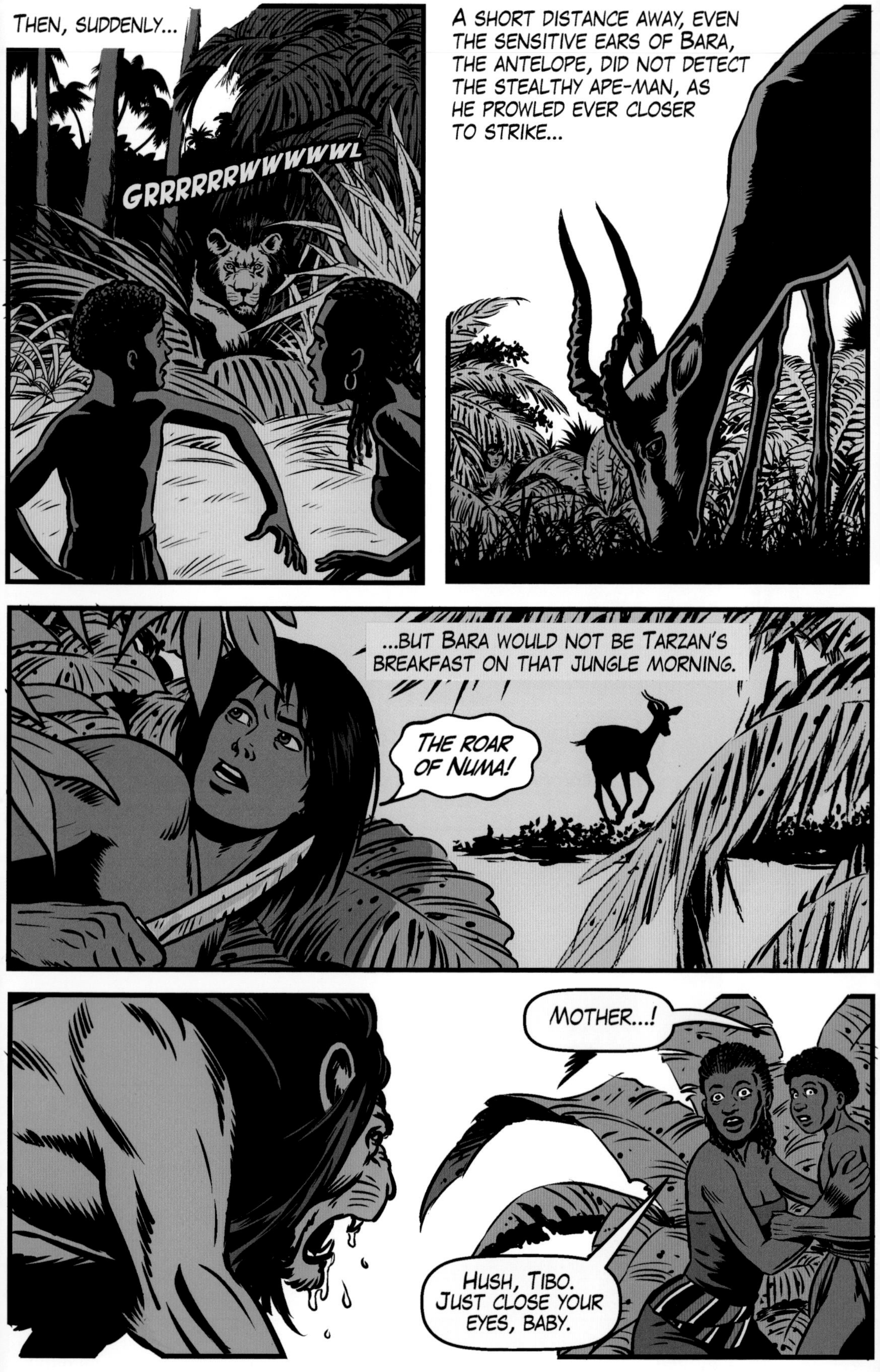
THEN, SUDDENLY...
GRRRRRRWWWWWL
A SHORT DISTANCE AWAY, EVEN THE SENSITIVE EARS OF BARA, THE ANTELOPE, DID NOT DETECT THE STEALTHY APE-MAN, AS HE PROWLED EVER CLOSER TO STRIKE...
...BUT BARA WOULD NOT BE TARZAN'S BREAKFAST ON THAT JUNGLE MORNING.
THE ROAR OF NUMA!
MOTHER...!
HUSH, TIBO. JUST CLOSE YOUR EYES, BABY.

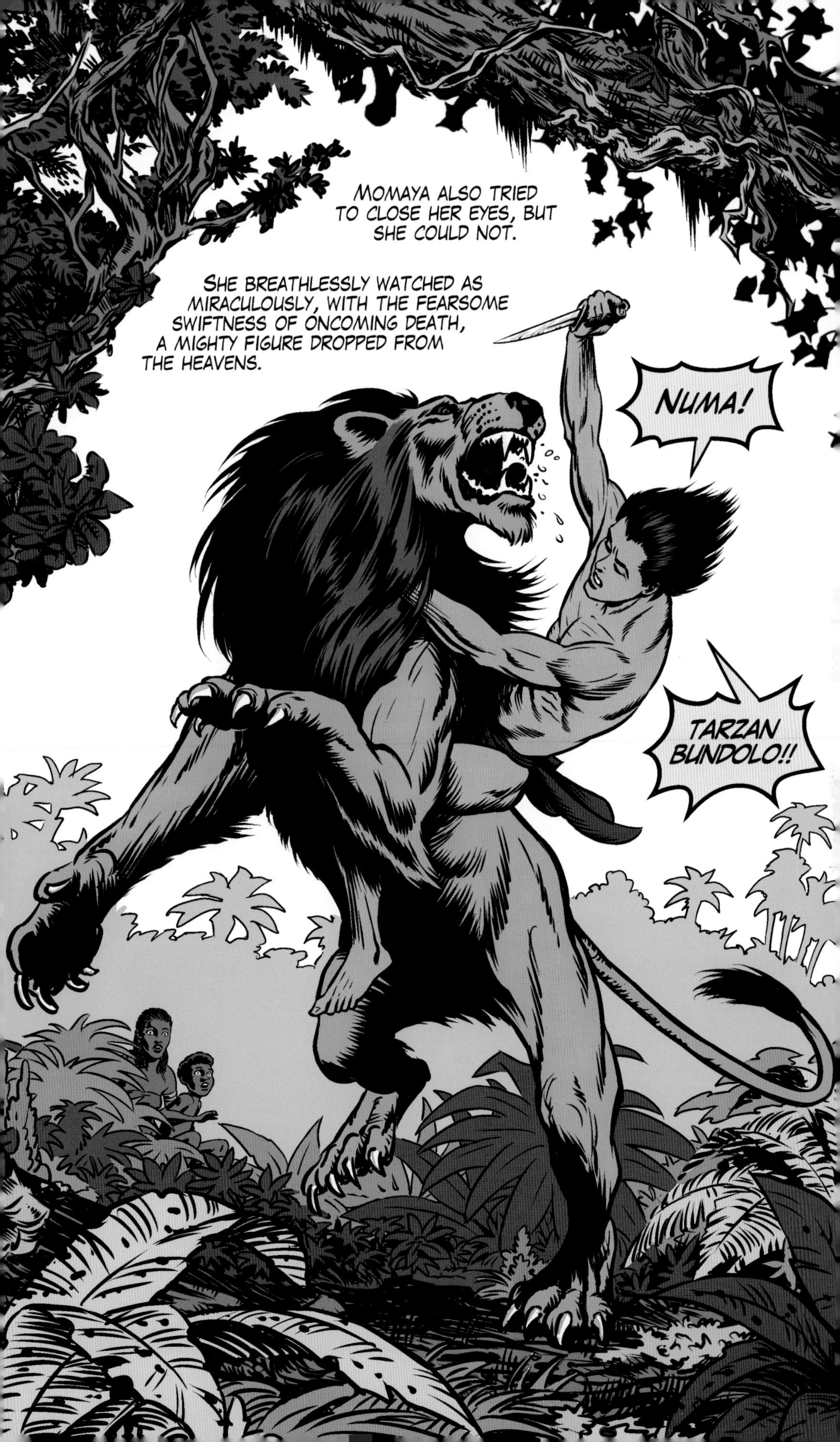
MOMAYA ALSO TRIED TO CLOSE HER EYES, BUT SHE COULD NOT.
SHE BREATHLESSLY WATCHED AS MIRACULOUSLY, WITH THE FEARSOME SWIFTNESS OF ONCOMING DEATH, A MIGHTY FIGURE DROPPED FROM THE HEAVENS.
NUMA!
TARZAN BUNDOLO!!

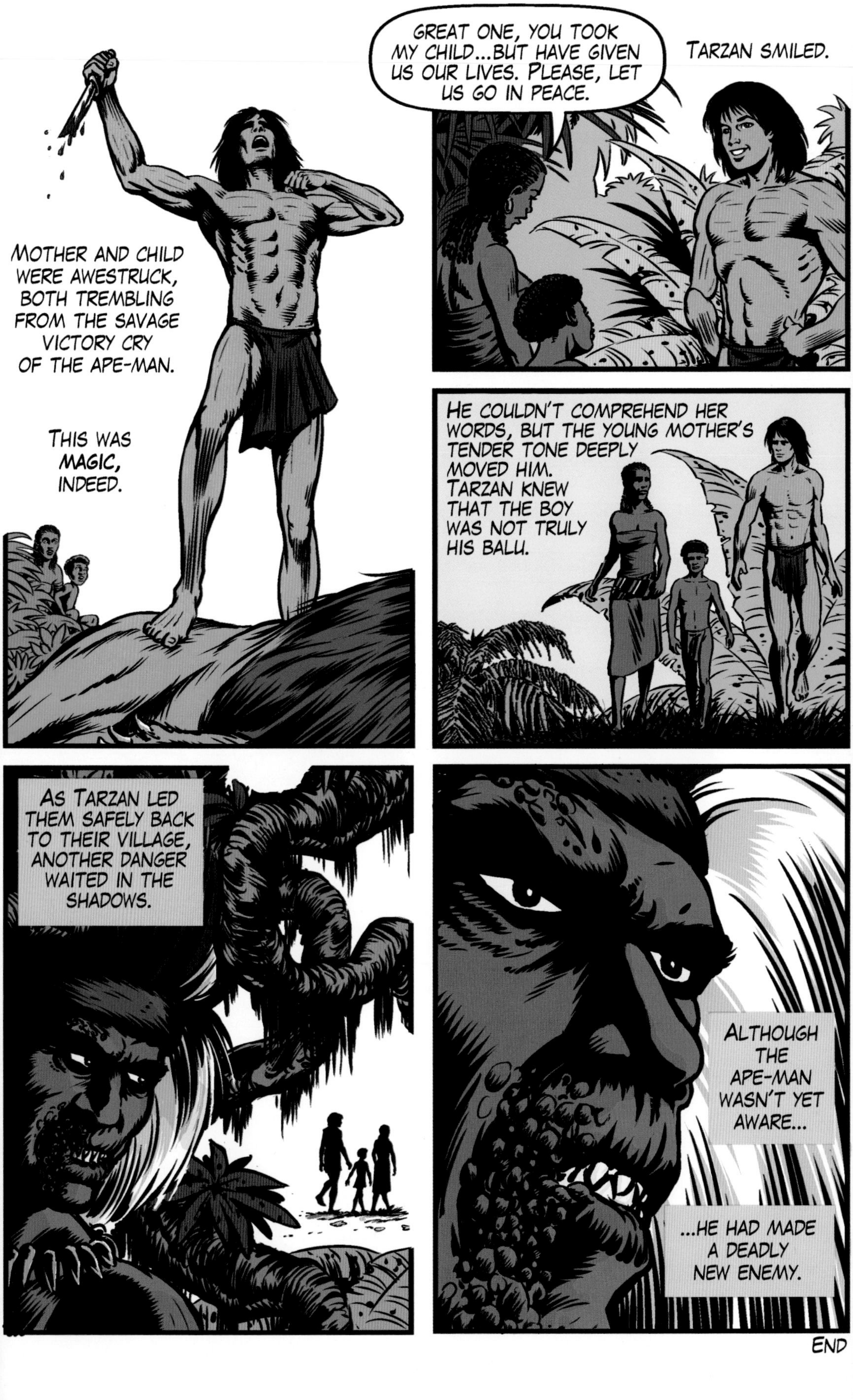
MOTHER AND CHILD WERE AWESTRUCK, BOTH TREMBLING FROM THE SAVAGE VICTORY CRY OF THE APE-MAN.
THIS WAS MAGIC, INDEED.
GREAT ONE, YOU TOOK MY CHILD...BUT HAVE GIVEN US OUR LIVES. PLEASE, LET US GO IN PEACE.
TARZAN SMILED.
HE COULDN'T COMPREHEND HER WORDS, BUT THE YOUNG MOTHER'S TENDER TONE DEEPLY MOVED HIM. TARZAN KNEW THAT THE BOY WAS NOT TRULY HIS BALU.
AS TARZAN LED THEM SAFELY BACK TO THEIR VILLAGE, ANOTHER DANGER WAITED IN THE SHADOWS.
ALTHOUGH THE APE-MAN WASN'T YET AWARE...
...HE HAD MADE A DEADLY NEW ENEMY.
END

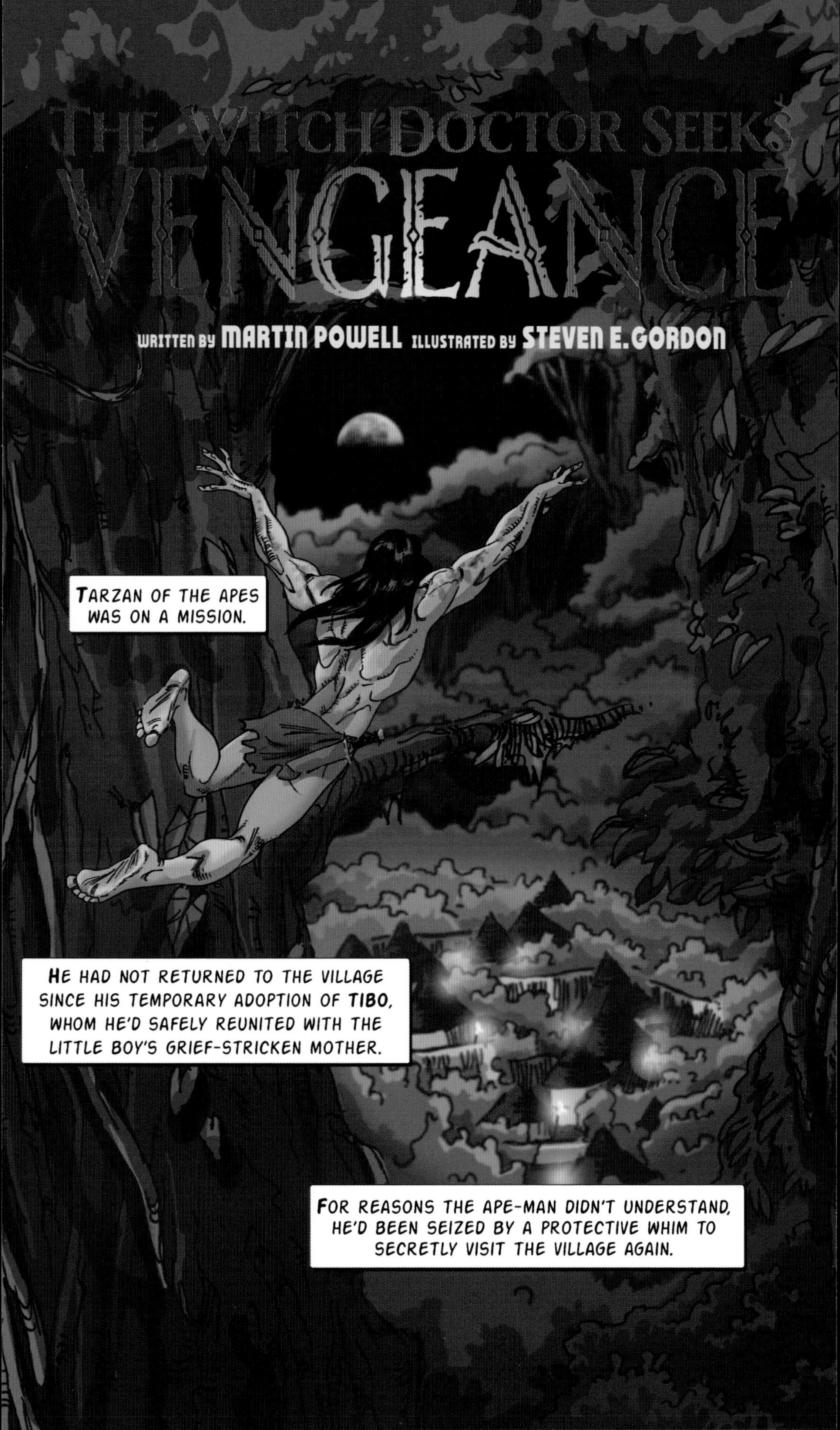
THE WITCH DOCTOR SEEKS
VENGEANCE
WRITTEN BY MARTIN POWELL ILLUSTRATED BY STEVEN E. GORDON
TARZAN OF THE APES WAS ON A MISSION.
HE HAD NOT RETURNED TO THE VILLAGE SINCE HIS TEMPORARY ADOPTION OF TIBO, WHOM HE'D SAFELY REUNITED WITH THE LITTLE BOY'S GRIEF-STRICKEN MOTHER.
FOR REASONS THE APE-MAN DIDN'T UNDERSTAND, HE'D BEEN SEIZED BY A PROTECTIVE WHIM TO SECRETLY VISIT THE VILLAGE AGAIN.

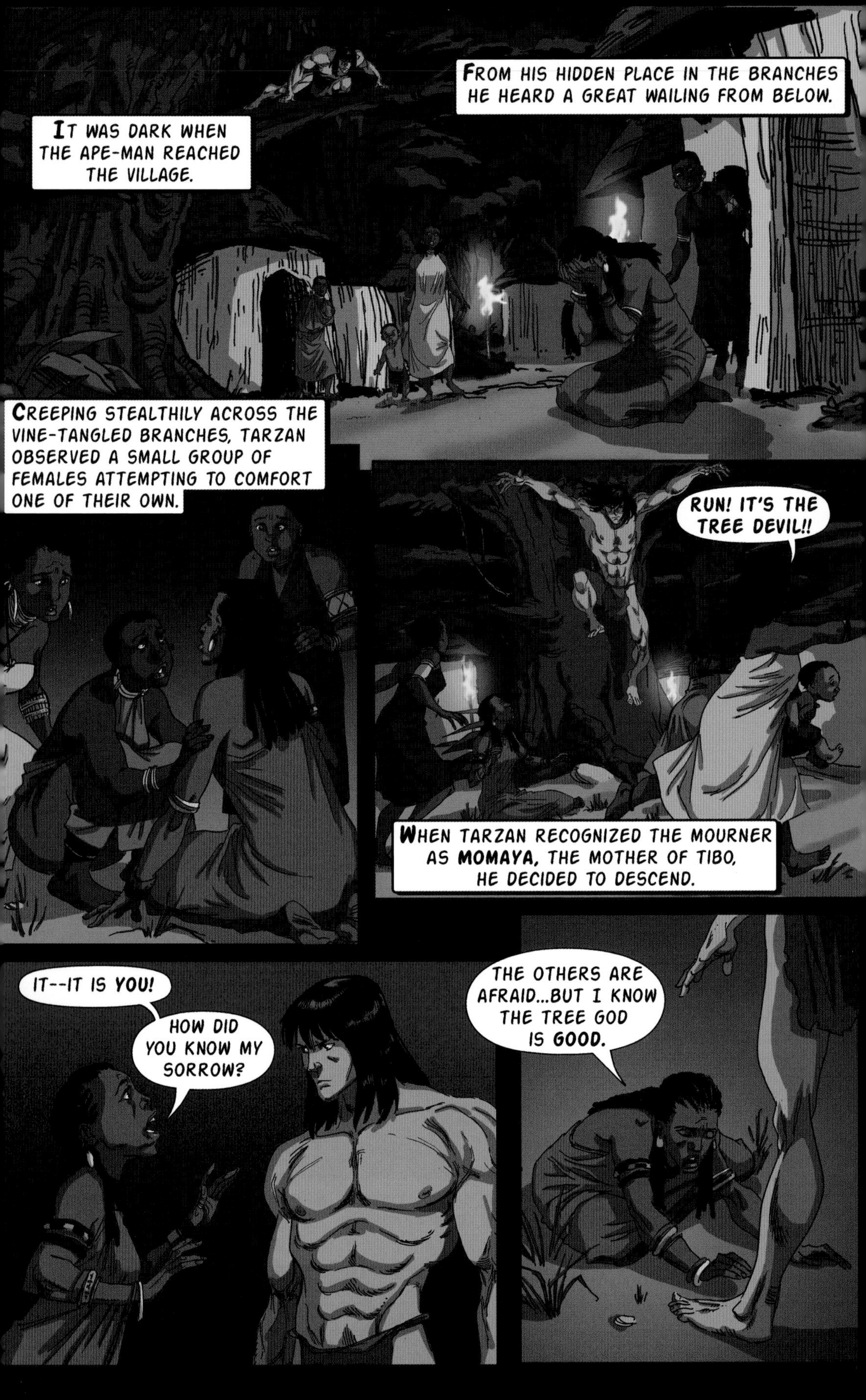

IT WAS DARK WHEN THE APE-MAN REACHED THE VILLAGE.
FROM HIS HIDDEN PLACE IN THE BRANCHES HE HEARD A GREAT WAILING FROM BELOW.
CREEPING STEALTHILY ACROSS THE VINE-TANGLED BRANCHES, TARZAN OBSERVED A SMALL GROUP OF FEMALES ATTEMPTING TO COMFORT ONE OF THEIR OWN.
RUN! IT'S THE TREE DEVIL!!
WHEN TARZAN RECOGNIZED THE MOURNER AS MOMAYA, THE MOTHER OF TIBO, HE DECIDED TO DESCEND.
IT--IT IS YOU!
HOW DID YOU KNOW MY SORROW?
THE OTHERS ARE AFRAID...BUT I KNOW THE TREE GOD IS GOOD.

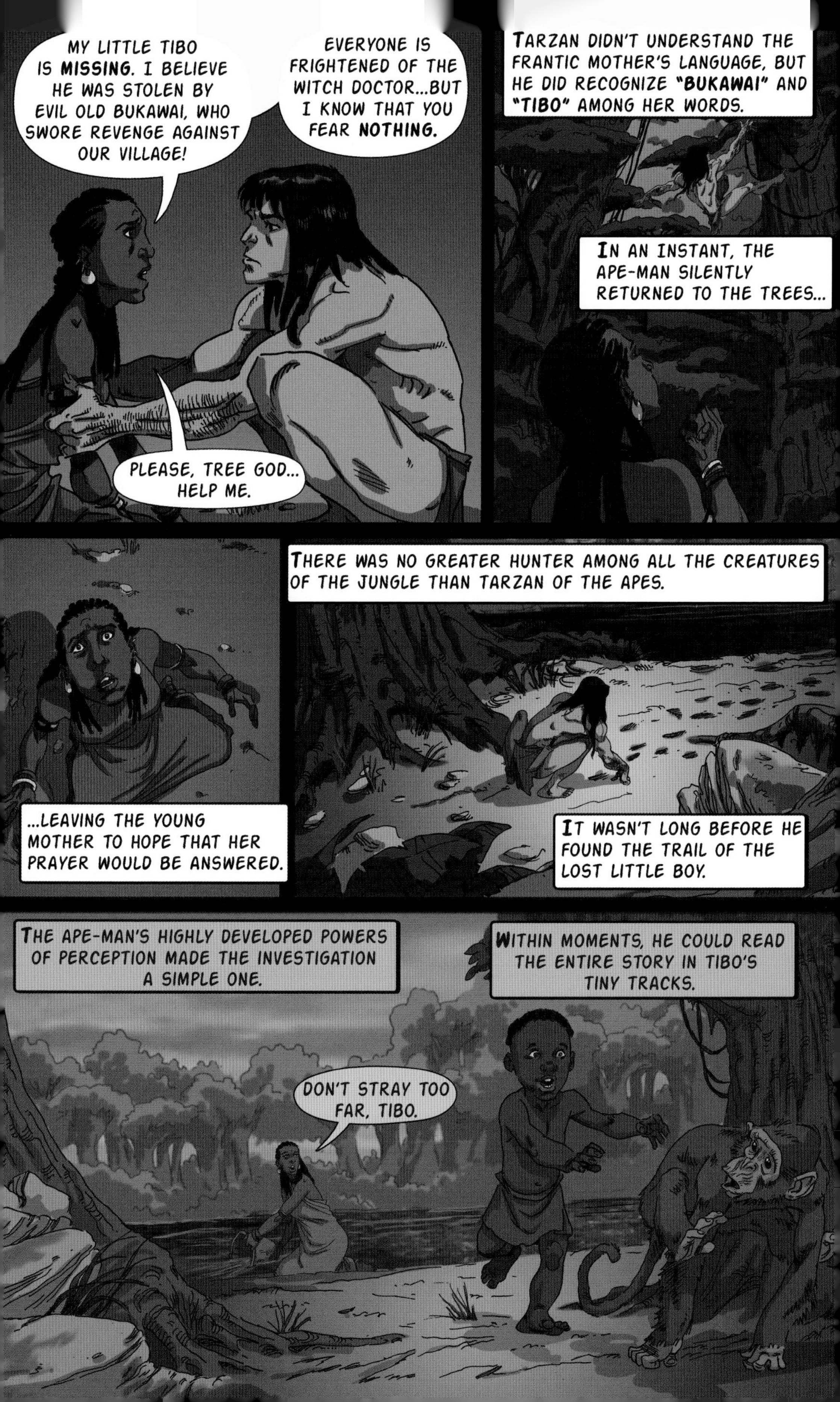
MY LITTLE TIBO IS MISSING. I BELIEVE HE WAS STOLEN BY EVIL OLD BUKAWAI, WHO SWORE REVENGE AGAINST OUR VILLAGE!
EVERYONE IS FRIGHTENED OF THE WITCH DOCTOR...BUT I KNOW THAT YOU FEAR NOTHING.
PLEASE, TREE GOD... HELP ME.
TARZAN DIDN'T UNDERSTAND THE FRANTIC MOTHER'S LANGUAGE, BUT HE DID RECOGNIZE "BUKAWAI" AND "TIBO" AMONG HER WORDS.
IN AN INSTANT, THE APE-MAN SILENTLY RETURNED TO THE TREES...
...LEAVING THE YOUNG MOTHER TO HOPE THAT HER PRAYER WOULD BE ANSWERED.
THERE WAS NO GREATER HUNTER AMONG ALL THE CREATURES OF THE JUNGLE THAN TARZAN OF THE APES.
IT WASN'T LONG BEFORE HE FOUND THE TRAIL OF THE LOST LITTLE BOY.
THE APE-MAN'S HIGHLY DEVELOPED POWERS OF PERCEPTION MADE THE INVESTIGATION A SIMPLE ONE.
WITHIN MOMENTS, HE COULD READ THE ENTIRE STORY IN TIBO'S TINY TRACKS.
DON'T STRAY TOO FAR, TIBO.

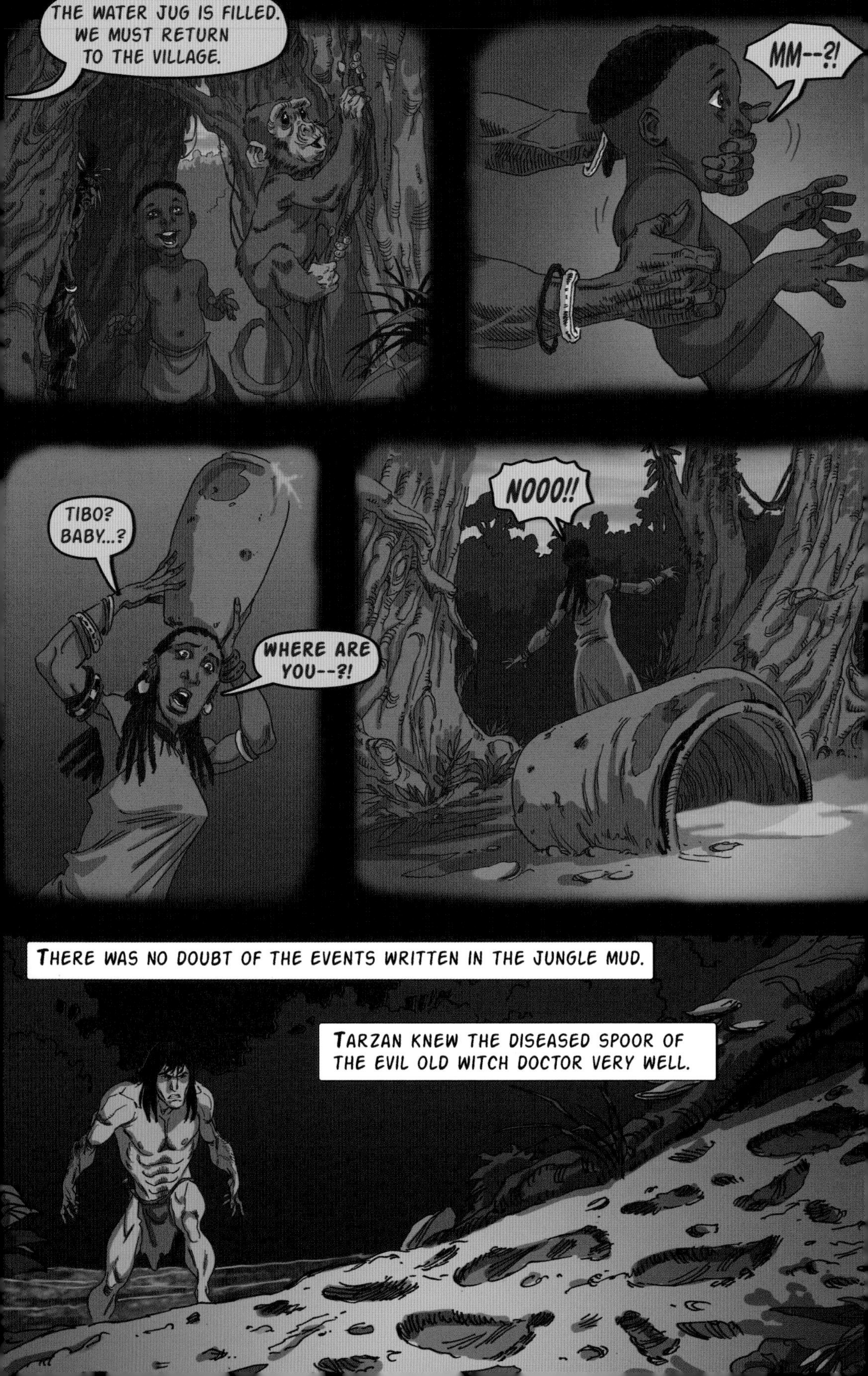
THE WATER JUG IS FILLED. WE MUST RETURN TO THE VILLAGE.
MM--?!
TIBO? BABY...?
WHERE ARE YOU--?!
NOOO!!
THERE WAS NO DOUBT OF THE EVENTS WRITTEN IN THE JUNGLE MUD.
TARZAN KNEW THE DISEASED SPOOR OF THE EVIL OLD WITCH DOCTOR VERY WELL.

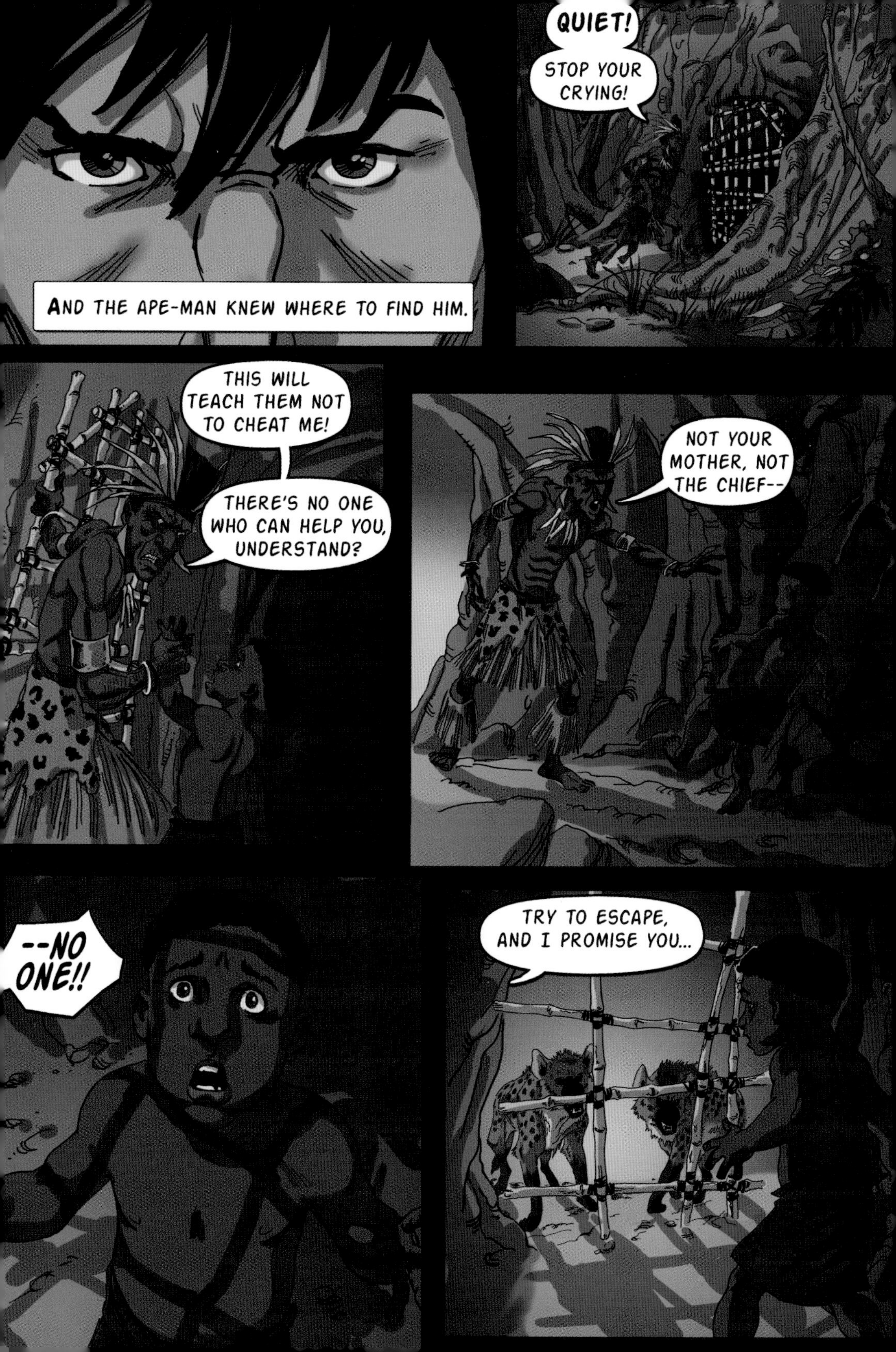
AND THE APE-MAN KNEW WHERE TO FIND HIM.
QUIET!
STOP YOUR CRYING!
THIS WILL TEACH THEM NOT TO CHEAT ME!
THERE'S NO ONE WHO CAN HELP YOU, UNDERSTAND?
NOT YOUR MOTHER, NOT THE CHIEF--
--NO ONE!!
TRY TO ESCAPE, AND I PROMISE YOU...

...THEY WON'T EVEN FIND YOUR BONES!

FRIGHTFUL TALES HAD BEEN WHISPERED OF THE CRUEL TORTURES THE WITCH DOCTOR INFLICTED UPON HIS VICTIMS...

...AND LITTLE TIBO HAD HEARD THE EVIL STORIES WITHOUT EVER FULLY BELIEVING.

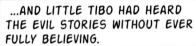

HE BELIEVED THEM NOW.

TARZAN ALSO KNEW, ONLY TOO WELL, THAT THE TERROR TALES WERE TRUE...

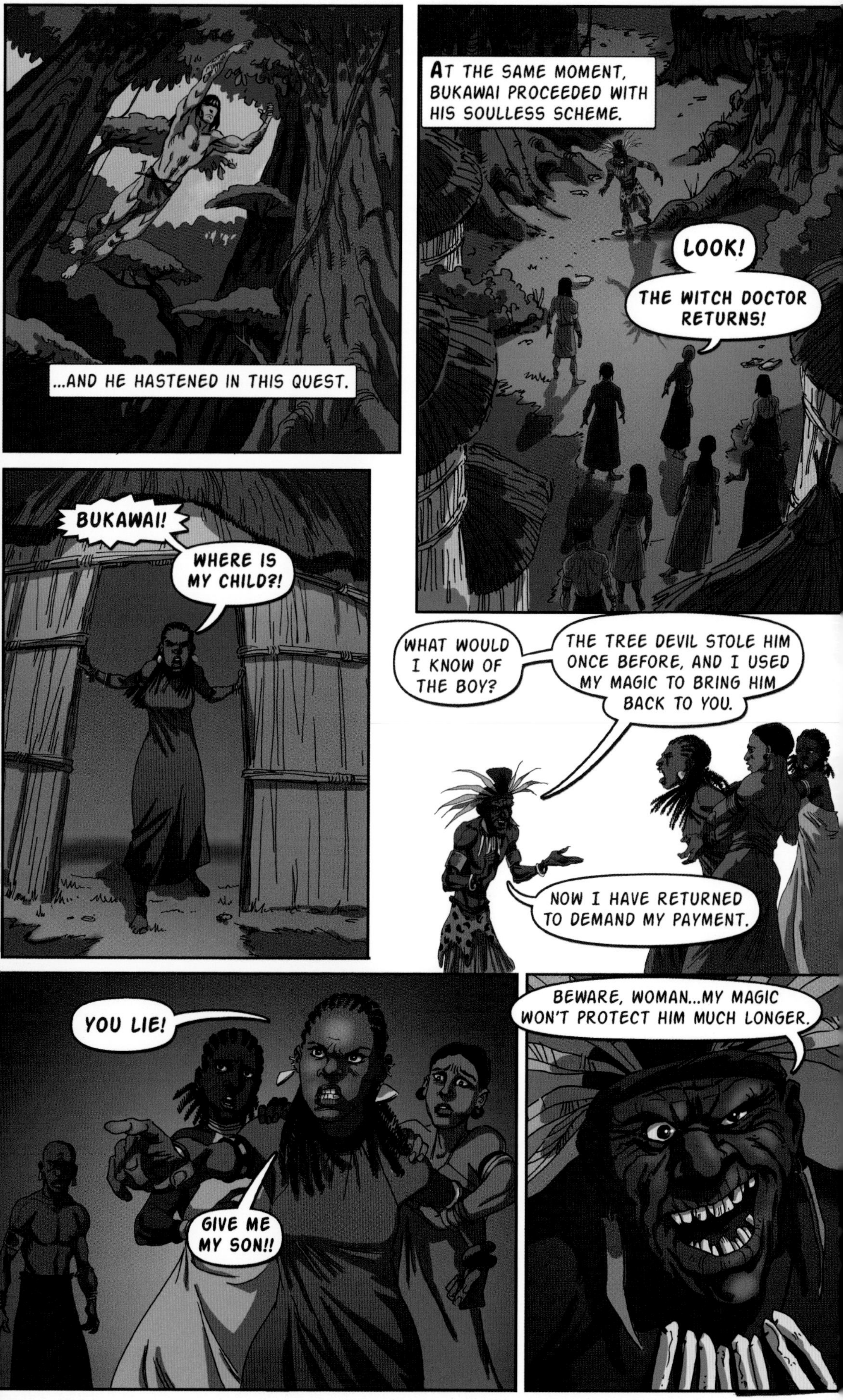
...AND HE HASTENED IN THIS QUEST.
AT THE SAME MOMENT, BUKAWAI PROCEEDED WITH HIS SOULLESS SCHEME.
LOOK!
THE WITCH DOCTOR RETURNS!
BUKAWAI!
WHERE IS MY CHILD?!
WHAT WOULD I KNOW OF THE BOY?
THE TREE DEVIL STOLE HIM ONCE BEFORE, AND I USED MY MAGIC TO BRING HIM BACK TO YOU.
NOW I HAVE RETURNED TO DEMAND MY PAYMENT.
YOU LIE!
GIVE ME MY SON!!
BEWARE, WOMAN...MY MAGIC WON'T PROTECT HIM MUCH LONGER.

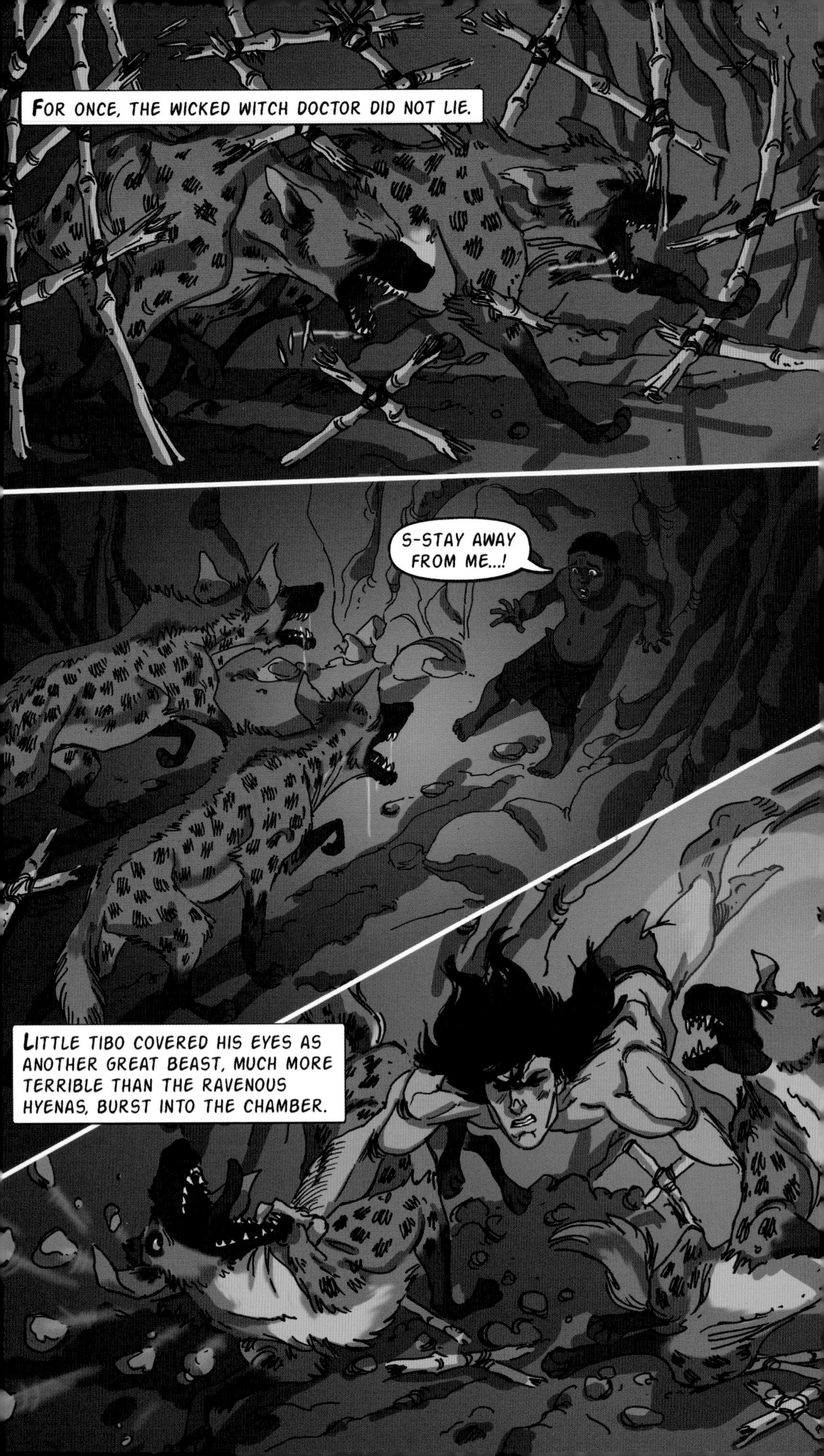
FOR ONCE, THE WICKED WITCH DOCTOR DID NOT LIE.
S-STAY AWAY FROM ME...!
LITTLE TIBO COVERED HIS EYES AS ANOTHER GREAT BEAST, MUCH MORE TERRIBLE THAN THE RAVENOUS HYENAS, BURST INTO THE CHAMBER.

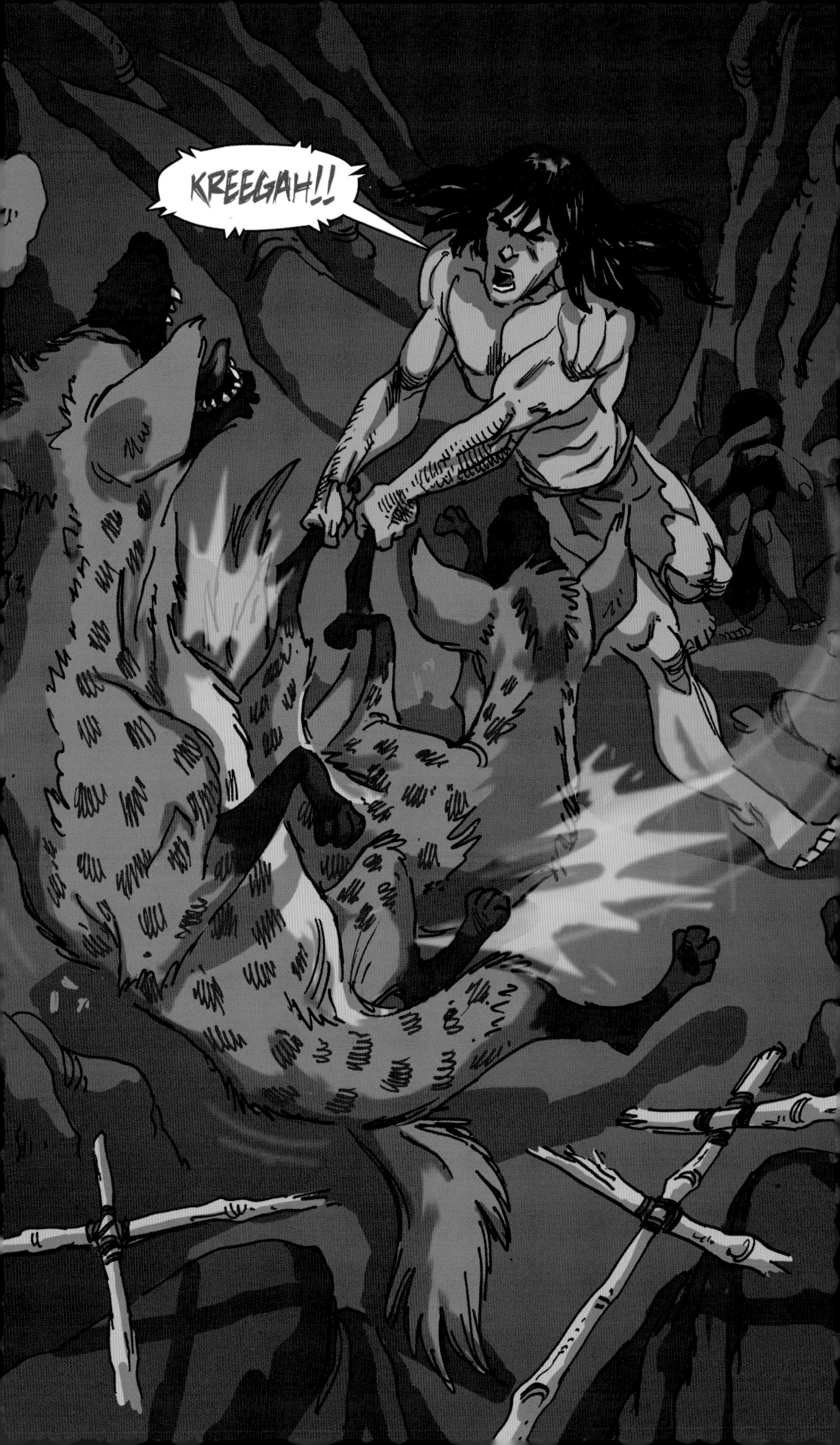
KREEGAH!!

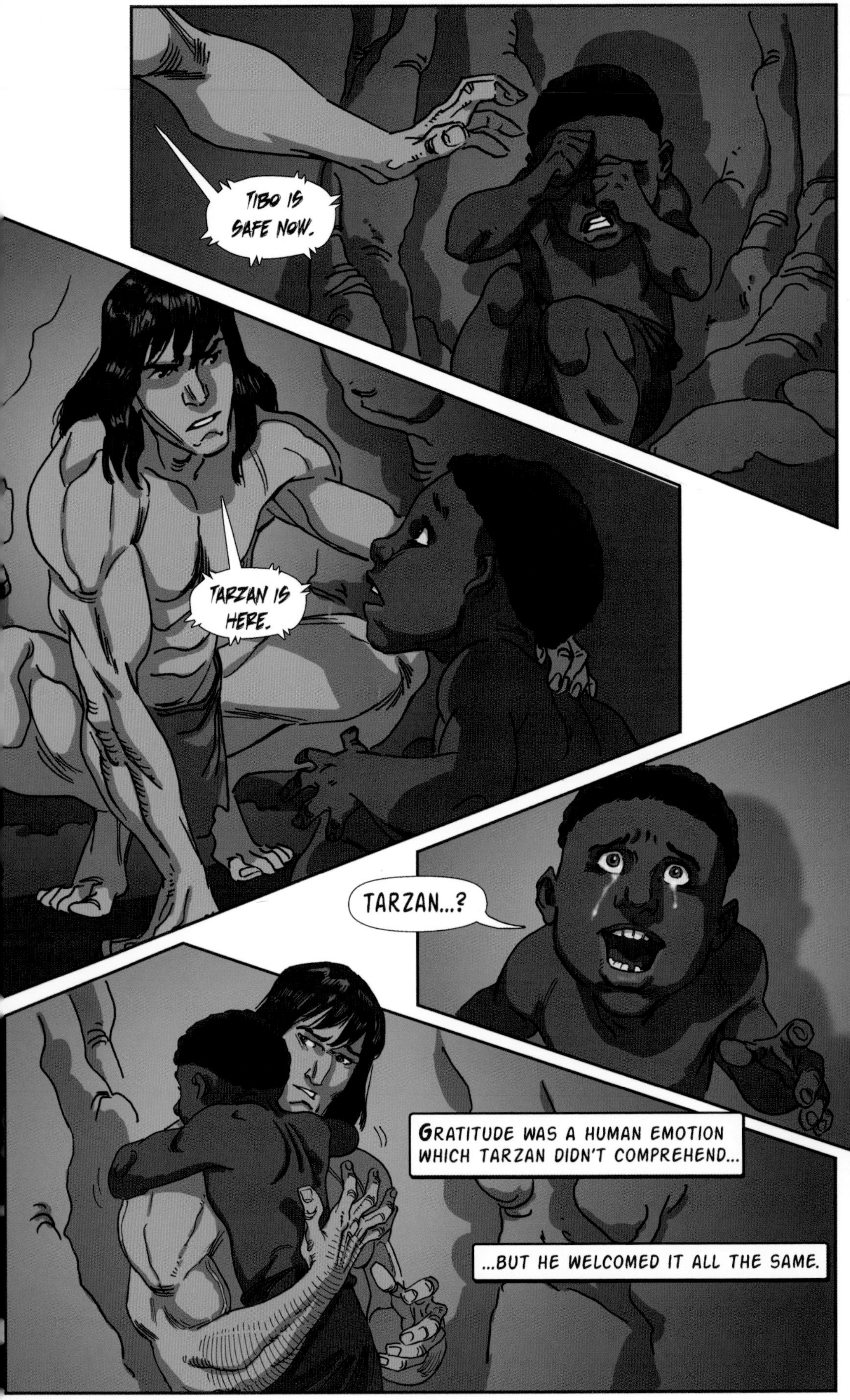
TIBO IS SAFE NOW.
TARZAN IS HERE.
TARZAN...?
GRATITUDE WAS A HUMAN EMOTION WHICH TARZAN DIDN'T COMPREHEND...
...BUT HE WELCOMED IT ALL THE SAME.

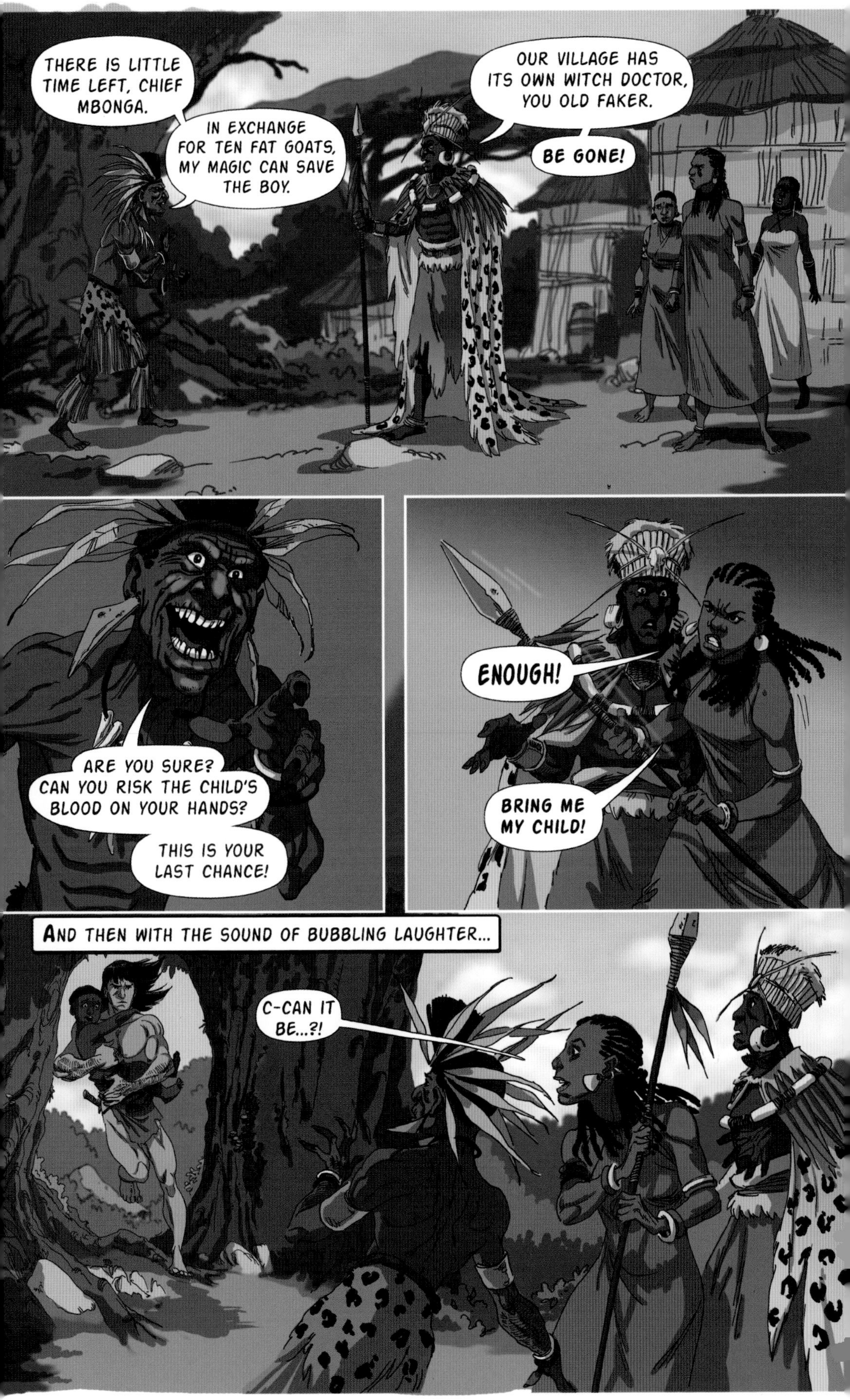
THERE IS LITTLE TIME LEFT, CHIEF MBONGA.
IN EXCHANGE FOR TEN FAT GOATS, MY MAGIC CAN SAVE THE BOY.
OUR VILLAGE HAS ITS OWN WITCH DOCTOR, YOU OLD FAKER.
BE GONE!
ARE YOU SURE? CAN YOU RISK THE CHILD'S BLOOD ON YOUR HANDS?
THIS IS YOUR LAST CHANCE!
ENOUGH!
BRING ME MY CHILD!
AND THEN WITH THE SOUND OF BUBBLING LAUGHTER...
C-CAN IT BE...?!

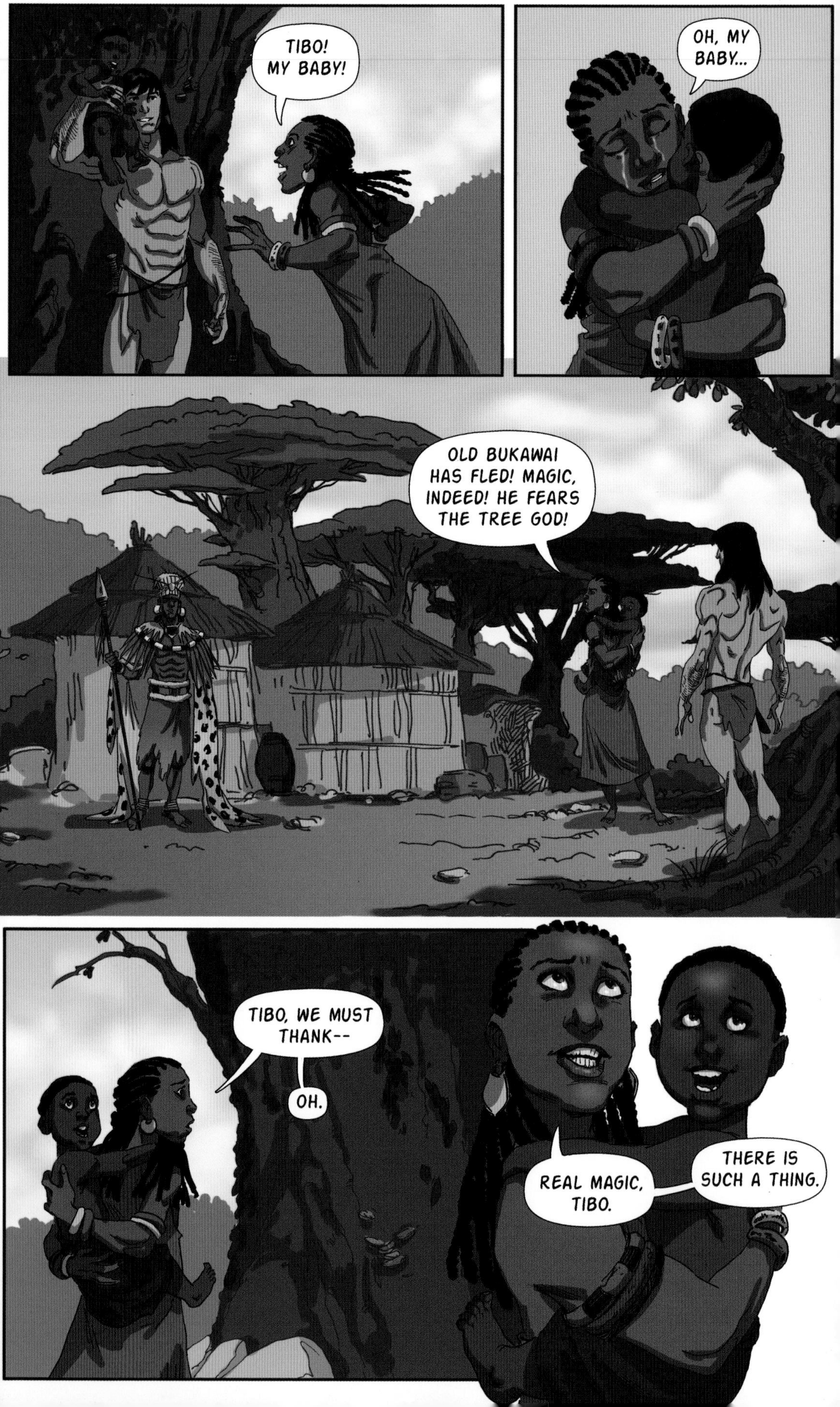
TIBO! MY BABY!
OH, MY BABY...
OLD BUKAWAI HAS FLED! MAGIC, INDEED! HE FEARS THE TREE GOD!
TIBO, WE MUST THANK--
OH.
REAL MAGIC, TIBO.
THERE IS SUCH A THING.

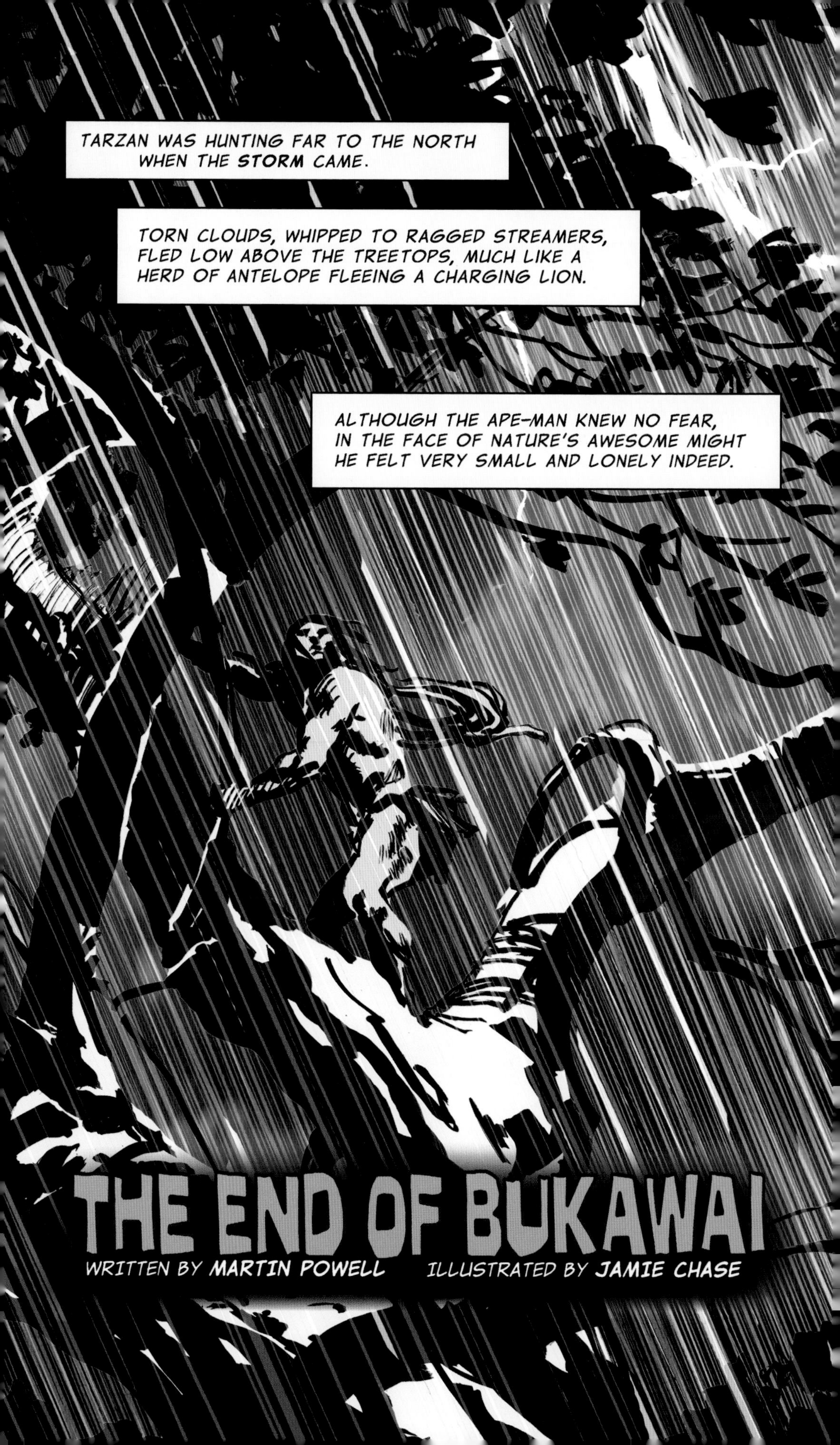
TARZAN WAS HUNTING FAR TO THE NORTH WHEN THE STORM CAME.
TORN CLOUDS, WHIPPED TO RAGGED STREAMERS, FLED LOW ABOVE THE TREETOPS, MUCH LIKE A HERD OF ANTELOPE FLEEING A CHARGING LION.
ALTHOUGH THE APE-MAN KNEW NO FEAR, IN THE FACE OF NATURE'S AWESOME MIGHT HE FELT VERY SMALL AND LONELY INDEED.
THE END OF BUKAWAI
WRITTEN BY MARTIN POWELL ILLUSTRATED BY JAMIE CHASE

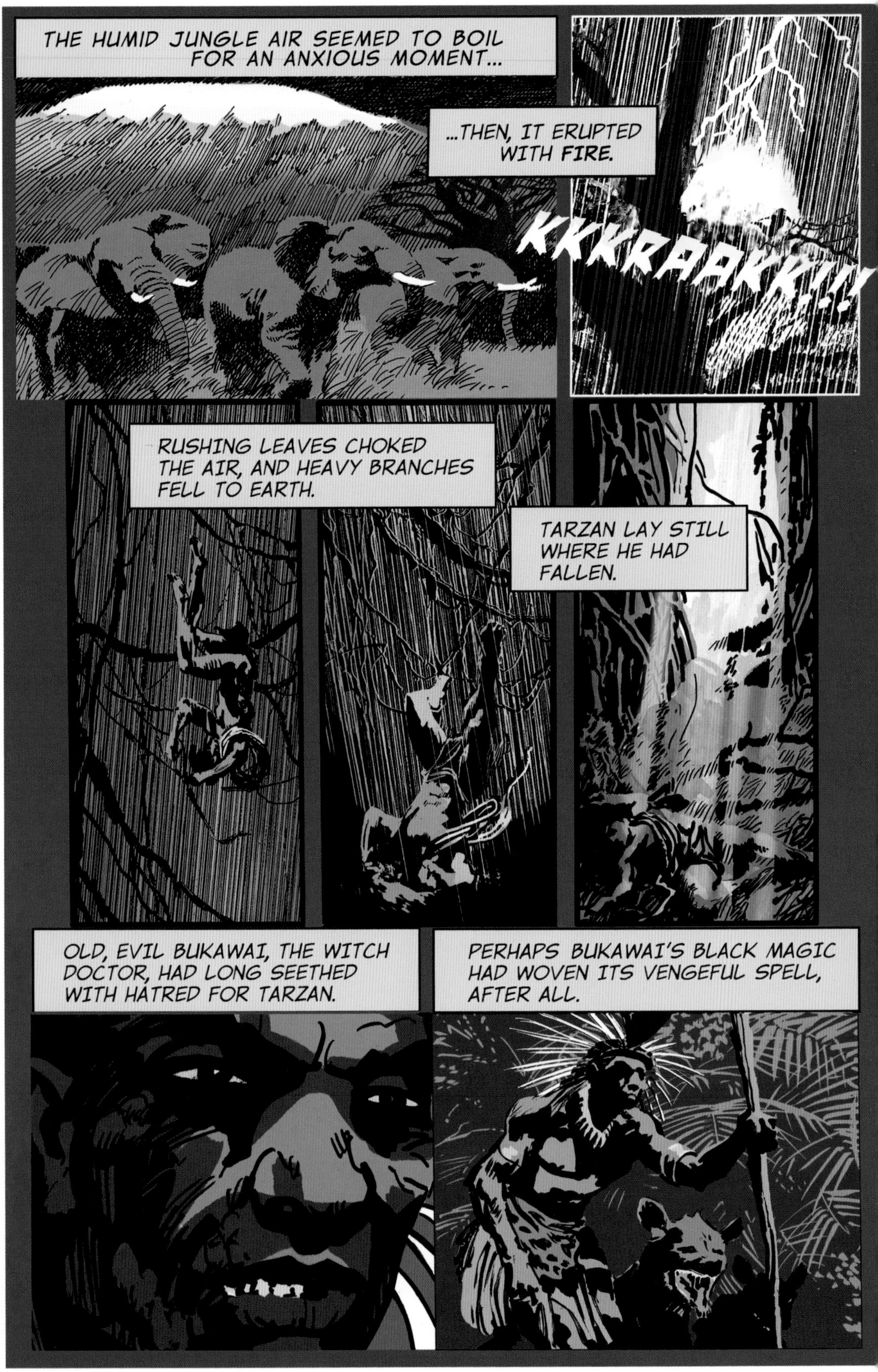
THE HUMID JUNGLE AIR SEEMED TO BOIL FOR AN ANXIOUS MOMENT...
...THEN, IT ERUPTED WITH FIRE.
KKKRAAKK!!!
RUSHING LEAVES CHOKED THE AIR, AND HEAVY BRANCHES FELL TO EARTH.
TARZAN LAY STILL WHERE HE HAD FALLEN.
OLD, EVIL BUKAWAI, THE WITCH DOCTOR, HAD LONG SEETHED WITH HATRED FOR TARZAN.
PERHAPS BUKAWAI'S BLACK MAGIC HAD WOVEN ITS VENGEFUL SPELL, AFTER ALL.

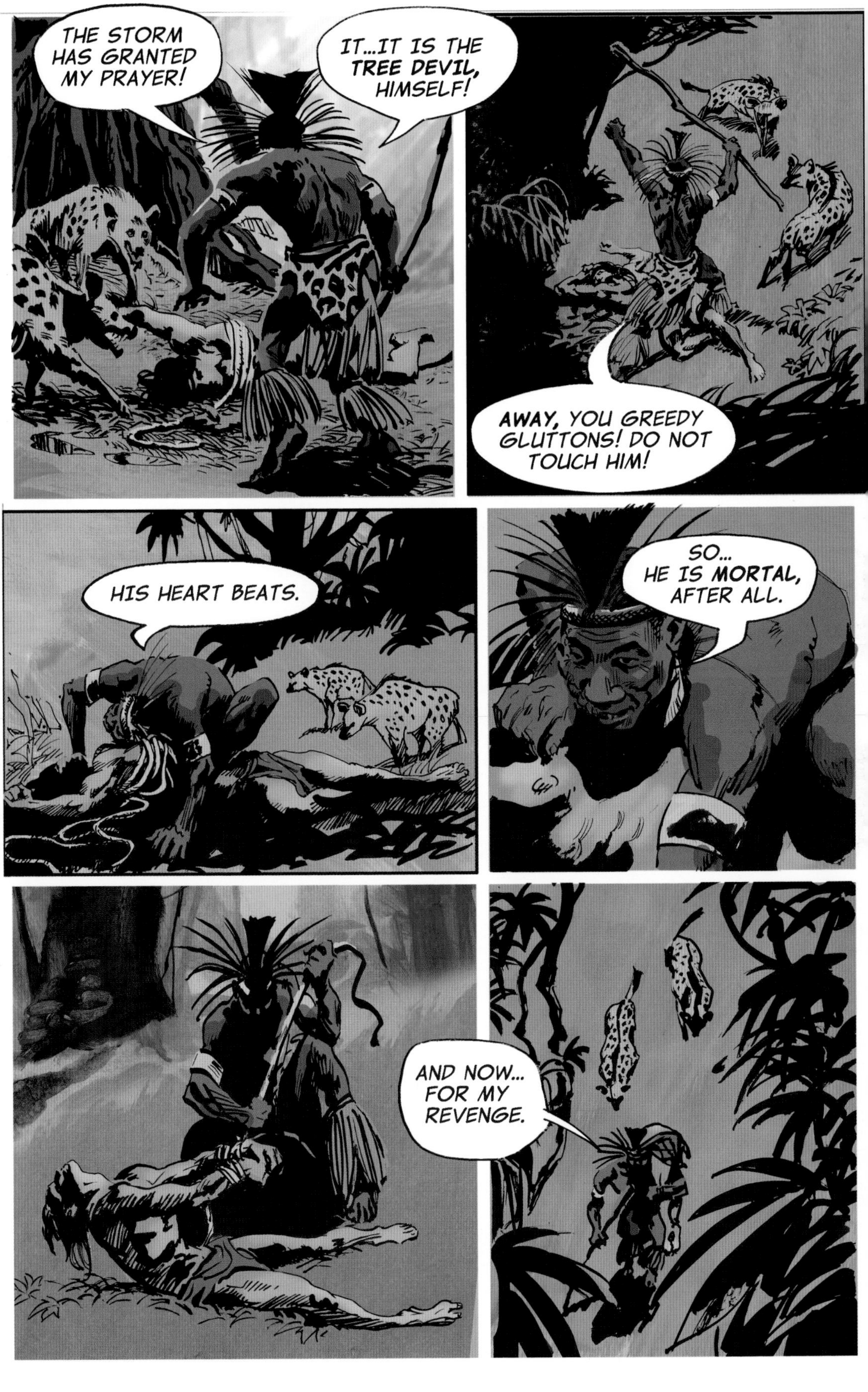
THE STORM HAS GRANTED MY PRAYER!
IT...IT IS THE TREE DEVIL, HIMSELF!
AWAY, YOU GREEDY GLUTTONS! DO NOT TOUCH HIM!
HIS HEART BEATS.
SO... HE IS MORTAL, AFTER ALL.
AND NOW... FOR MY REVENGE.

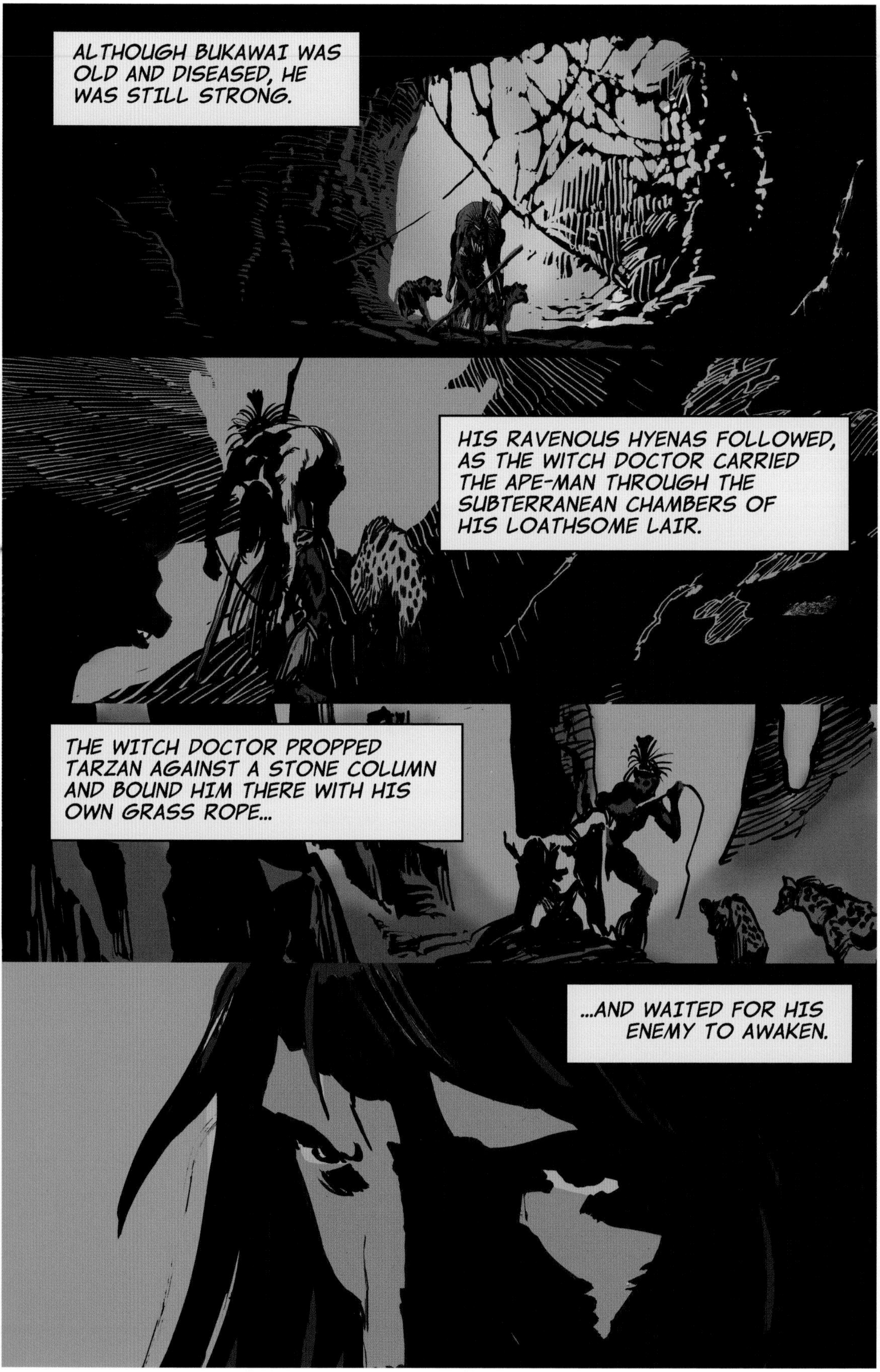
ALTHOUGH BUKAWAI WAS OLD AND DISEASED, HE WAS STILL STRONG.
HIS RAVENOUS HYENAS FOLLOWED, AS THE WITCH DOCTOR CARRIED THE APE-MAN THROUGH THE SUBTERRANEAN CHAMBERS OF HIS LOATHSOME LAIR.
THE WITCH DOCTOR PROPPED TARZAN AGAINST A STONE COLUMN AND BOUND HIM THERE WITH HIS OWN GRASS ROPE...
...AND WAITED FOR HIS ENEMY TO AWAKEN.

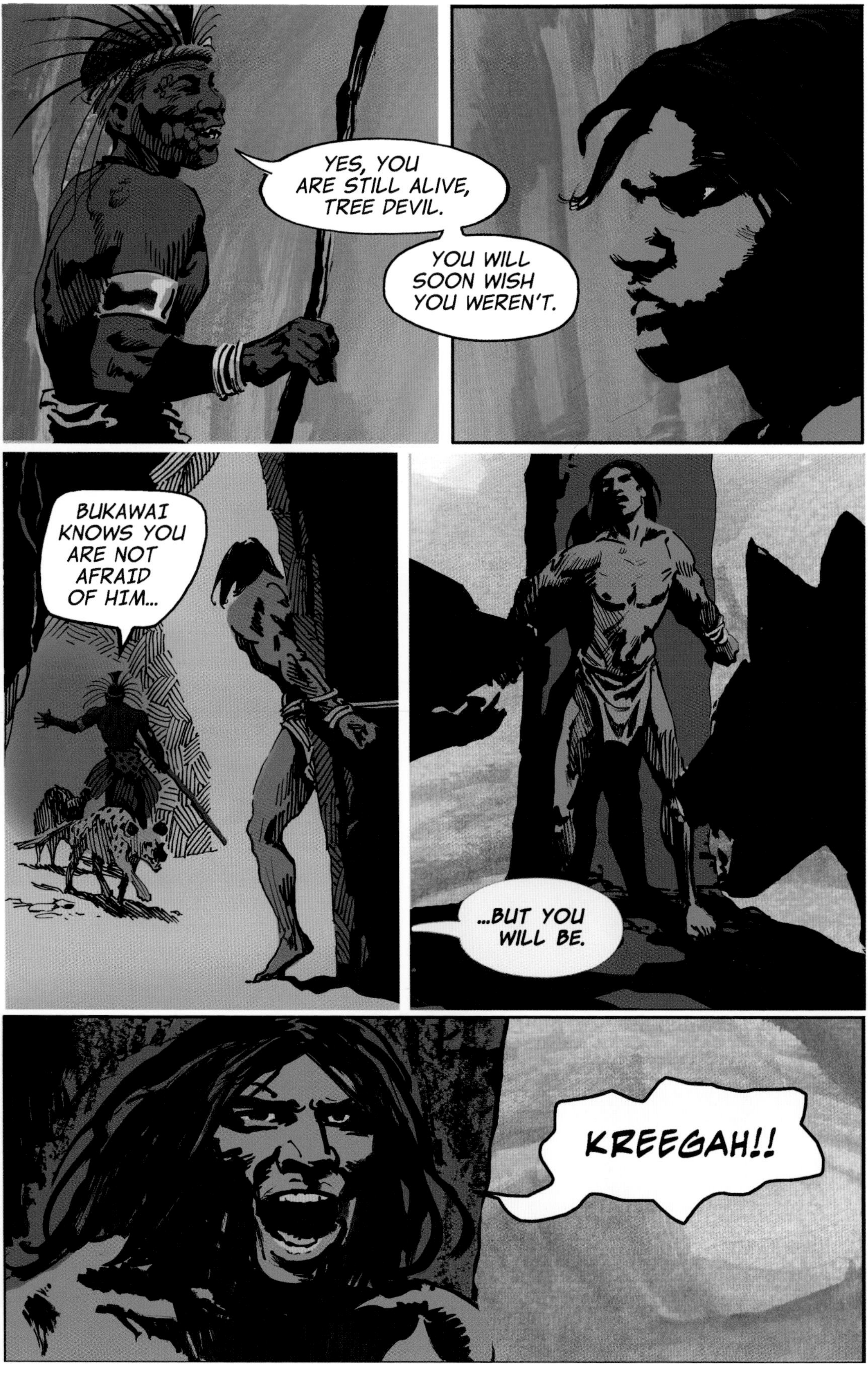
YES, YOU ARE STILL ALIVE, TREE DEVIL.
YOU WILL SOON WISH YOU WEREN'T.
BUKAWAI KNOWS YOU ARE NOT AFRAID OF HIM...
...BUT YOU WILL BE.
KREEGAH!!

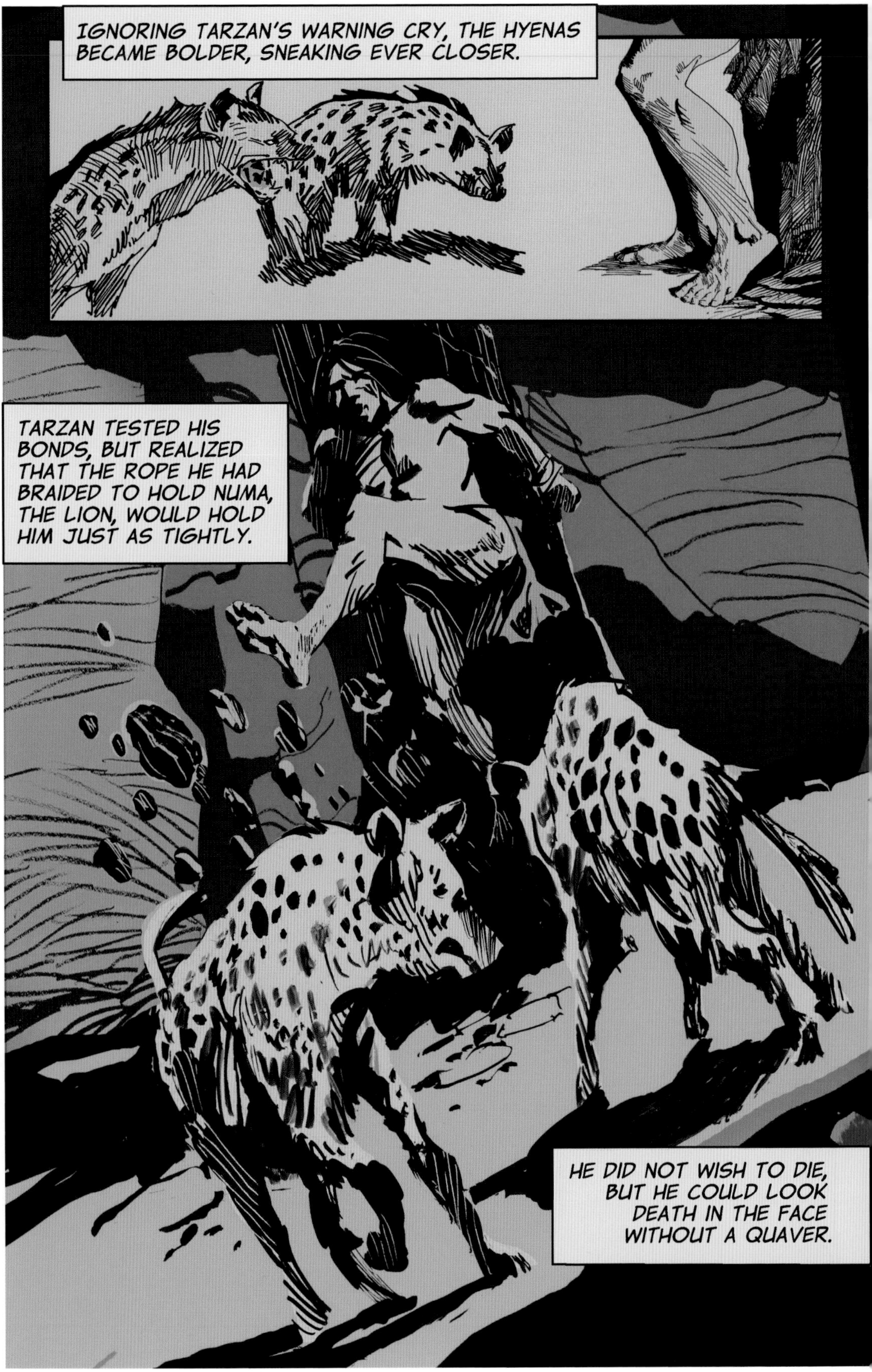
IGNORING TARZAN'S WARNING CRY, THE HYENAS BECAME BOLDER, SNEAKING EVER CLOSER.
TARZAN TESTED HIS BONDS, BUT REALIZED THAT THE ROPE HE HAD BRAIDED TO HOLD NUMA, THE LION, WOULD HOLD HIM JUST AS TIGHTLY.
HE DID NOT WISH TO DIE, BUT HE COULD LOOK DEATH IN THE FACE WITHOUT A QUAVER.

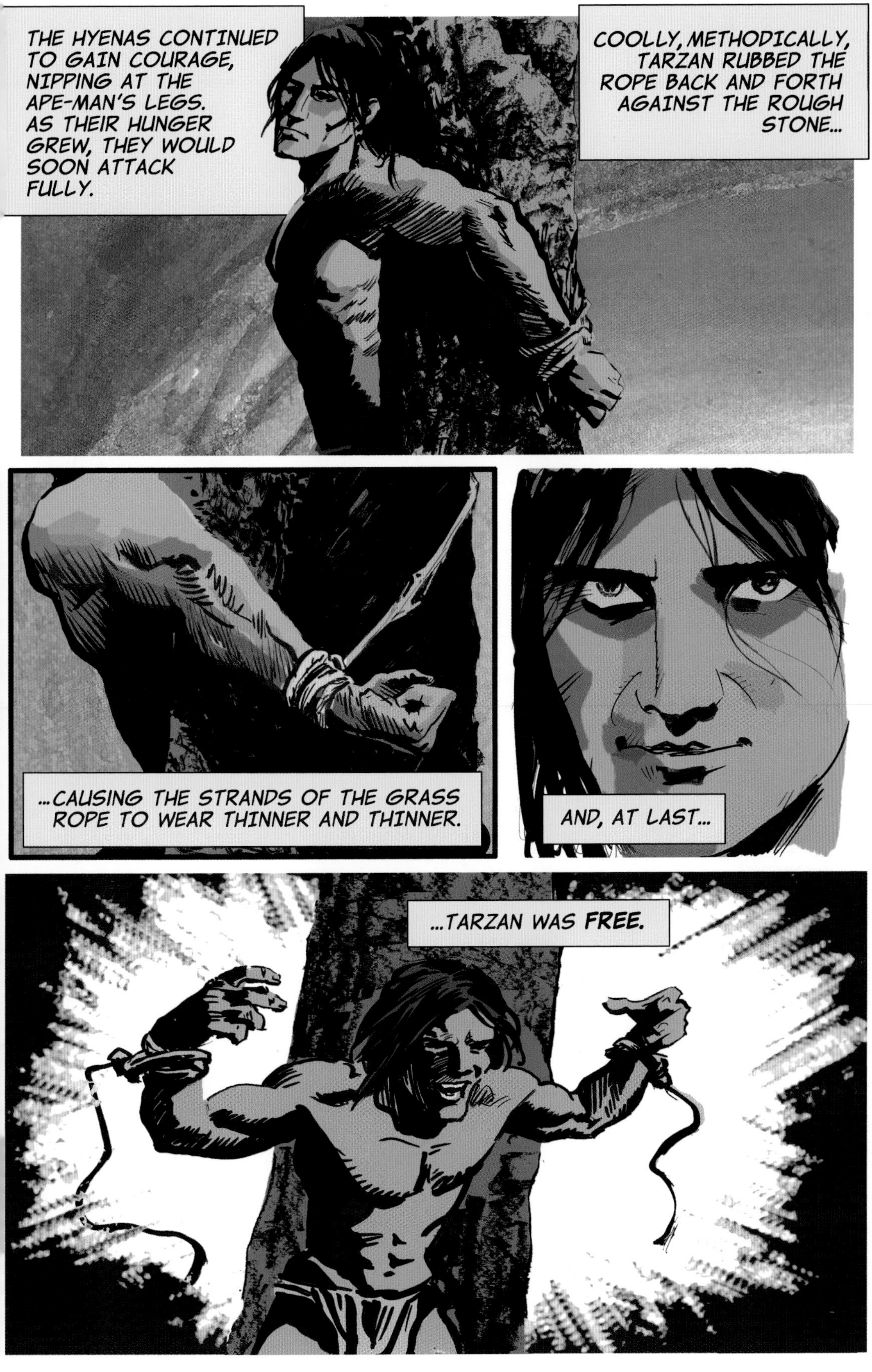
THE HYENAS CONTINUED TO GAIN COURAGE, NIPPING AT THE APE-MAN'S LEGS. AS THEIR HUNGER GREW, THEY WOULD SOON ATTACK FULLY.
COOLLY, METHODICALLY, TARZAN RUBBED THE ROPE BACK AND FORTH AGAINST THE ROUGH STONE...
...CAUSING THE STRANDS OF THE GRASS ROPE TO WEAR THINNER AND THINNER.
AND, AT LAST...
...TARZAN WAS **FREE.**

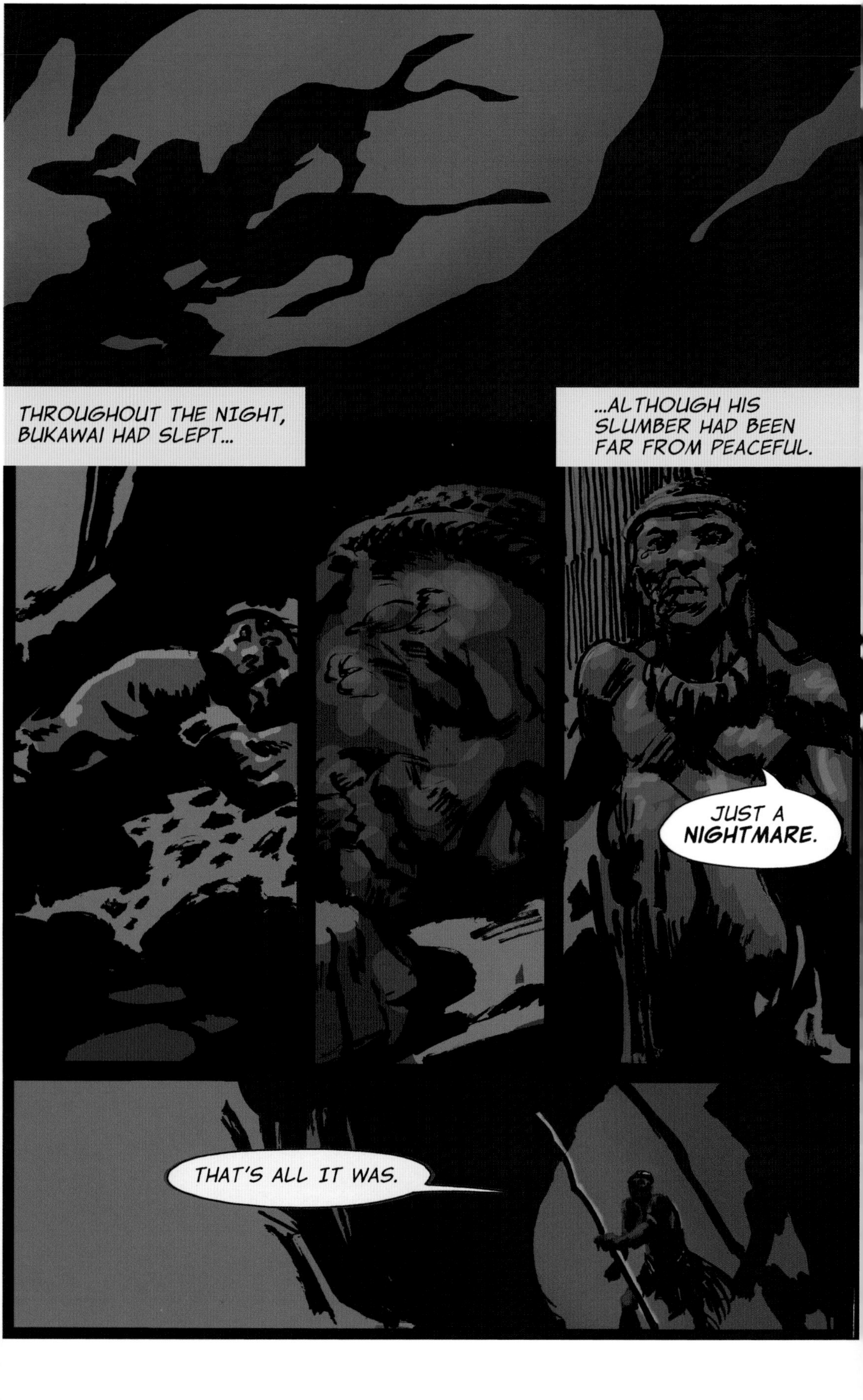
THROUGHOUT THE NIGHT, BUKAWAI HAD SLEPT...
...ALTHOUGH HIS SLUMBER HAD BEEN FAR FROM PEACEFUL.
JUST A NIGHTMARE.
THAT'S ALL IT WAS.

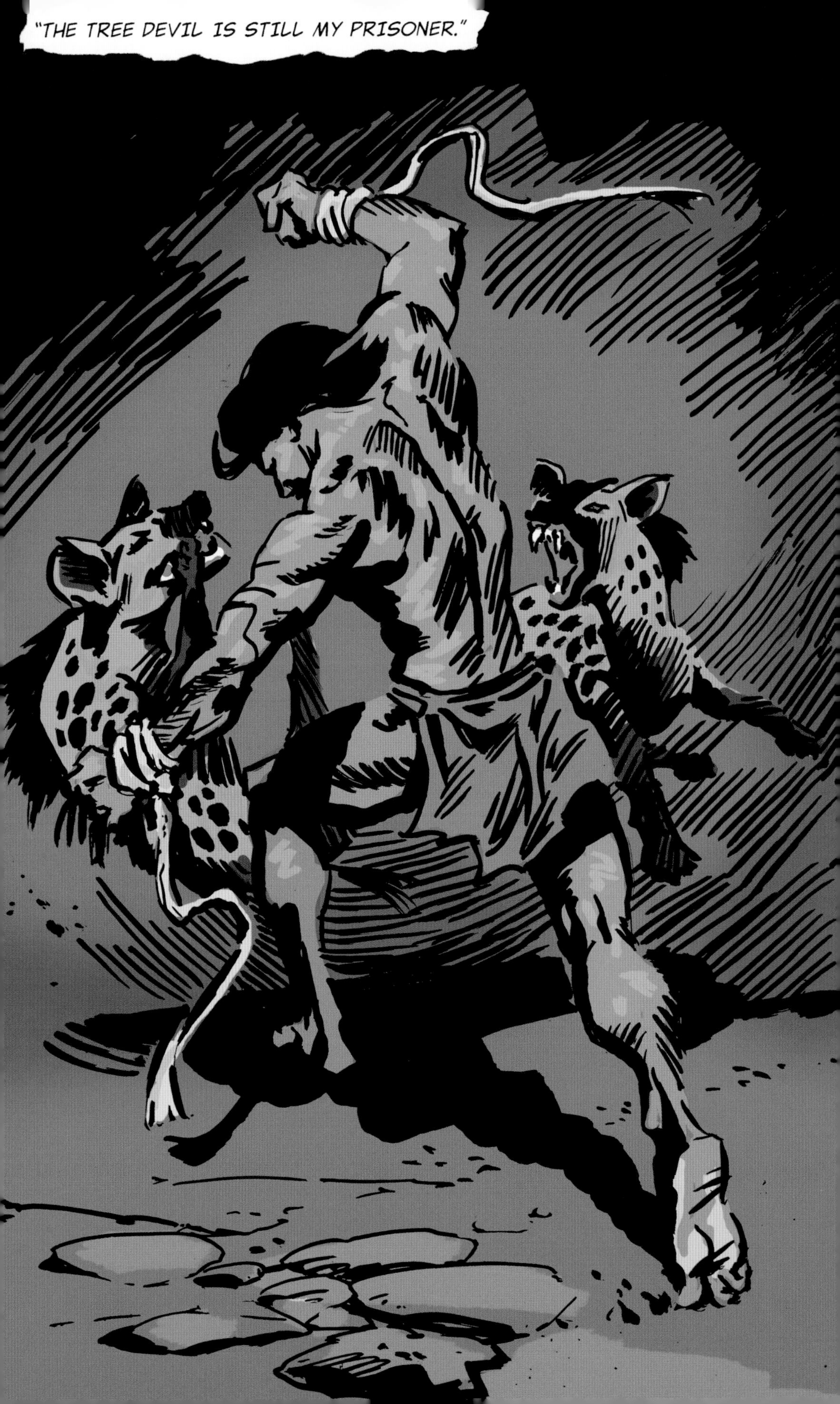
"THE TREE DEVIL IS STILL MY PRISONER."

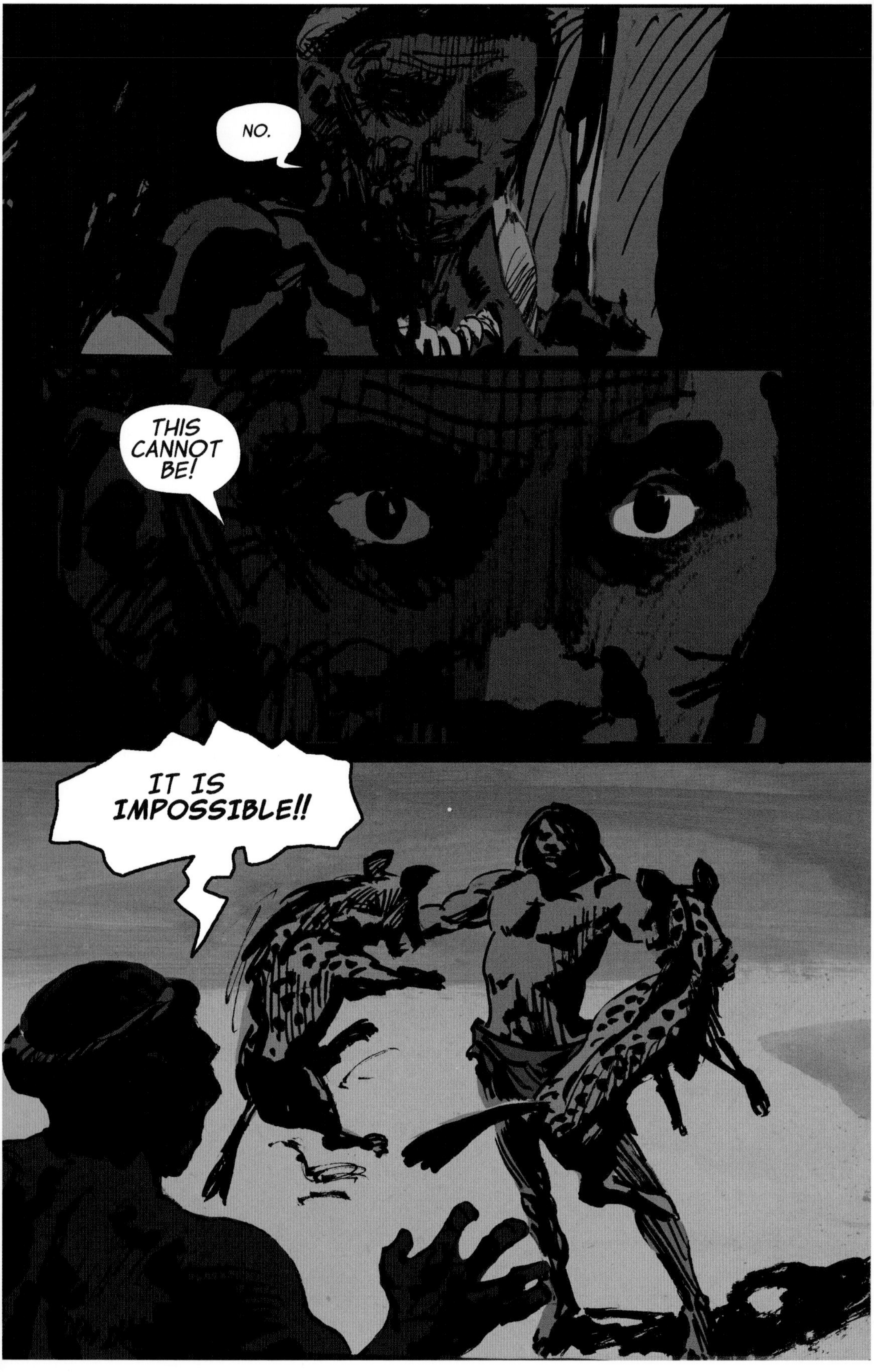
NO.
THIS CANNOT BE!
IT IS IMPOSSIBLE!!

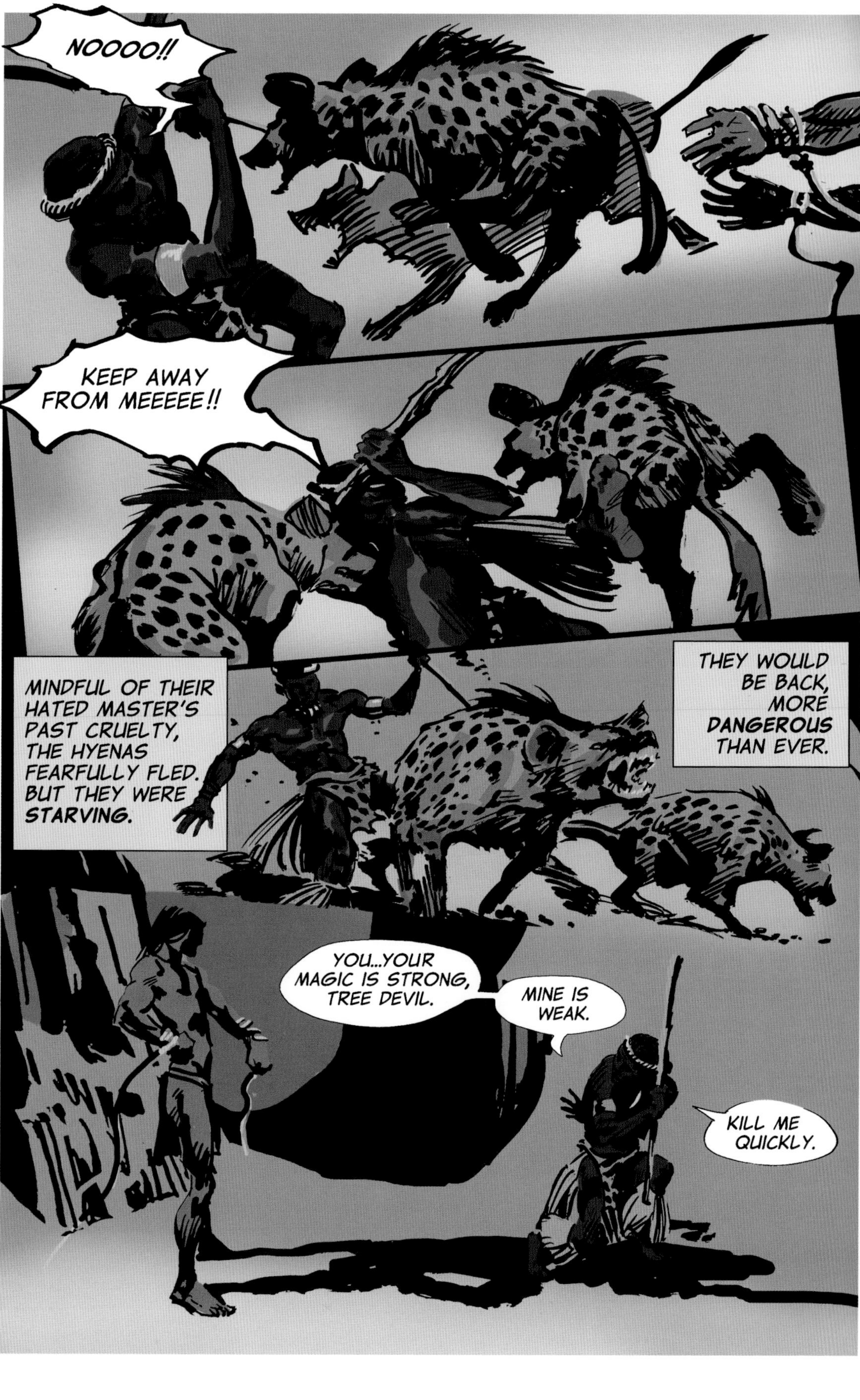
NOOOO!!
KEEP AWAY FROM MEEEEE!!
MINDFUL OF THEIR HATED MASTER'S PAST CRUELTY, THE HYENAS FEARFULLY FLED. BUT THEY WERE STARVING.
THEY WOULD BE BACK, MORE DANGEROUS THAN EVER.
YOU...YOUR MAGIC IS STRONG, TREE DEVIL.
MINE IS WEAK.
KILL ME QUICKLY.

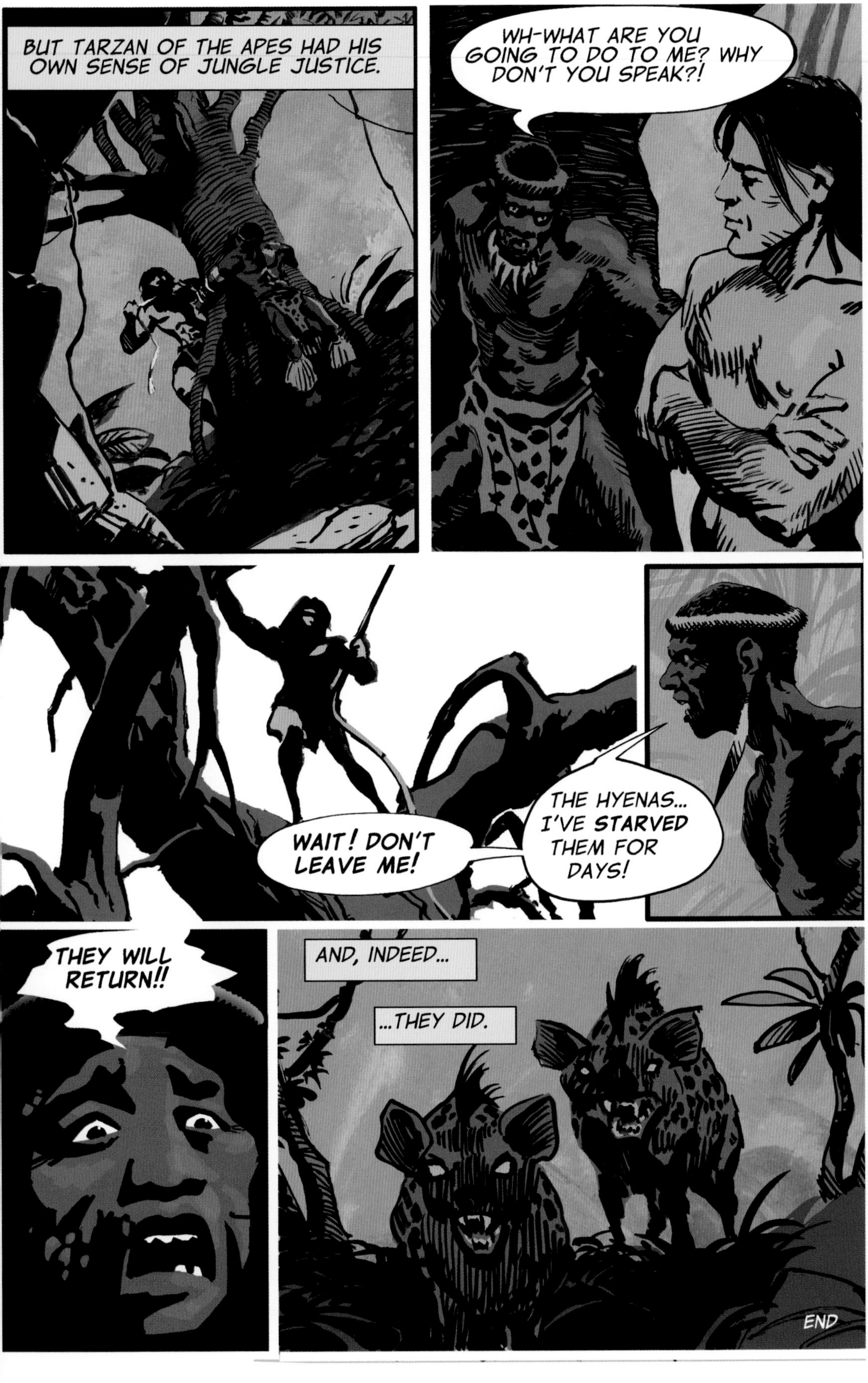

BUT TARZAN OF THE APES HAD HIS OWN SENSE OF JUNGLE JUSTICE.
WH-WHAT ARE YOU GOING TO DO TO ME? WHY DON'T YOU SPEAK?!
WAIT! DON'T LEAVE ME!
THE HYENAS... I'VE STARVED THEM FOR DAYS!
THEY WILL RETURN!!
AND, INDEED...
...THEY DID.
END

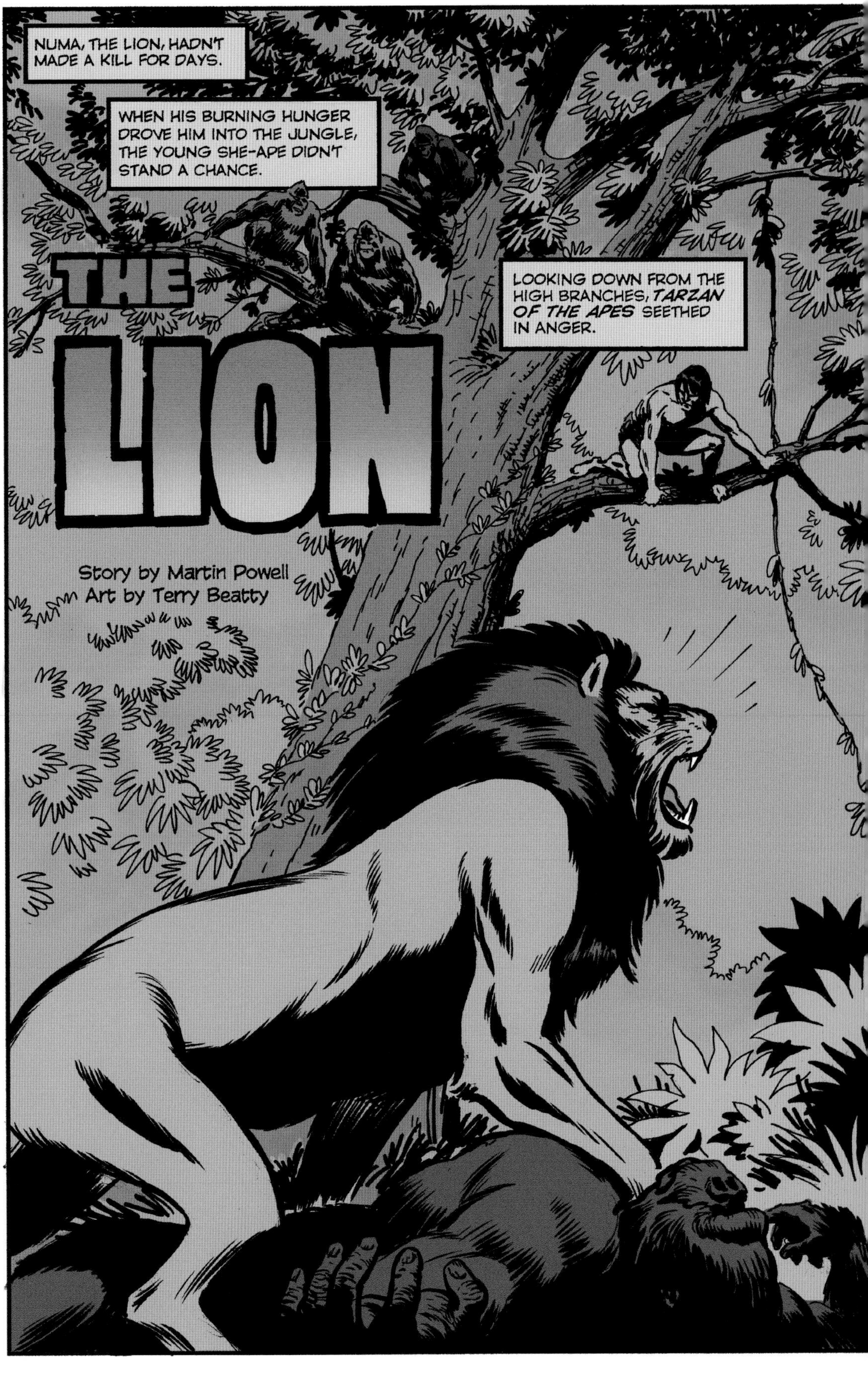
NUMA, THE LION, HADN'T MADE A KILL FOR DAYS.
WHEN HIS BURNING HUNGER DROVE HIM INTO THE JUNGLE, THE YOUNG SHE-APE DIDN'T STAND A CHANCE.
THE LION
LOOKING DOWN FROM THE HIGH BRANCHES, *TARZAN OF THE APES* SEETHED IN ANGER.
Story by Martin Powell
Art by Terry Beatty

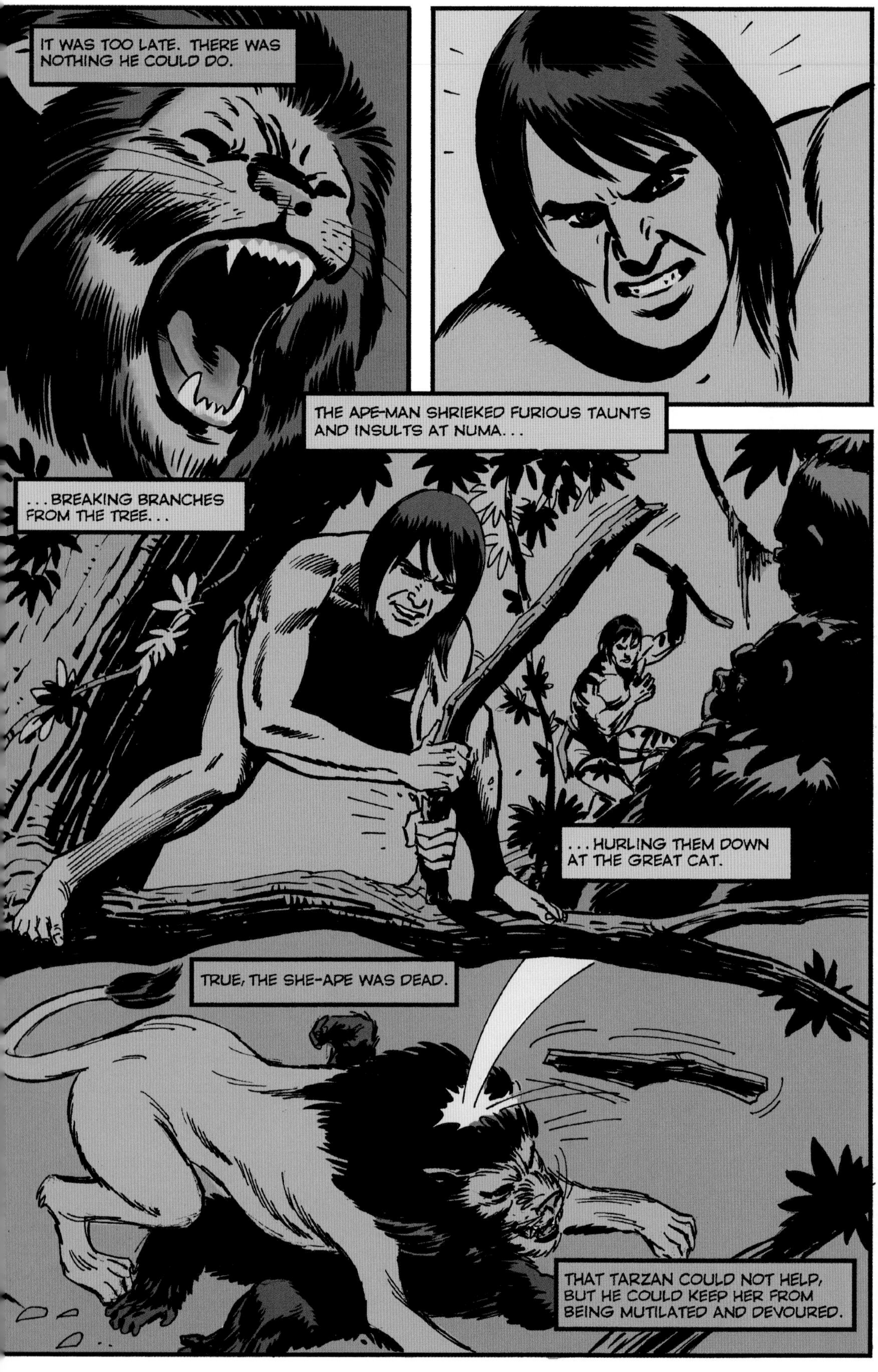
IT WAS TOO LATE. THERE WAS NOTHING HE COULD DO.
THE APE-MAN SHRIEKED FURIOUS TAUNTS AND INSULTS AT NUMA...
...BREAKING BRANCHES FROM THE TREE...
...HURLING THEM DOWN AT THE GREAT CAT.
TRUE, THE SHE-APE WAS DEAD.
THAT TARZAN COULD NOT HELP, BUT HE COULD KEEP HER FROM BEING MUTILATED AND DEVOURED.

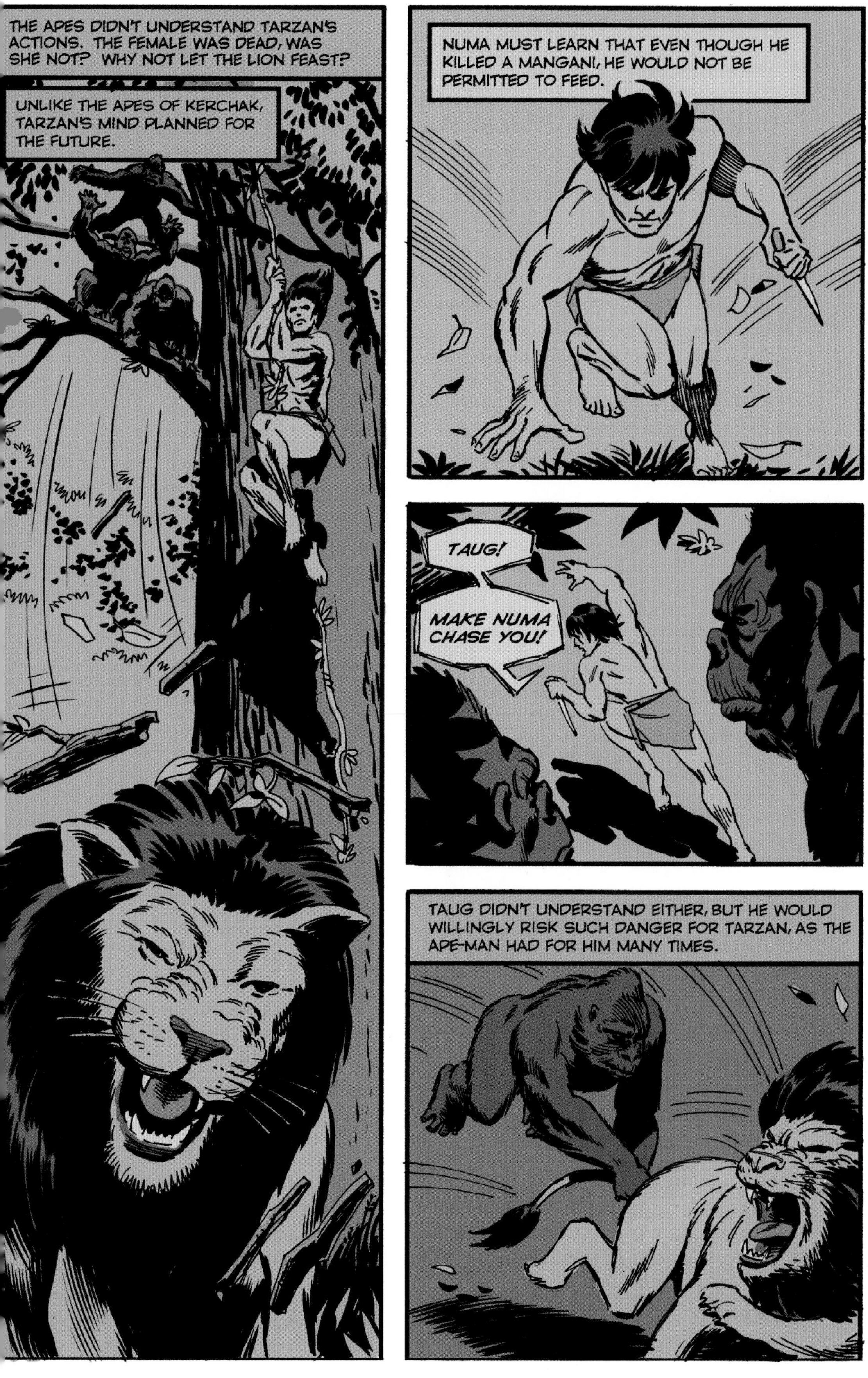
THE APES DIDN'T UNDERSTAND TARZAN'S ACTIONS. THE FEMALE WAS DEAD, WAS SHE NOT? WHY NOT LET THE LION FEAST?
UNLIKE THE APES OF KERCHAK, TARZAN'S MIND PLANNED FOR THE FUTURE.
NUMA MUST LEARN THAT EVEN THOUGH HE KILLED A MANGANI, HE WOULD NOT BE PERMITTED TO FEED.
TAUG!
MAKE NUMA CHASE YOU!
TAUG DIDN'T UNDERSTAND EITHER, BUT HE WOULD WILLINGLY RISK SUCH DANGER FOR TARZAN, AS THE APE-MAN HAD FOR HIM MANY TIMES.

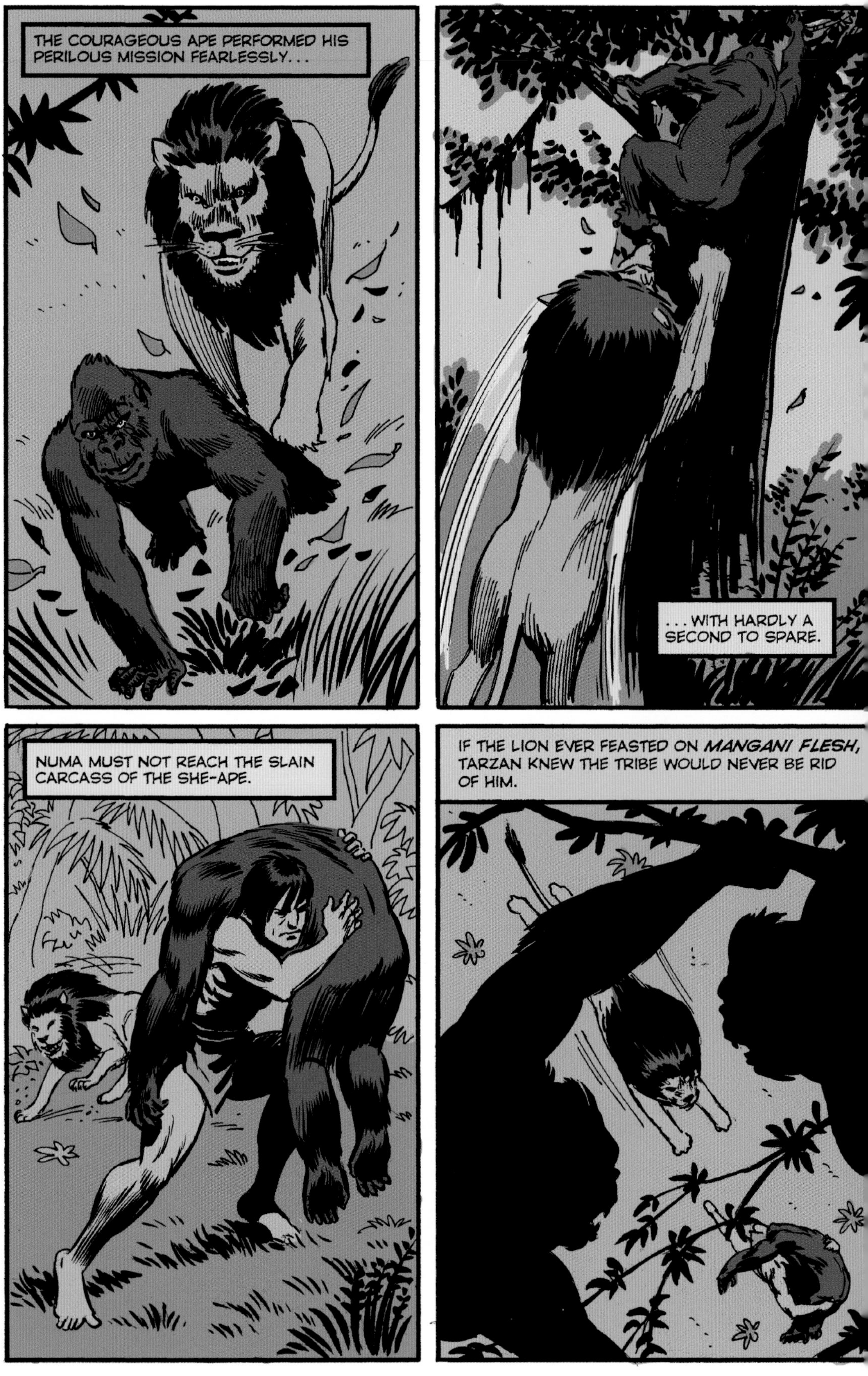
THE COURAGEOUS APE PERFORMED HIS PERILOUS MISSION FEARLESSLY...
...WITH HARDLY A SECOND TO SPARE.
NUMA MUST NOT REACH THE SLAIN CARCASS OF THE SHE-APE.
IF THE LION EVER FEASTED ON *MANGANI FLESH,* TARZAN KNEW THE TRIBE WOULD NEVER BE RID OF HIM.

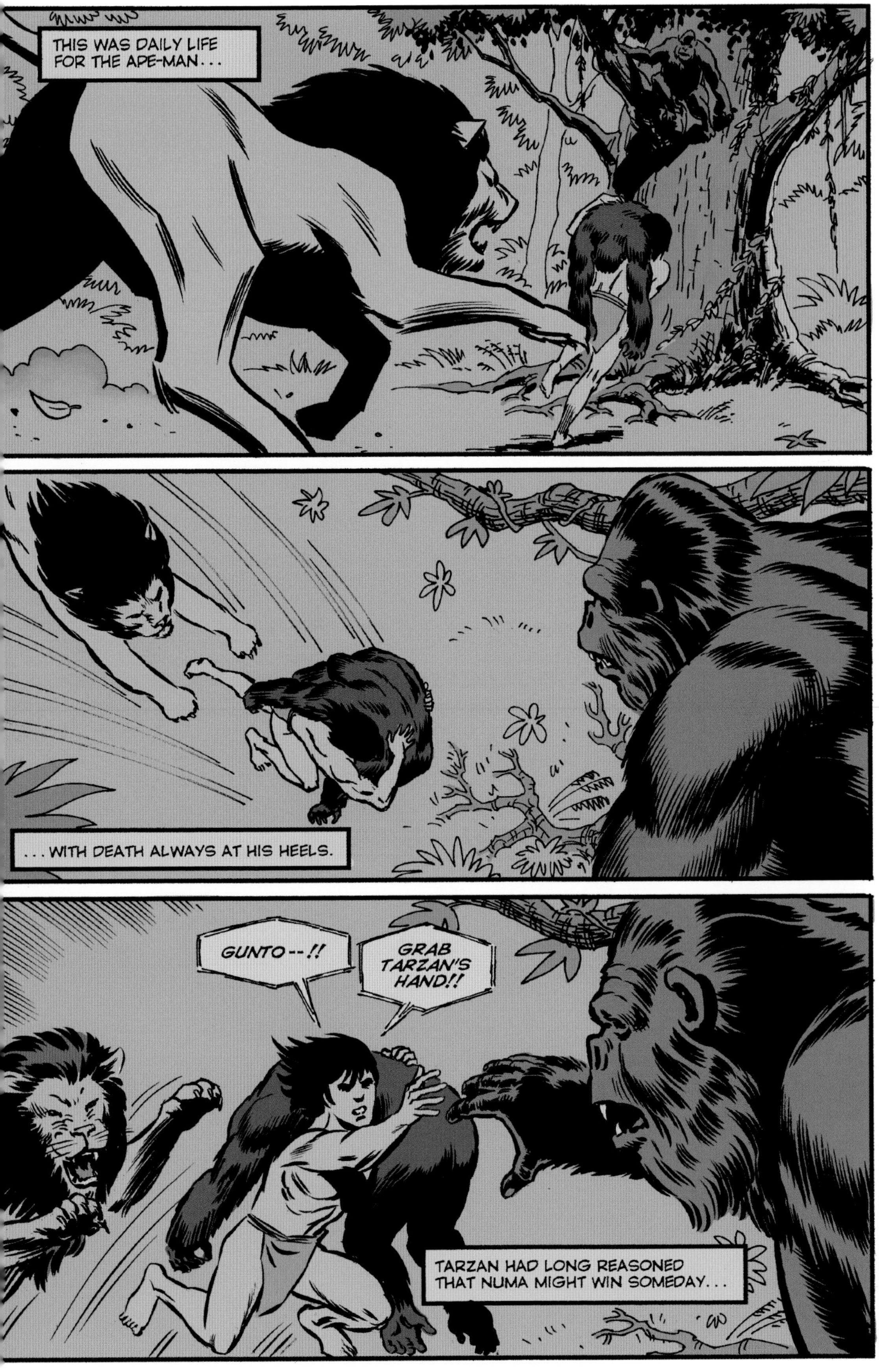
THIS WAS DAILY LIFE FOR THE APE-MAN . . .
. . . WITH DEATH ALWAYS AT HIS HEELS.
GUNTO- -!!
GRAB TARZAN'S HAND!!
TARZAN HAD LONG REASONED THAT NUMA MIGHT WIN SOMEDAY . . .

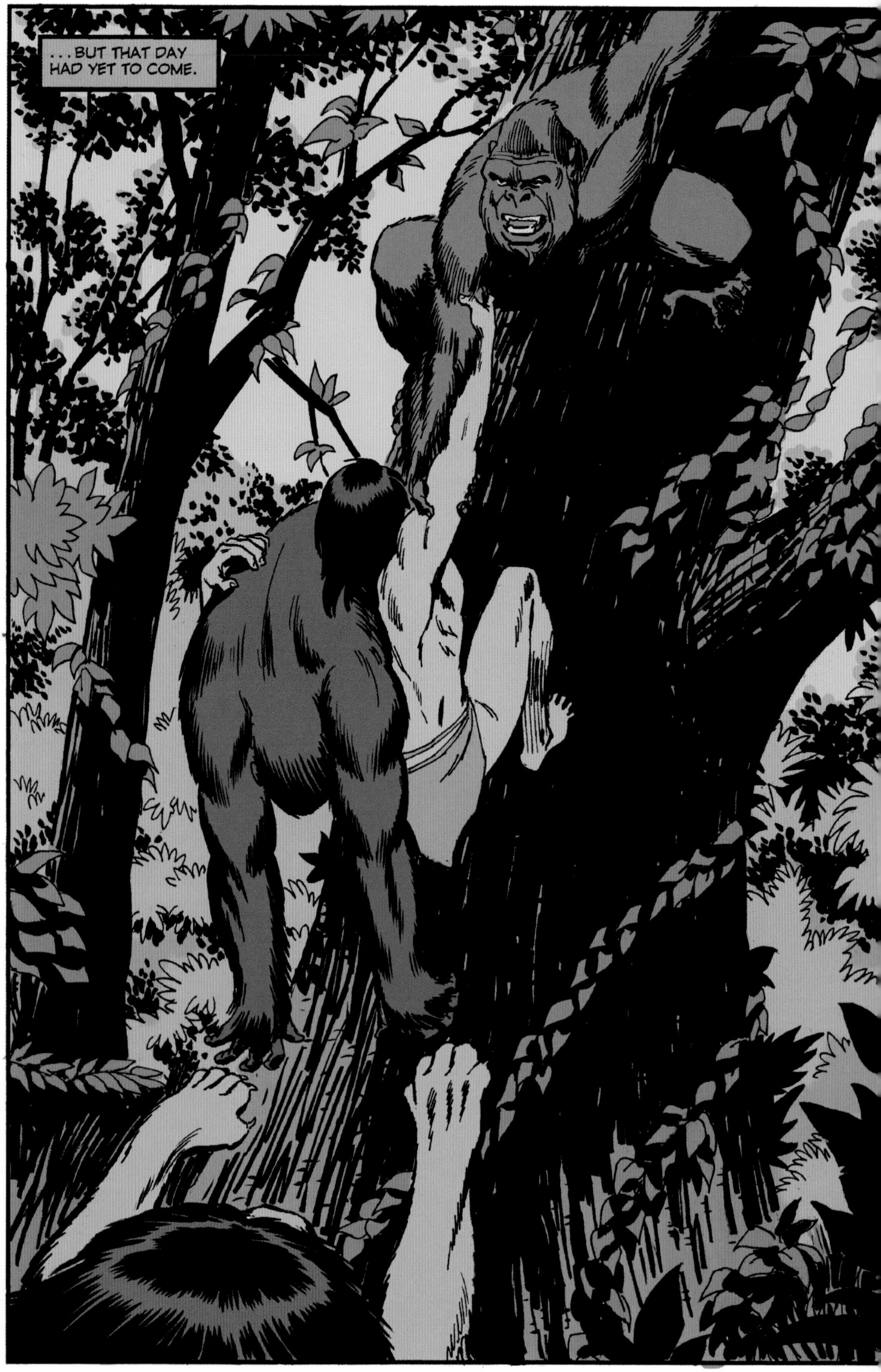
. . . BUT THAT DAY HAD YET TO COME.

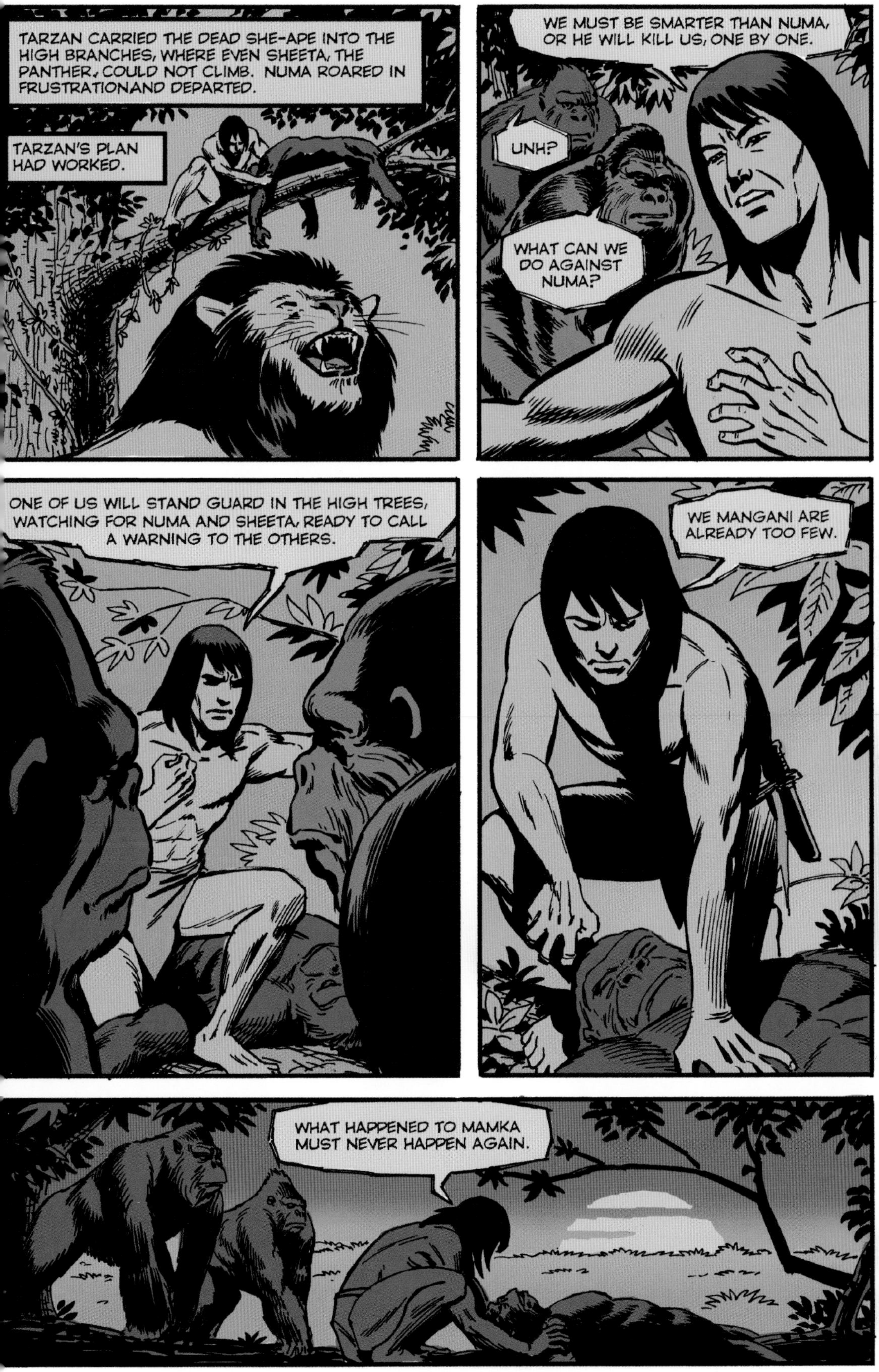
TARZAN CARRIED THE DEAD SHE-APE INTO THE HIGH BRANCHES, WHERE EVEN SHEETA, THE PANTHER, COULD NOT CLIMB. NUMA ROARED IN FRUSTRATIONAND DEPARTED.
TARZAN'S PLAN HAD WORKED.
WE MUST BE SMARTER THAN NUMA, OR HE WILL KILL US, ONE BY ONE.
UNH?
WHAT CAN WE DO AGAINST NUMA?
ONE OF US WILL STAND GUARD IN THE HIGH TREES, WATCHING FOR NUMA AND SHEETA, READY TO CALL A WARNING TO THE OTHERS.
WE MANGANI ARE ALREADY TOO FEW.
WHAT HAPPENED TO MAMKA MUST NEVER HAPPEN AGAIN.

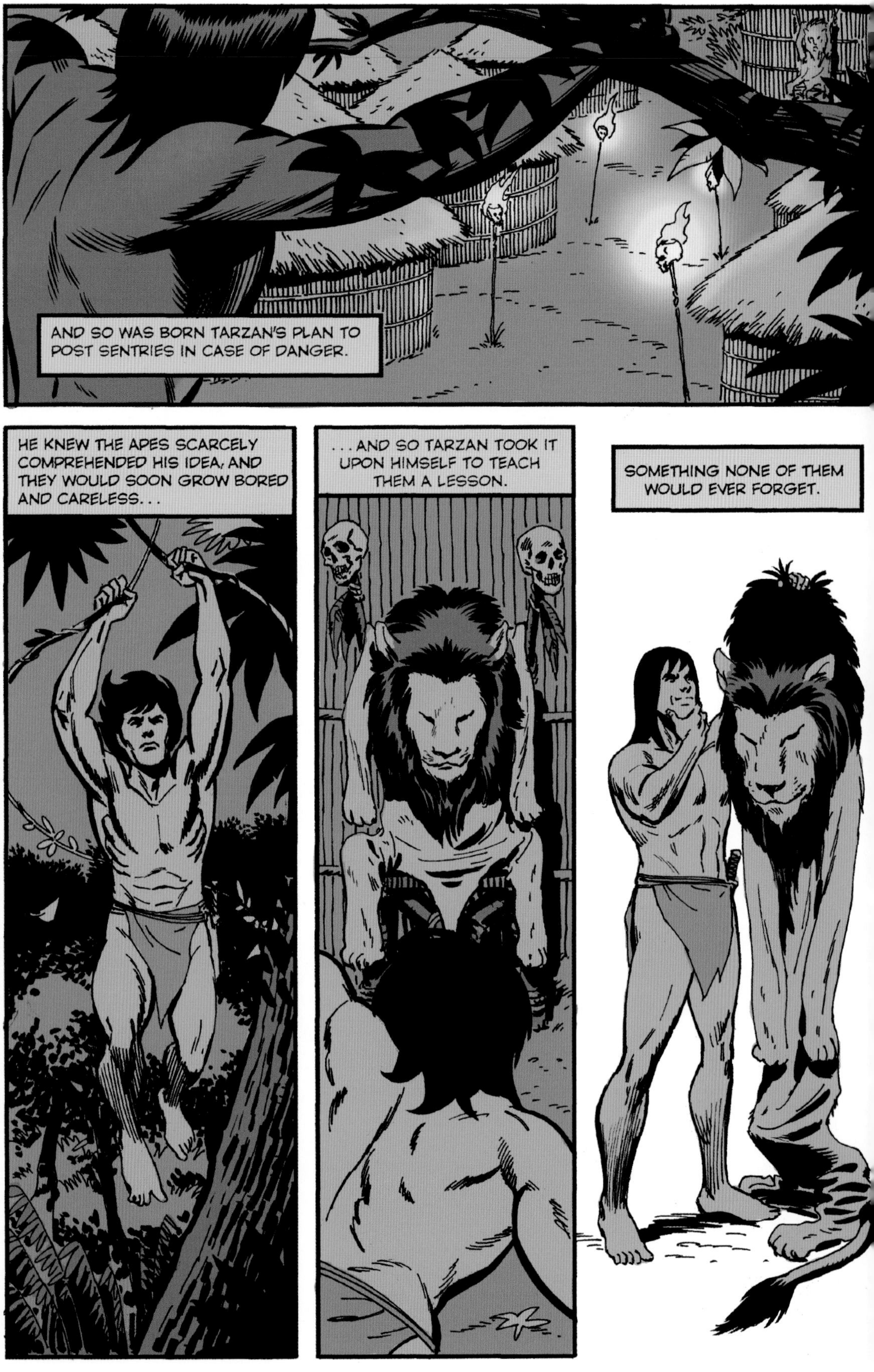
AND SO WAS BORN TARZAN'S PLAN TO POST SENTRIES IN CASE OF DANGER.
HE KNEW THE APES SCARCELY COMPREHENDED HIS IDEA, AND THEY WOULD SOON GROW BORED AND CARELESS...
...AND SO TARZAN TOOK IT UPON HIMSELF TO TEACH THEM A LESSON.
SOMETHING NONE OF THEM WOULD EVER FORGET.

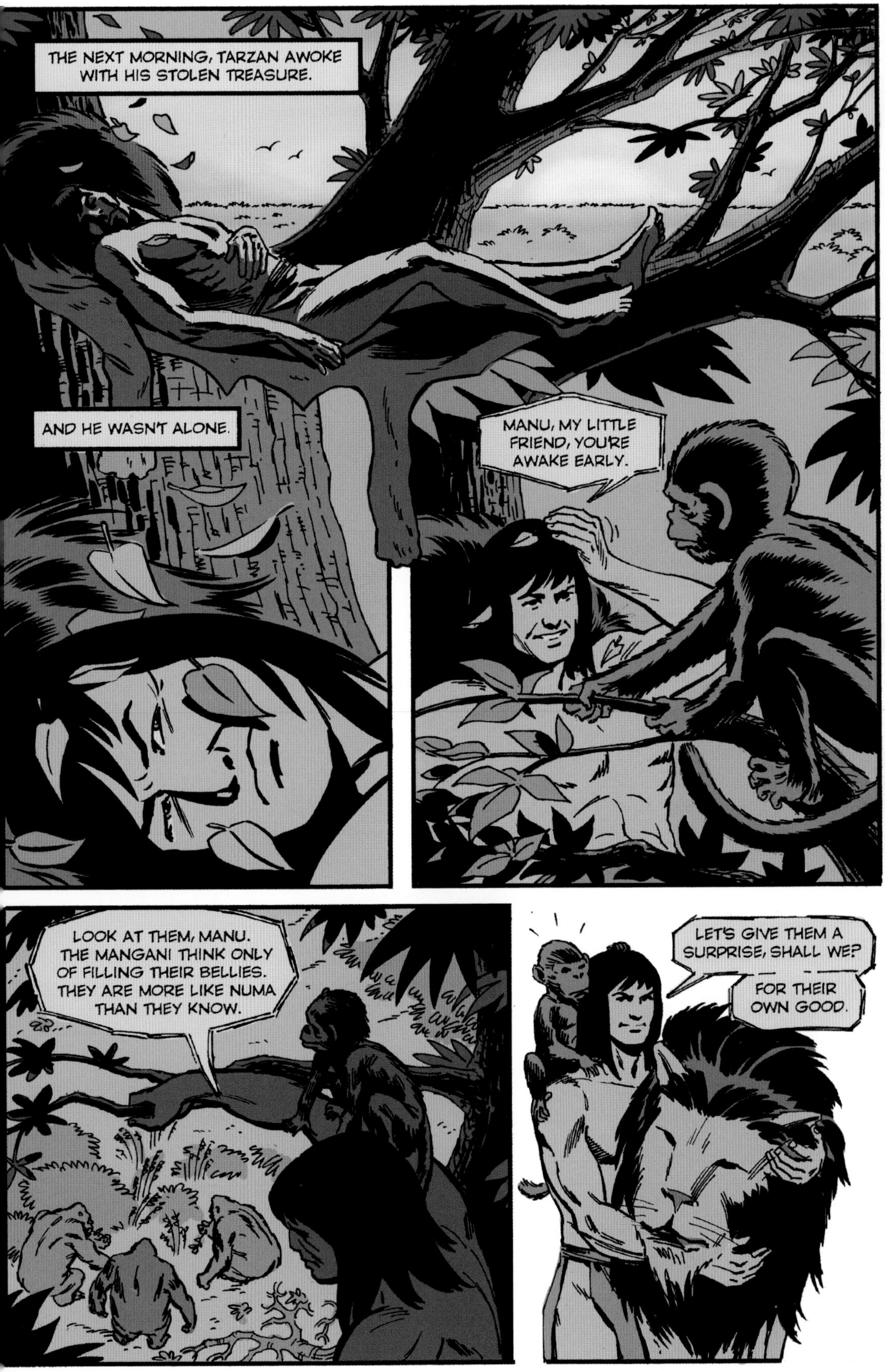
THE NEXT MORNING, TARZAN AWOKE WITH HIS STOLEN TREASURE.
AND HE WASN'T ALONE.
MANU, MY LITTLE FRIEND, YOU'RE AWAKE EARLY.
LOOK AT THEM, MANU. THE MANGANI THINK ONLY OF FILLING THEIR BELLIES. THEY ARE MORE LIKE NUMA THAN THEY KNOW.
LET'S GIVE THEM A SURPRISE, SHALL WE?
FOR THEIR OWN GOOD.

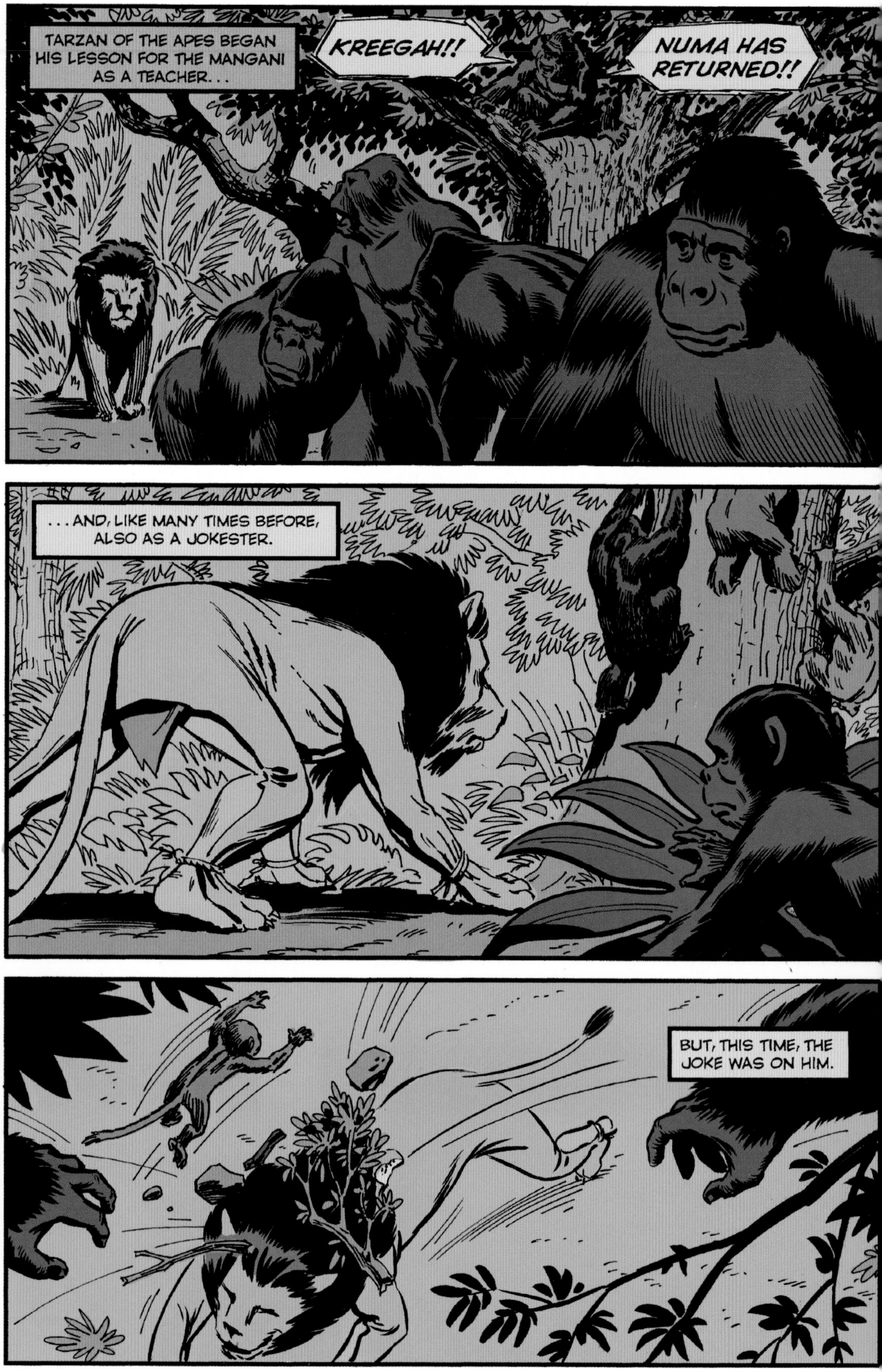
TARZAN OF THE APES BEGAN HIS LESSON FOR THE MANGANI AS A TEACHER...
KREEGAH!!
NUMA HAS RETURNED!!
...AND, LIKE MANY TIMES BEFORE, ALSO AS A JOKESTER.
BUT, THIS TIME, THE JOKE WAS ON HIM.

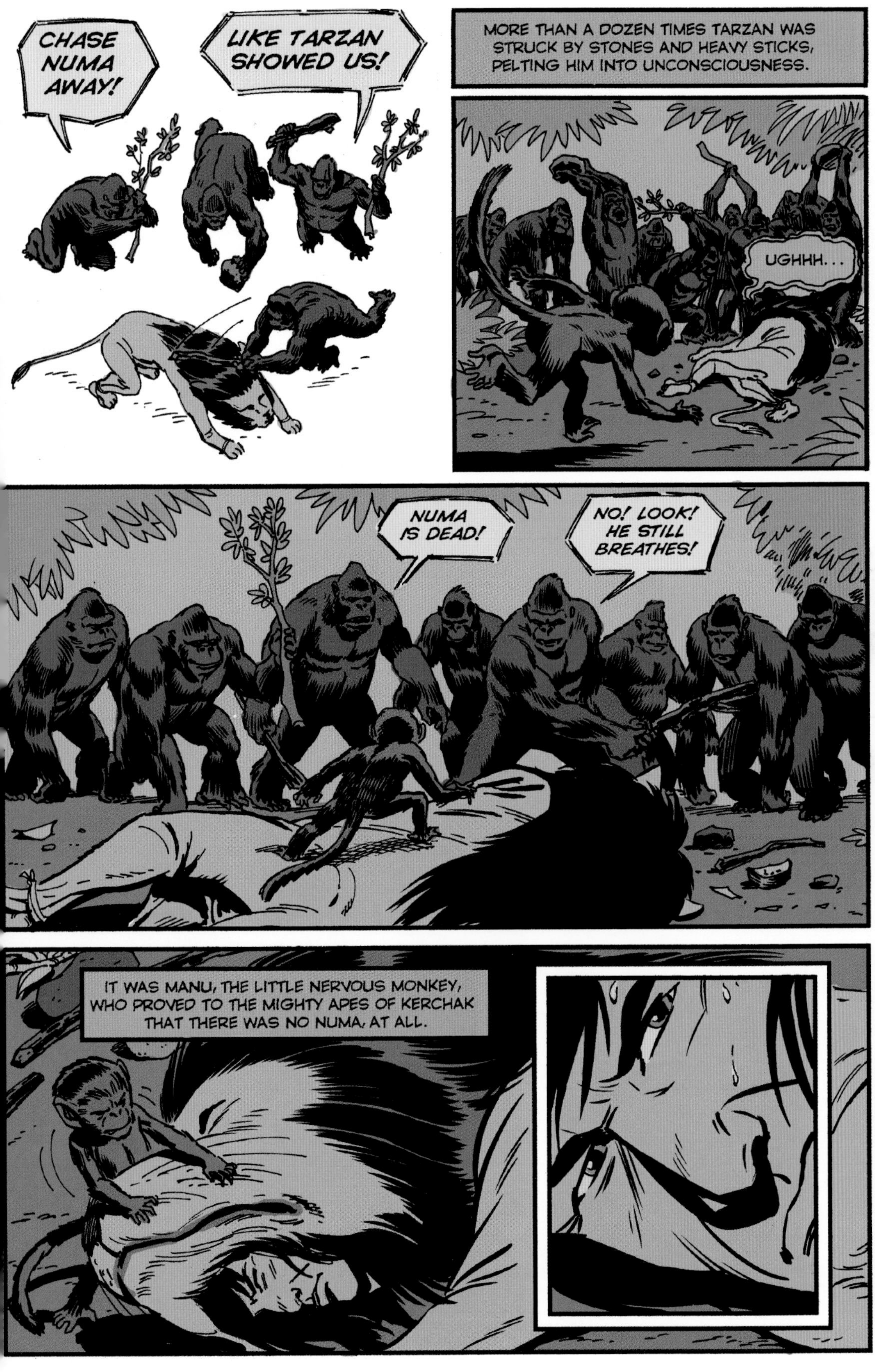
CHASE NUMA AWAY!
LIKE TARZAN SHOWED US!
MORE THAN A DOZEN TIMES TARZAN WAS STRUCK BY STONES AND HEAVY STICKS, PELTING HIM INTO UNCONSCIOUSNESS.
UGHHH...
NUMA IS DEAD!
NO! LOOK! HE STILL BREATHES!
IT WAS MANU, THE LITTLE NERVOUS MONKEY, WHO PROVED TO THE MIGHTY APES OF KERCHAK THAT THERE WAS NO NUMA, AT ALL.

DEVOID OF ALL HUMOR, THE ILL-TEMPERED APES WERE READY TO FINISH WHAT THEY HAD COMMENCED...

...BUT TAUG, AND TEEKA, HIS MATE, STOOD FEARLESSLY BY TARZAN, BARING THEIR FIGHTING FANGS AGAINST THE SULLEN MOB.

SUDDENLY, THE APE-MAN REALIZED THAT HE, TOO, HAD LEARNED SOMETHING. TAUG AND TEEKA HAD EXPRESSED A SENTIMENT OF LOYALTY WHICH HE'D NEVER SEEN IN THE MANGANI BEFORE. AND BETTER STILL...

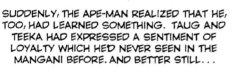

...THE APES OF KERCHAK HAD UNDERSTOOD AND HEEDED HIS ADVICE, AS GRUFF OLD GUNTO RESUMED HIS POSITION AS SENTRY.

TARZAN WAS VERY GLAD TO SEE THESE THINGS, AMID ALL HIS ACHES AND HURTS THAT DAY. HE ALMOST SWORE AN OATH TO GIVE UP PRACTICAL JOKES.

ALMOST...BUT NOT QUITE.

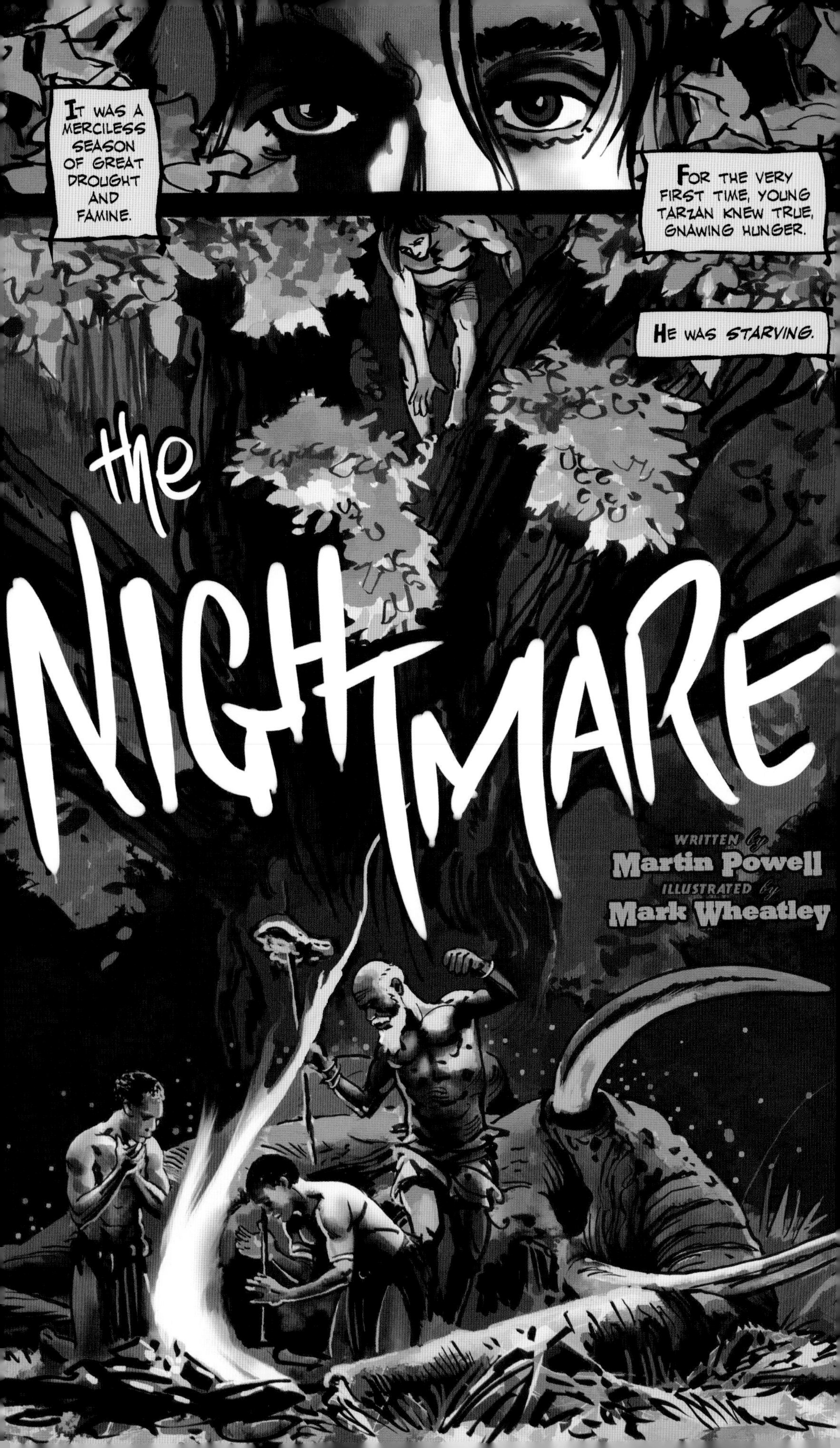

IT WAS A MERCILESS SEASON OF GREAT DROUGHT AND FAMINE.
FOR THE VERY FIRST TIME, YOUNG TARZAN KNEW TRUE, GNAWING HUNGER.
HE WAS STARVING.
the NIGHTMARE
WRITTEN by Martin Powell
ILLUSTRATED by Mark Wheatley

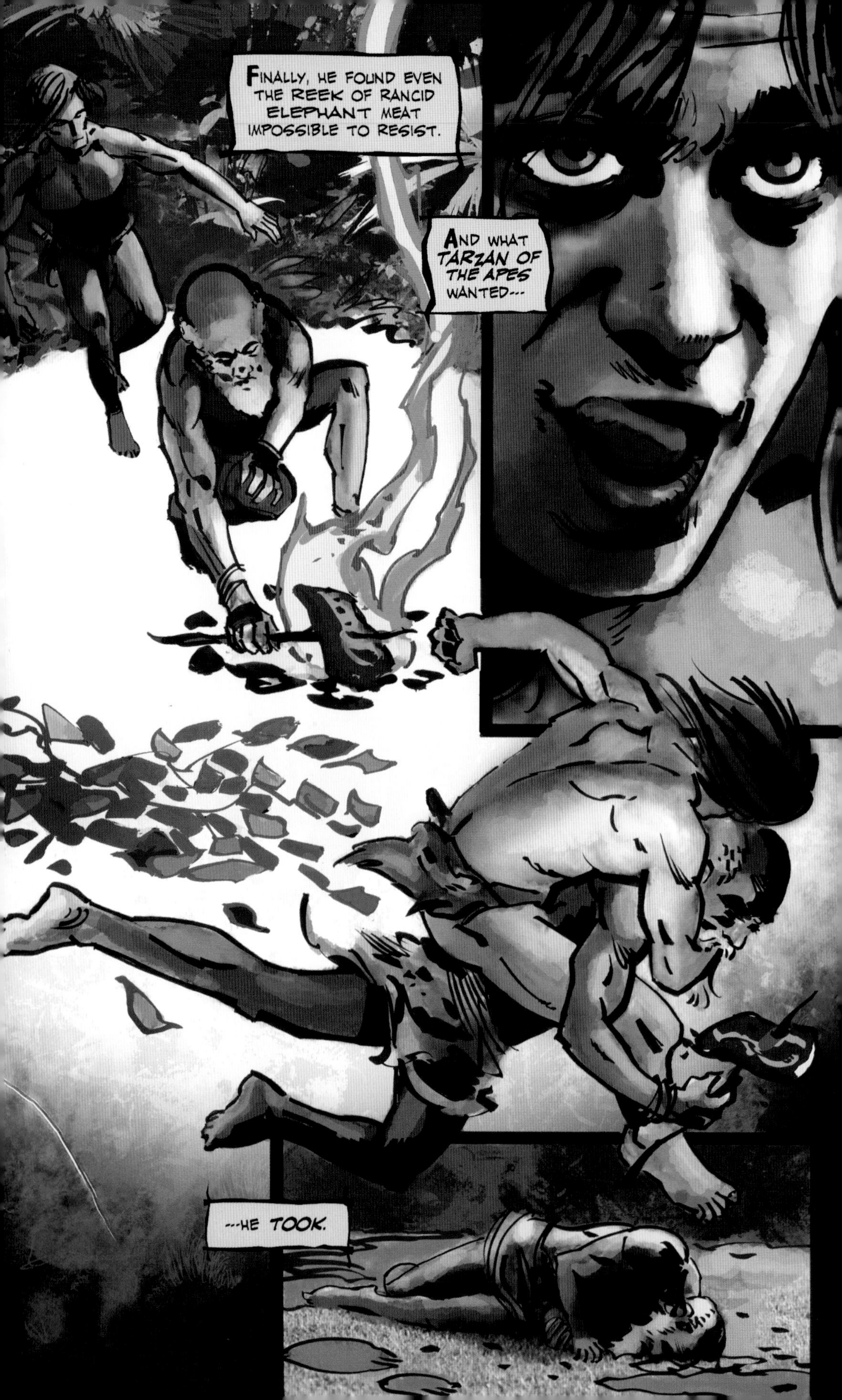
FINALLY, HE FOUND EVEN THE REEK OF RANCID ELEPHANT MEAT IMPOSSIBLE TO RESIST.
AND WHAT *TARZAN OF THE APES* WANTED---
---HE *TOOK.*

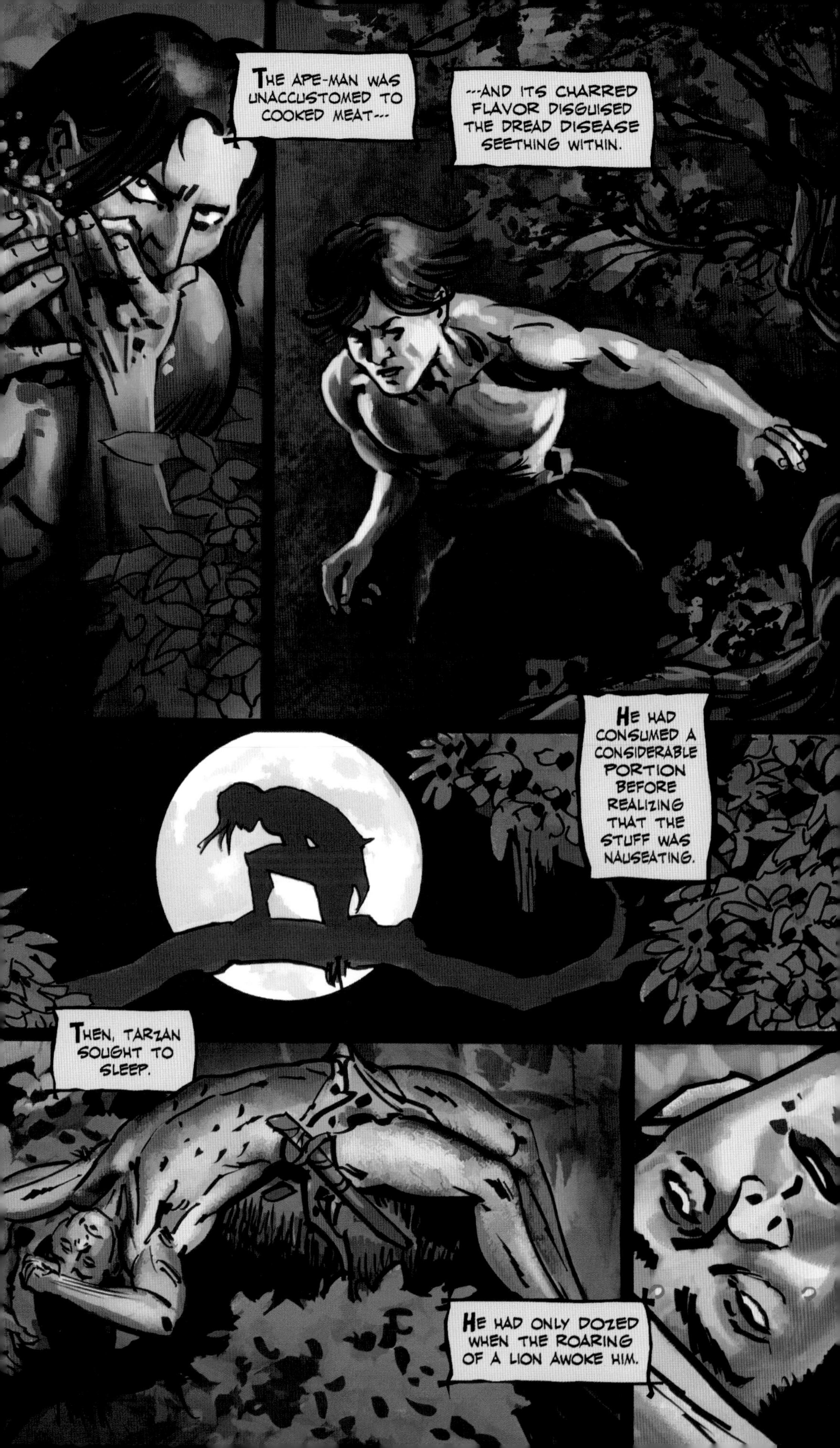

THE APE-MAN WAS UNACCUSTOMED TO COOKED MEAT---
---AND ITS CHARRED FLAVOR DISGUISED THE DREAD DISEASE SEETHING WITHIN.
HE HAD CONSUMED A CONSIDERABLE PORTION BEFORE REALIZING THAT THE STUFF WAS NAUSEATING.
THEN, TARZAN SOUGHT TO SLEEP.
HE HAD ONLY DOZED WHEN THE ROARING OF A LION AWOKE HIM.

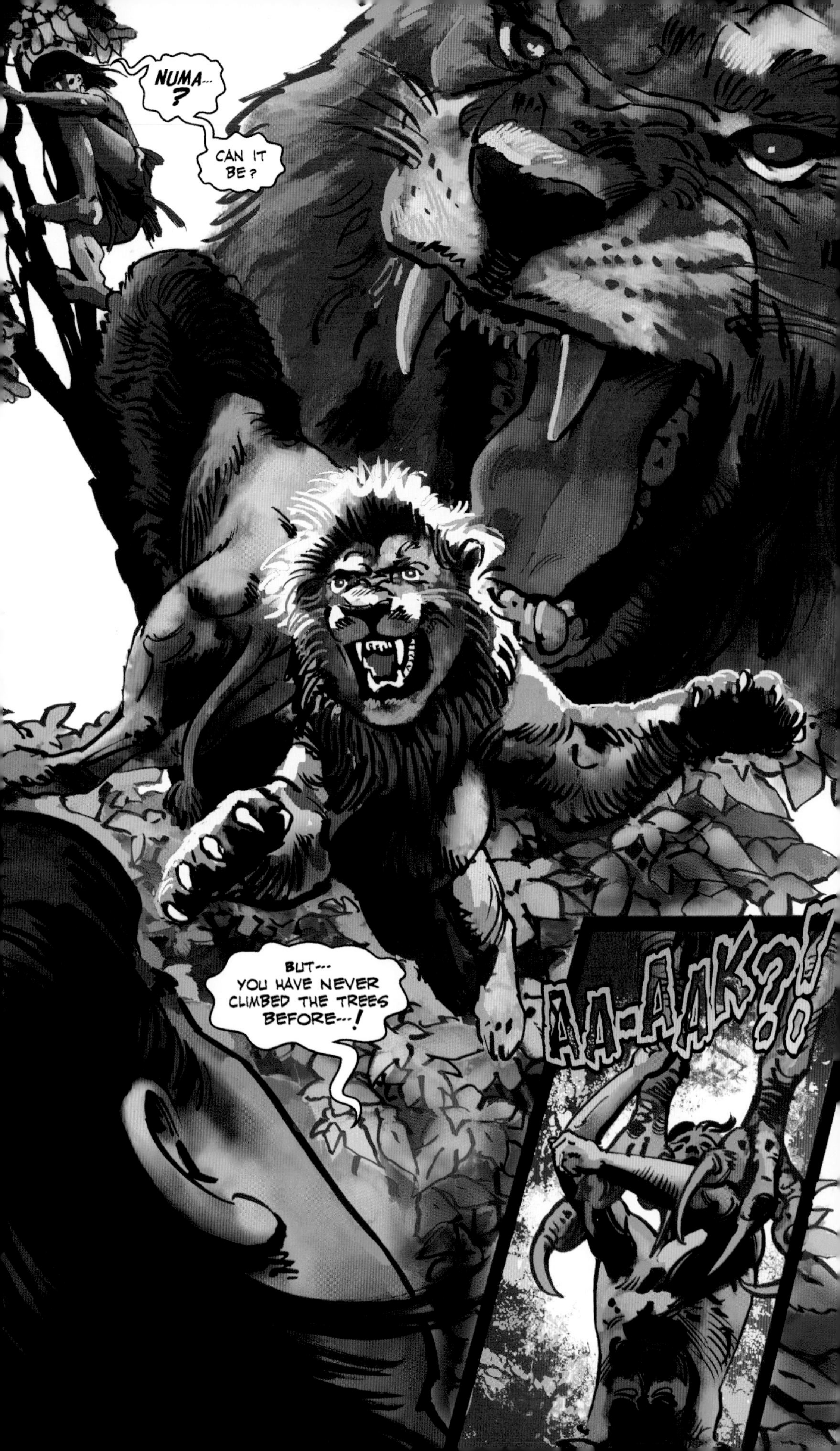
NUMA... ?
CAN IT BE?
BUT--- YOU HAVE NEVER CLIMBED THE TREES BEFORE---!
AA-AAK?!

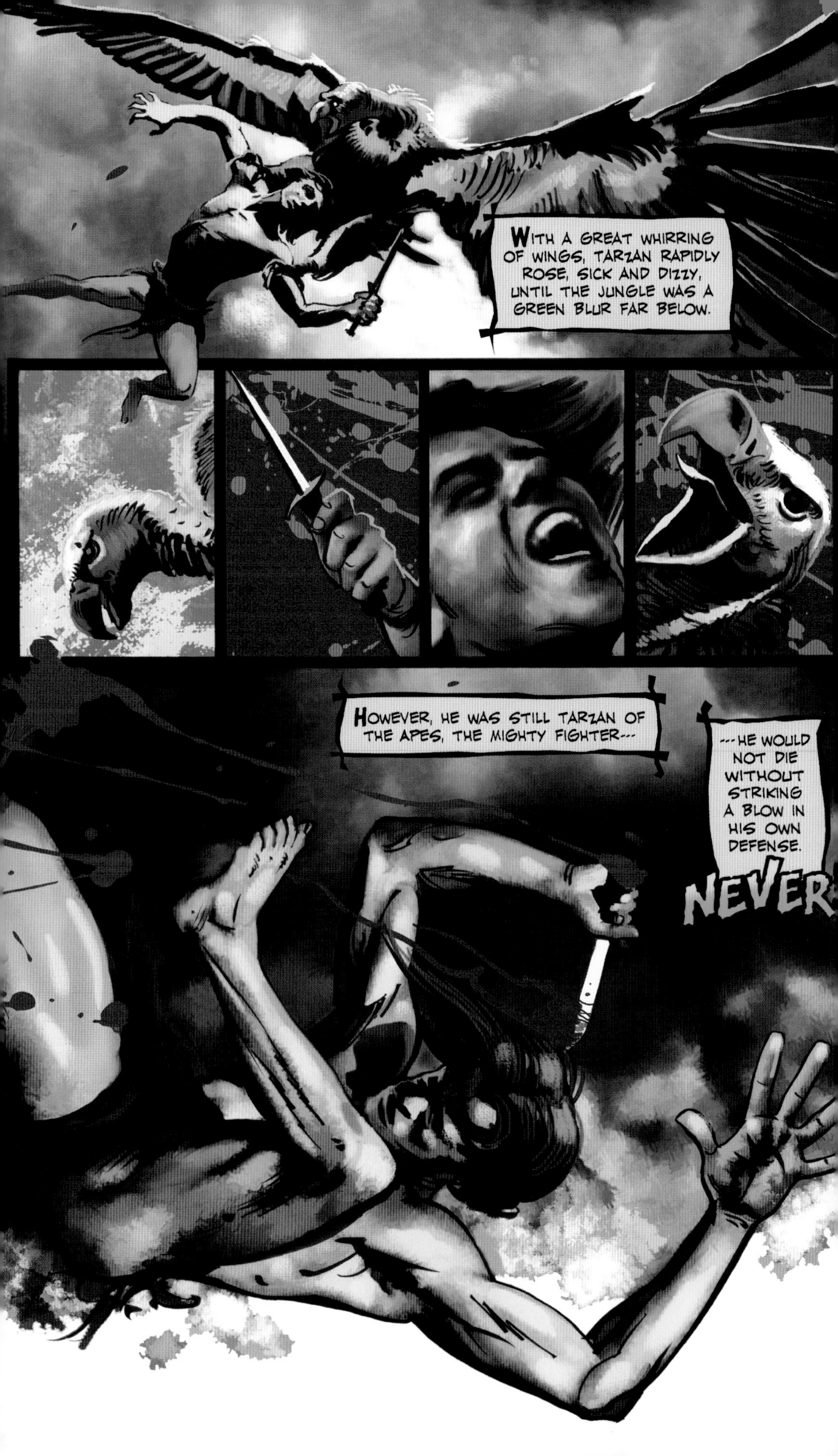
WITH A GREAT WHIRRING OF WINGS, TARZAN RAPIDLY ROSE, SICK AND DIZZY, UNTIL THE JUNGLE WAS A GREEN BLUR FAR BELOW.
HOWEVER, HE WAS STILL TARZAN OF THE APES, THE MIGHTY FIGHTER---
---HE WOULD NOT DIE WITHOUT STRIKING A BLOW IN HIS OWN DEFENSE.
NEVER

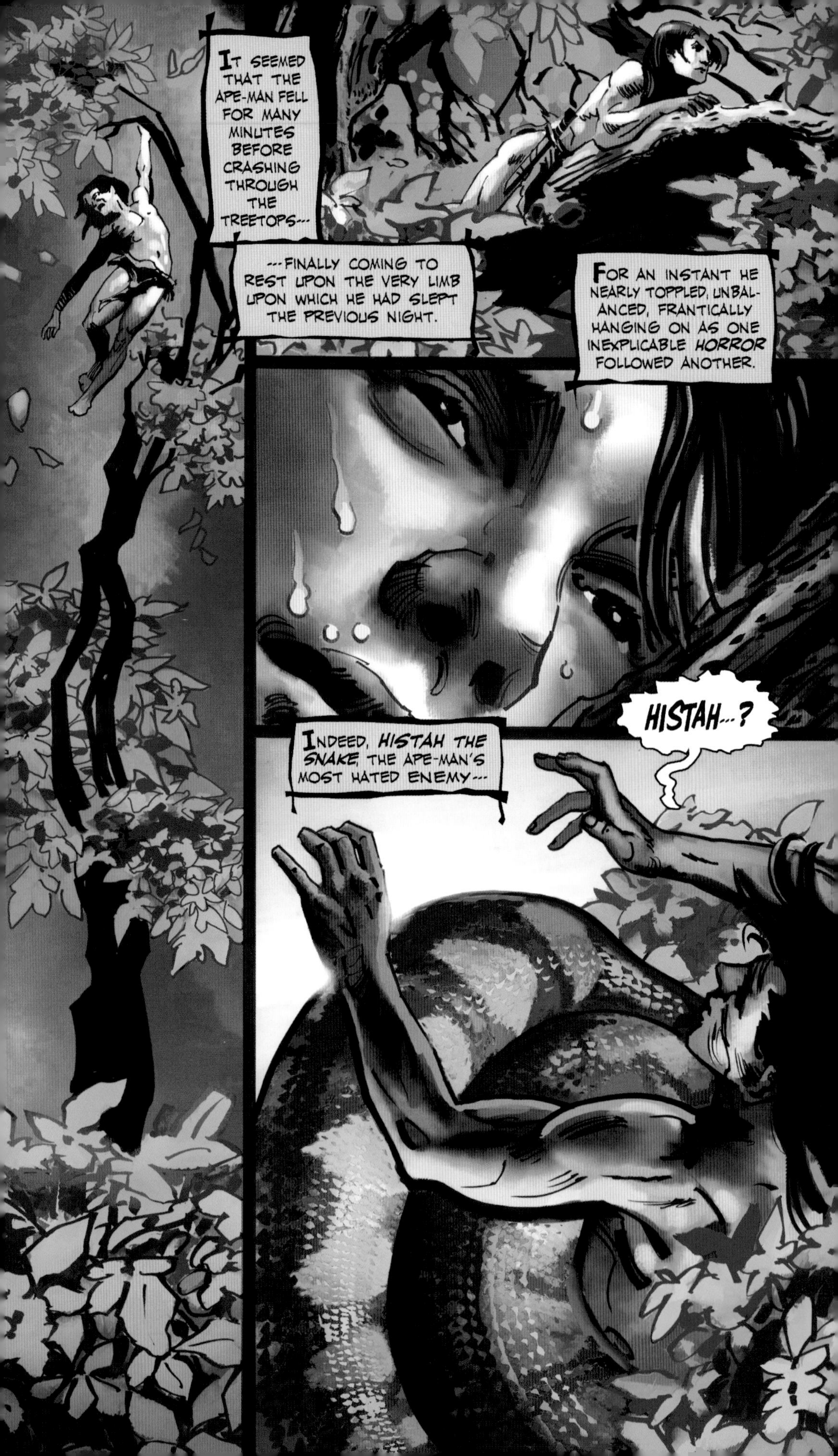
IT SEEMED THAT THE APE-MAN FELL FOR MANY MINUTES BEFORE CRASHING THROUGH THE TREETOPS---
---FINALLY COMING TO REST UPON THE VERY LIMB UPON WHICH HE HAD SLEPT THE PREVIOUS NIGHT.
FOR AN INSTANT HE NEARLY TOPPLED, UNBAL-ANCED, FRANTICALLY HANGING ON AS ONE INEXPLICABLE HORROR FOLLOWED ANOTHER.
HISTAH...?
INDEED, HISTAH THE SNAKE, THE APE-MAN'S MOST HATED ENEMY---

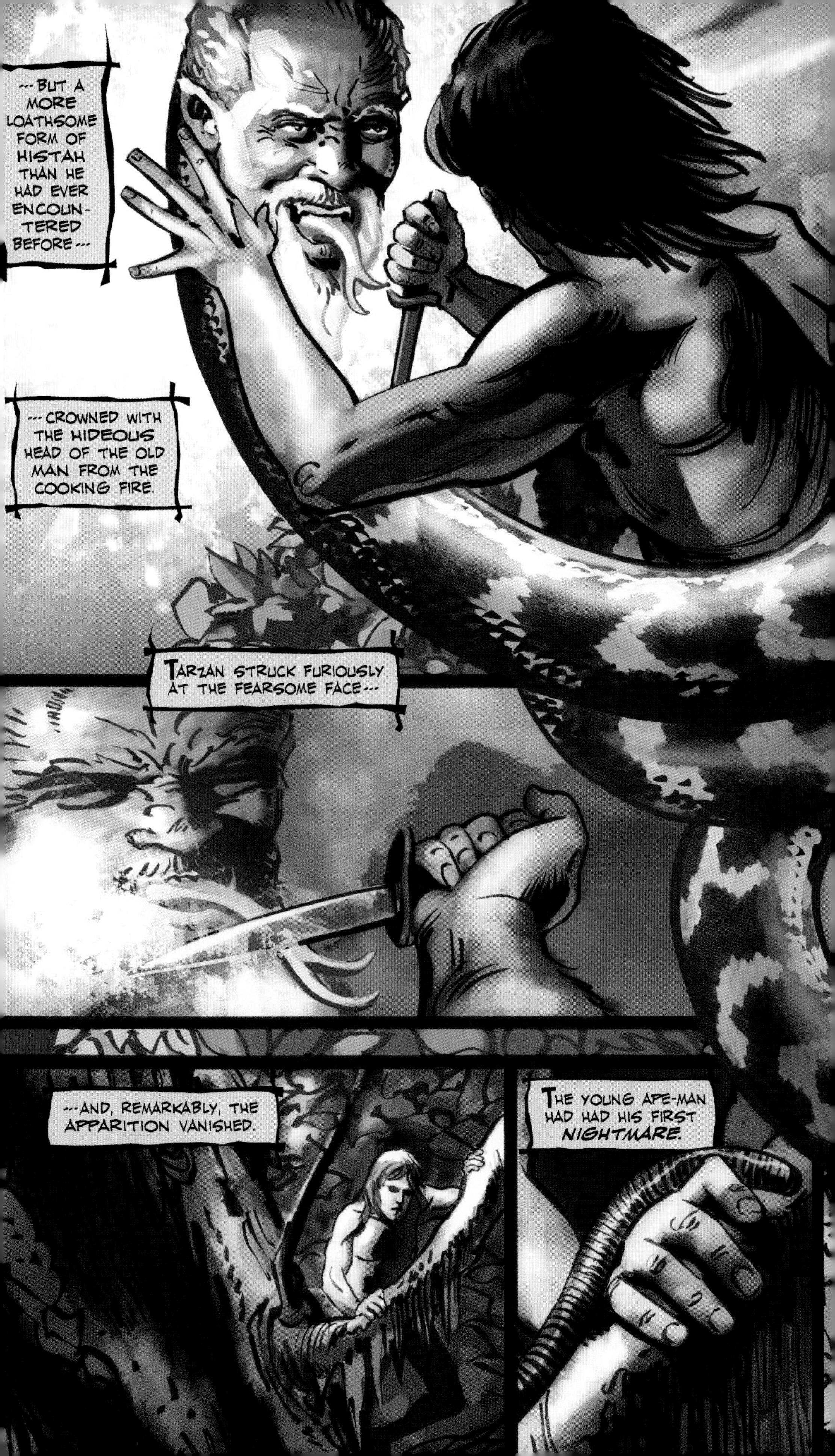
---BUT A MORE LOATHSOME FORM OF HISTAH THAN HE HAD EVER ENCOUNTERED BEFORE---
---CROWNED WITH THE HIDEOUS HEAD OF THE OLD MAN FROM THE COOKING FIRE.
TARZAN STRUCK FURIOUSLY AT THE FEARSOME FACE---
---AND, REMARKABLY, THE APPARITION VANISHED.
THE YOUNG APE-MAN HAD HAD HIS FIRST NIGHTMARE.

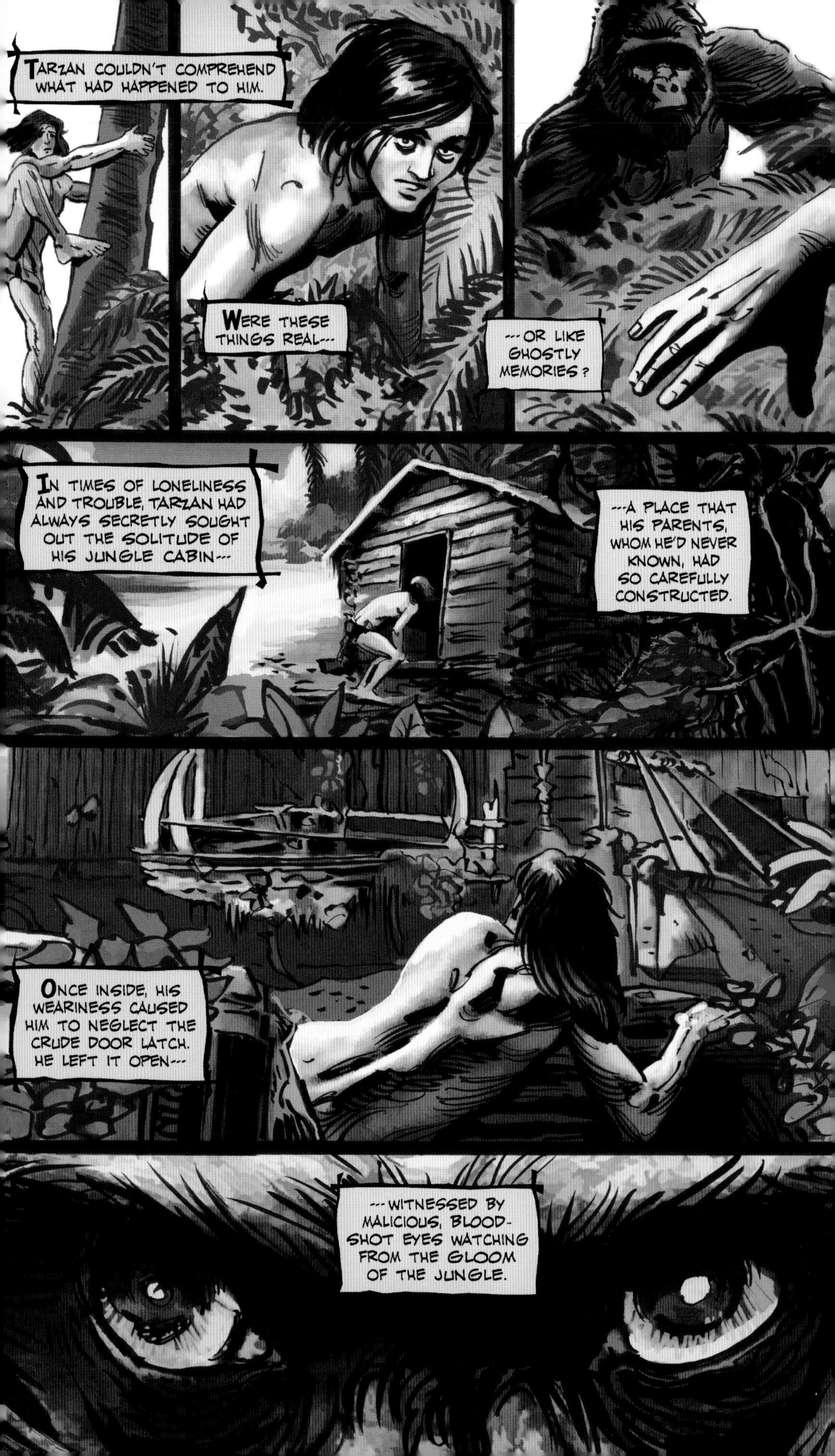
TARZAN COULDN'T COMPREHEND WHAT HAD HAPPENED TO HIM.
WERE THESE THINGS REAL---
---OR LIKE GHOSTLY MEMORIES?
IN TIMES OF LONELINESS AND TROUBLE, TARZAN HAD ALWAYS SECRETLY SOUGHT OUT THE SOLITUDE OF HIS JUNGLE CABIN---
---A PLACE THAT HIS PARENTS, WHOM HE'D NEVER KNOWN, HAD SO CAREFULLY CONSTRUCTED.
ONCE INSIDE, HIS WEARINESS CAUSED HIM TO NEGLECT THE CRUDE DOOR LATCH. HE LEFT IT OPEN---
---WITNESSED BY MALICIOUS, BLOOD-SHOT EYES WATCHING FROM THE GLOOM OF THE JUNGLE.

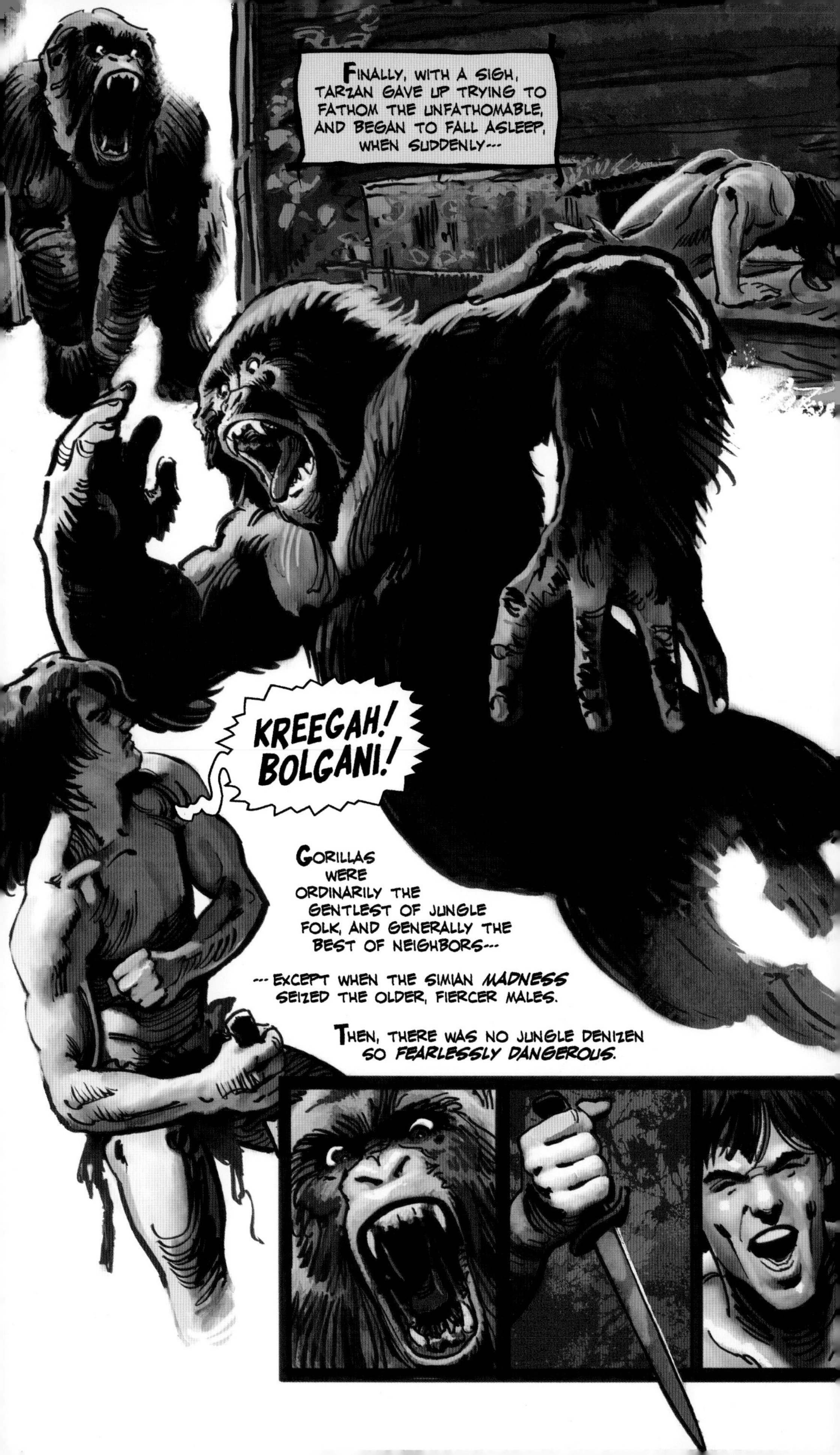
FINALLY, WITH A SIGH, TARZAN GAVE UP TRYING TO FATHOM THE UNFATHOMABLE, AND BEGAN TO FALL ASLEEP, WHEN SUDDENLY---
KREEGAH! BOLGANI!
GORILLAS WERE ORDINARILY THE GENTLEST OF JUNGLE FOLK, AND GENERALLY THE BEST OF NEIGHBORS---
--- EXCEPT WHEN THE SIMIAN MADNESS SEIZED THE OLDER, FIERCER MALES.
THEN, THERE WAS NO JUNGLE DENIZEN SO FEARLESSLY DANGEROUS.

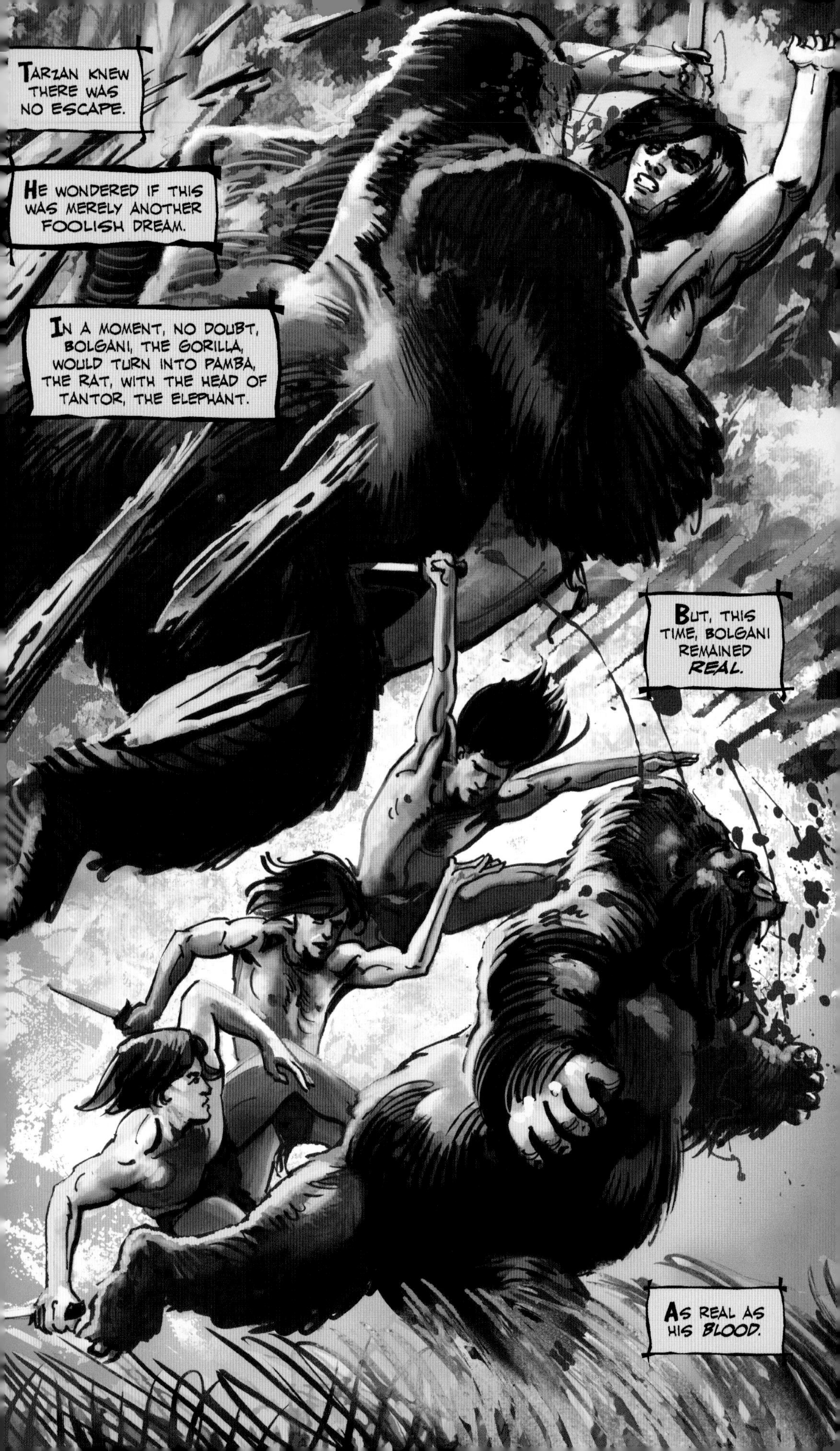
TARZAN KNEW THERE WAS NO ESCAPE.
HE WONDERED IF THIS WAS MERELY ANOTHER FOOLISH DREAM.
IN A MOMENT, NO DOUBT, BOLGANI, THE GORILLA, WOULD TURN INTO PAMBA, THE RAT, WITH THE HEAD OF TANTOR, THE ELEPHANT.
BUT, THIS TIME, BOLGANI REMAINED *REAL*.
AS REAL AS HIS *BLOOD*.

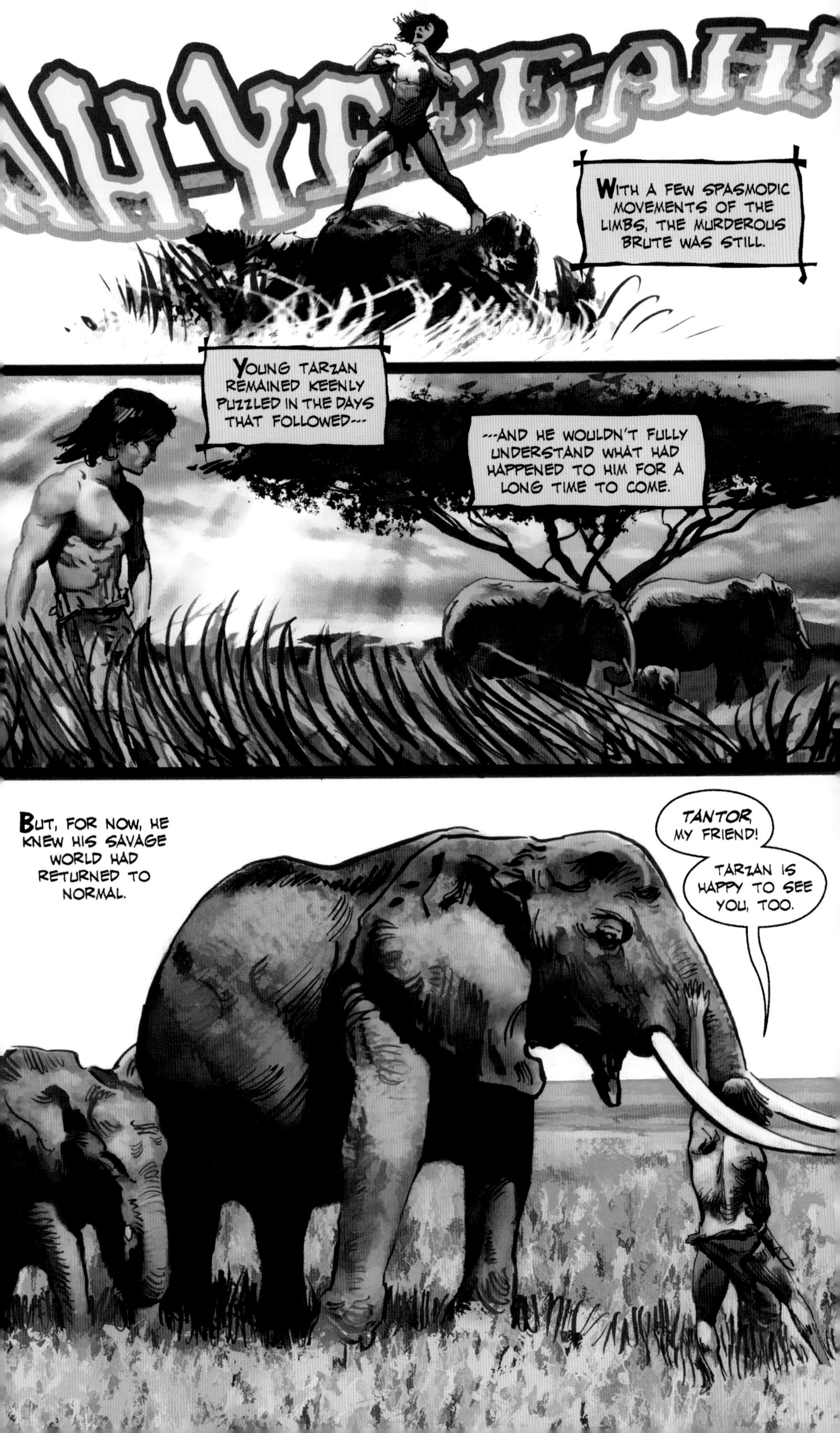
WITH A FEW SPASMODIC MOVEMENTS OF THE LIMBS, THE MURDEROUS BRUTE WAS STILL.
YOUNG TARZAN REMAINED KEENLY PUZZLED IN THE DAYS THAT FOLLOWED---
---AND HE WOULDN'T FULLY UNDERSTAND WHAT HAD HAPPENED TO HIM FOR A LONG TIME TO COME.
BUT, FOR NOW, HE KNEW HIS SAVAGE WORLD HAD RETURNED TO NORMAL.
TANTOR, MY FRIEND!
TARZAN IS HAPPY TO SEE YOU, TOO.

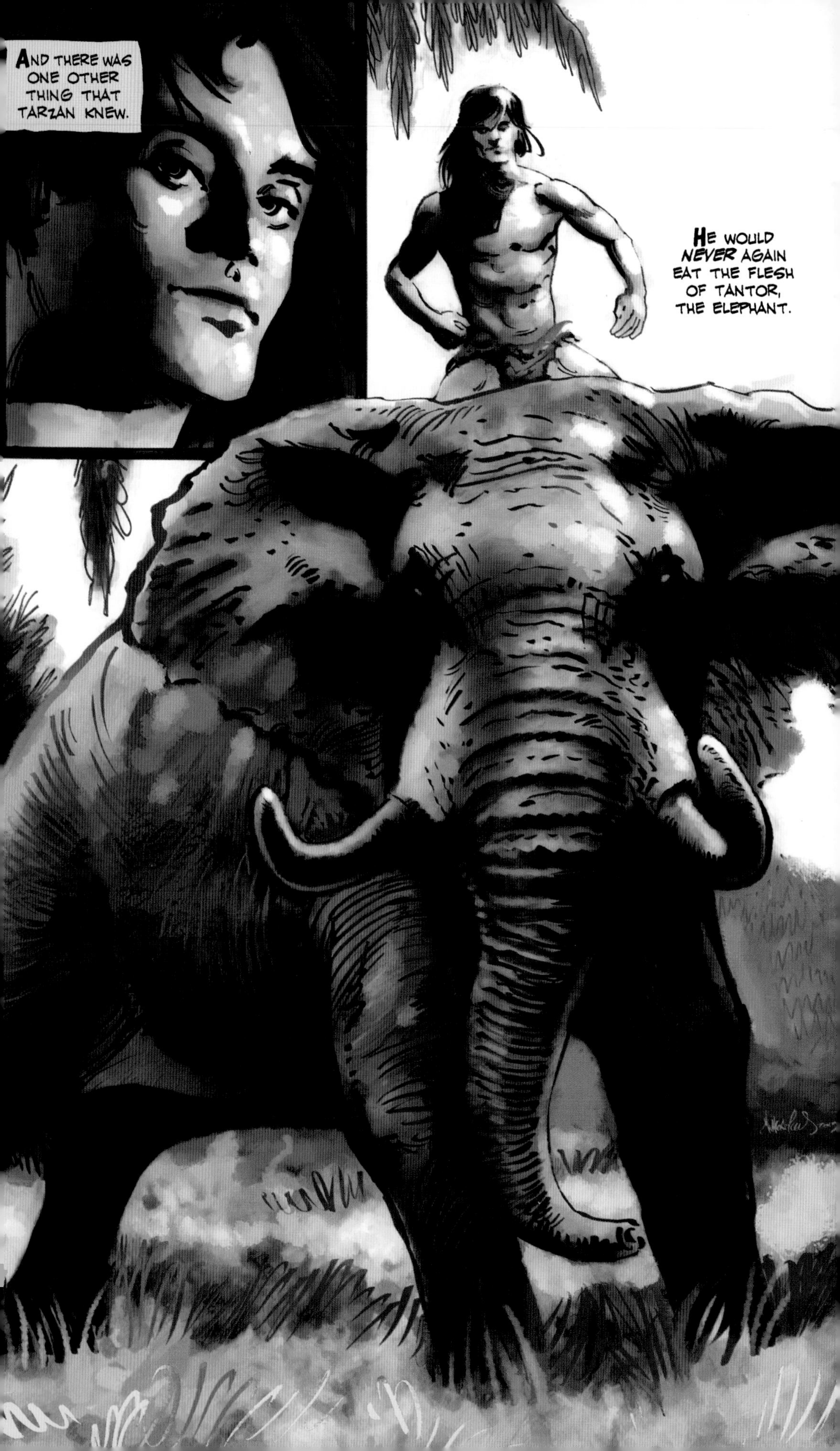
AND THERE WAS ONE OTHER THING THAT TARZAN KNEW.
HE WOULD NEVER AGAIN EAT THE FLESH OF TANTOR, THE ELEPHANT.

WRITTEN BY MARTIN POWELL • ILLUSTRATED BY SERGIO CARIELLO
COLORED BY PATRICK GAMA • LETTERED BY DAVE LANPHEAR

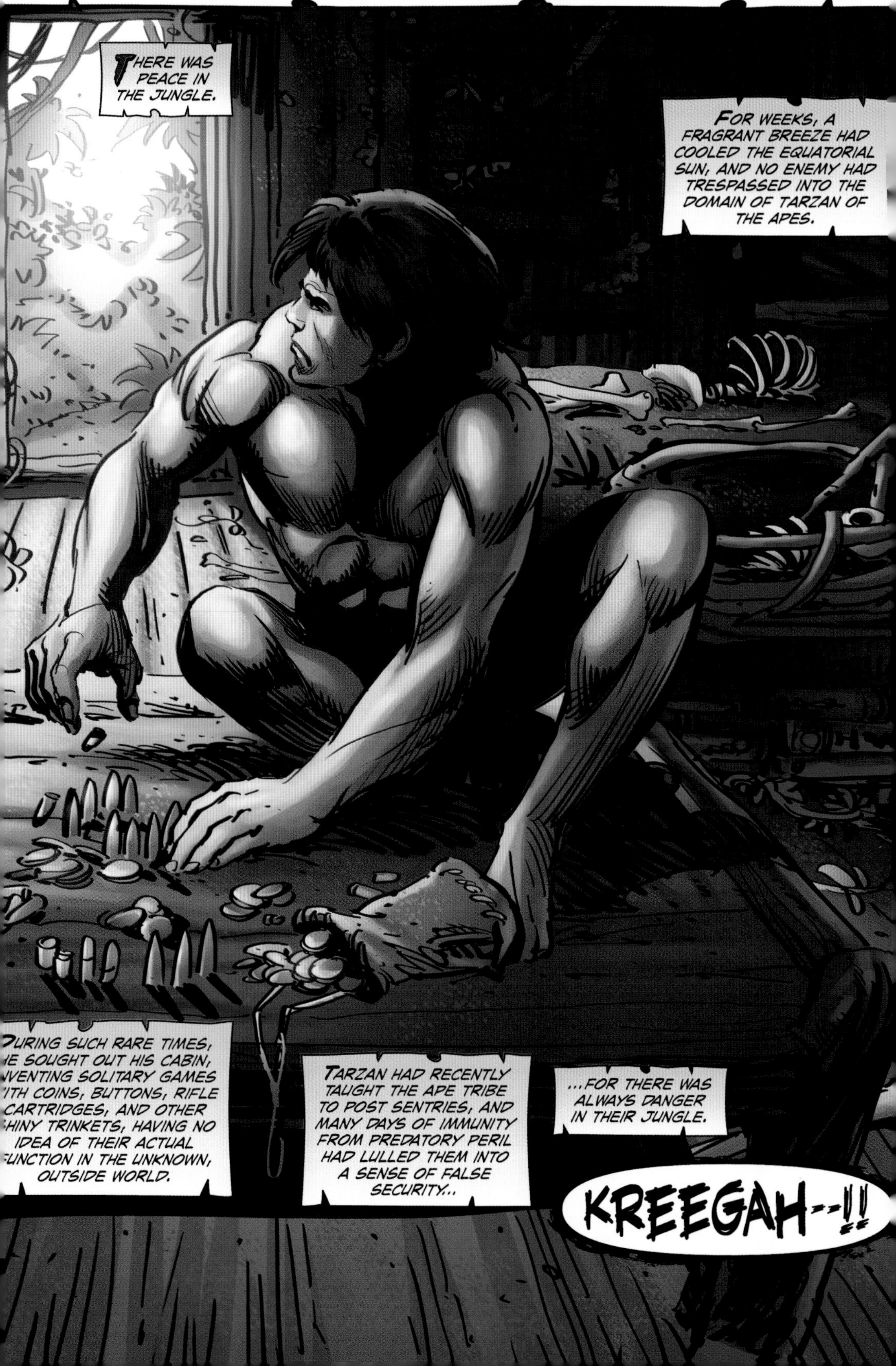
THERE WAS PEACE IN THE JUNGLE.
FOR WEEKS, A FRAGRANT BREEZE HAD COOLED THE EQUATORIAL SUN, AND NO ENEMY HAD TRESPASSED INTO THE DOMAIN OF TARZAN OF THE APES.
DURING SUCH RARE TIMES, E SOUGHT OUT HIS CABIN, NVENTING SOLITARY GAMES ITH COINS, BUTTONS, RIFLE CARTRIDGES, AND OTHER HINY TRINKETS, HAVING NO IDEA OF THEIR ACTUAL UNCTION IN THE UNKNOWN, OUTSIDE WORLD.
TARZAN HAD RECENTLY TAUGHT THE APE TRIBE TO POST SENTRIES, AND MANY DAYS OF IMMUNITY FROM PREDATORY PERIL HAD LULLED THEM INTO A SENSE OF FALSE SECURITY...
...FOR THERE WAS ALWAYS DANGER IN THEIR JUNGLE.
KREEGAH--!!

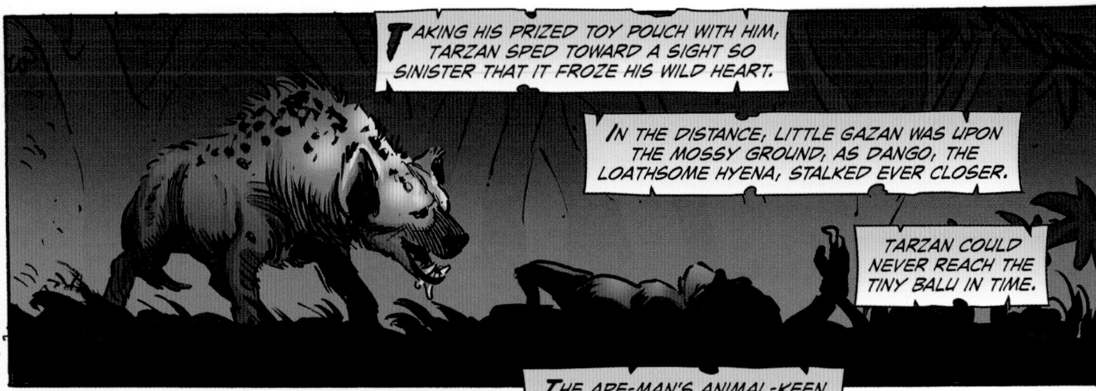
TAKING HIS PRIZED TOY POUCH WITH HIM, TARZAN SPED TOWARD A SIGHT SO SINISTER THAT IT FROZE HIS WILD HEART.
IN THE DISTANCE, LITTLE GAZAN WAS UPON THE MOSSY GROUND, AS DANGO, THE LOATHSOME HYENA, STALKED EVER CLOSER.
TARZAN COULD NEVER REACH THE TINY BALU IN TIME.

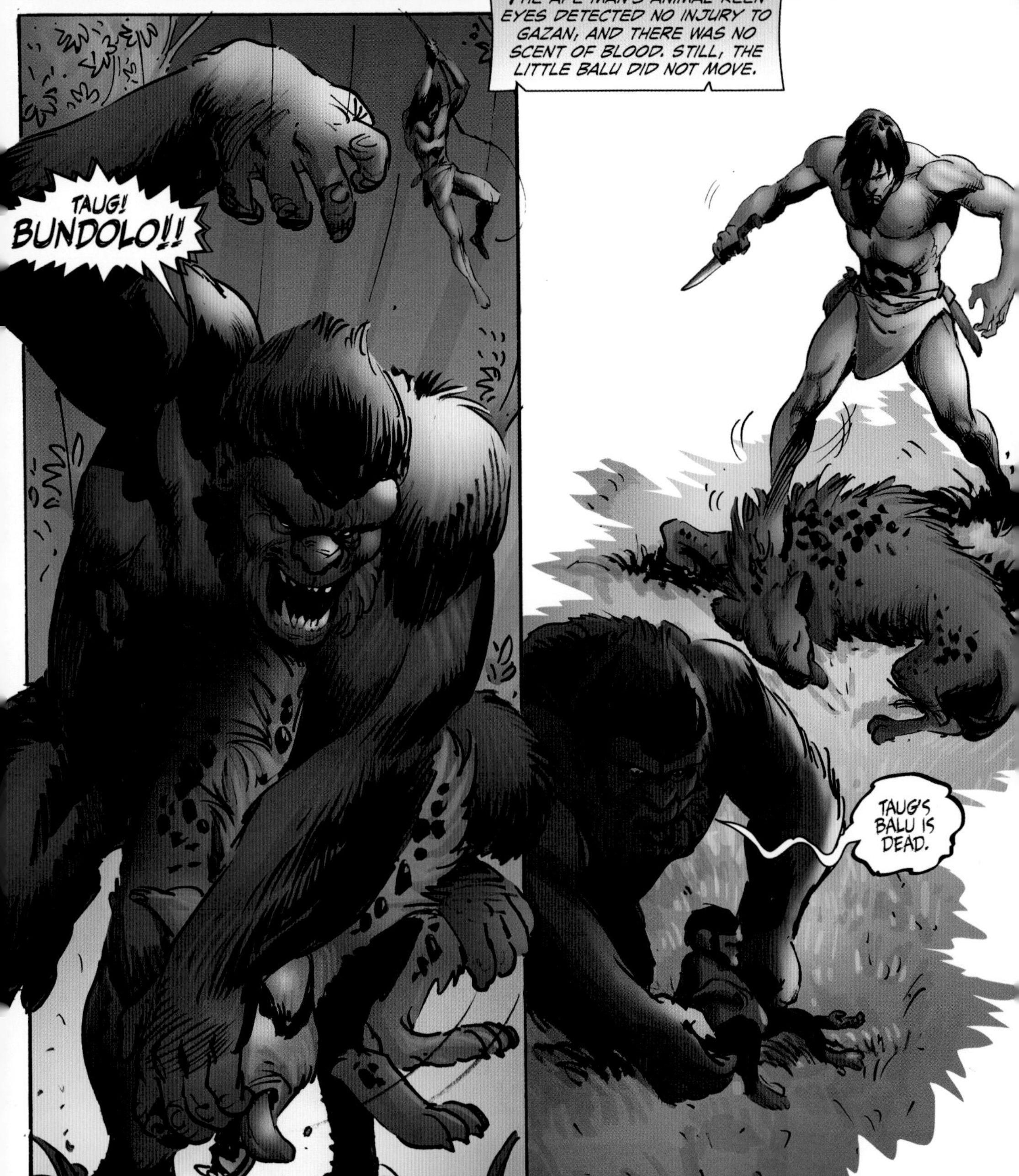
TAUG! BUNDOLO!!
THE APE-MAN'S ANIMAL-KEEN EYES DETECTED NO INJURY TO GAZAN, AND THERE WAS NO SCENT OF BLOOD. STILL, THE LITTLE BALU DID NOT MOVE.
TAUG'S BALU IS DEAD.

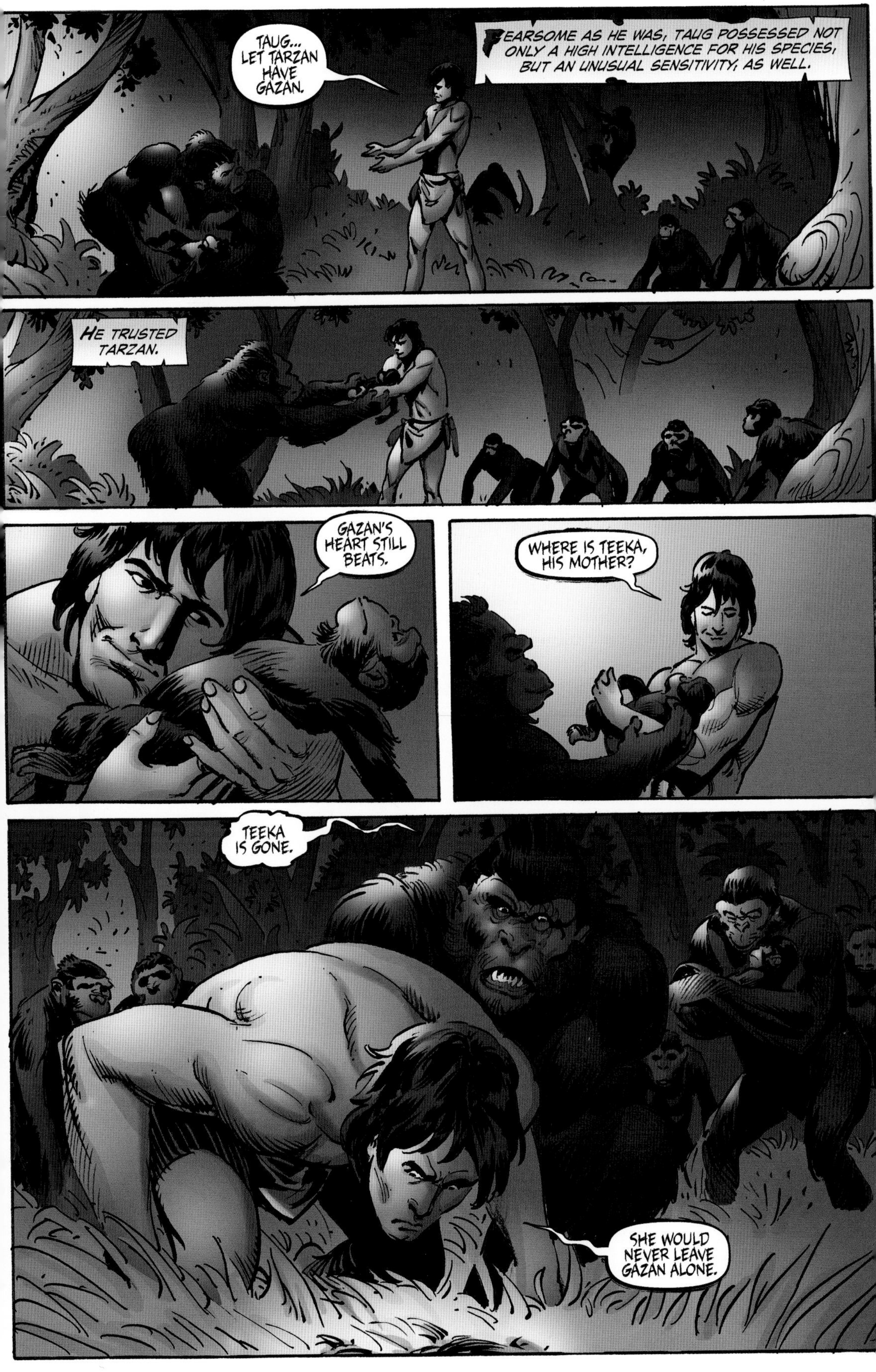
TAUG... LET TARZAN HAVE GAZAN.
FEARSOME AS HE WAS, TAUG POSSESSED NOT ONLY A HIGH INTELLIGENCE FOR HIS SPECIES, BUT AN UNUSUAL SENSITIVITY, AS WELL.
HE TRUSTED TARZAN.
GAZAN'S HEART STILL BEATS.
WHERE IS TEEKA, HIS MOTHER?
TEEKA IS GONE.
SHE WOULD NEVER LEAVE GAZAN ALONE.

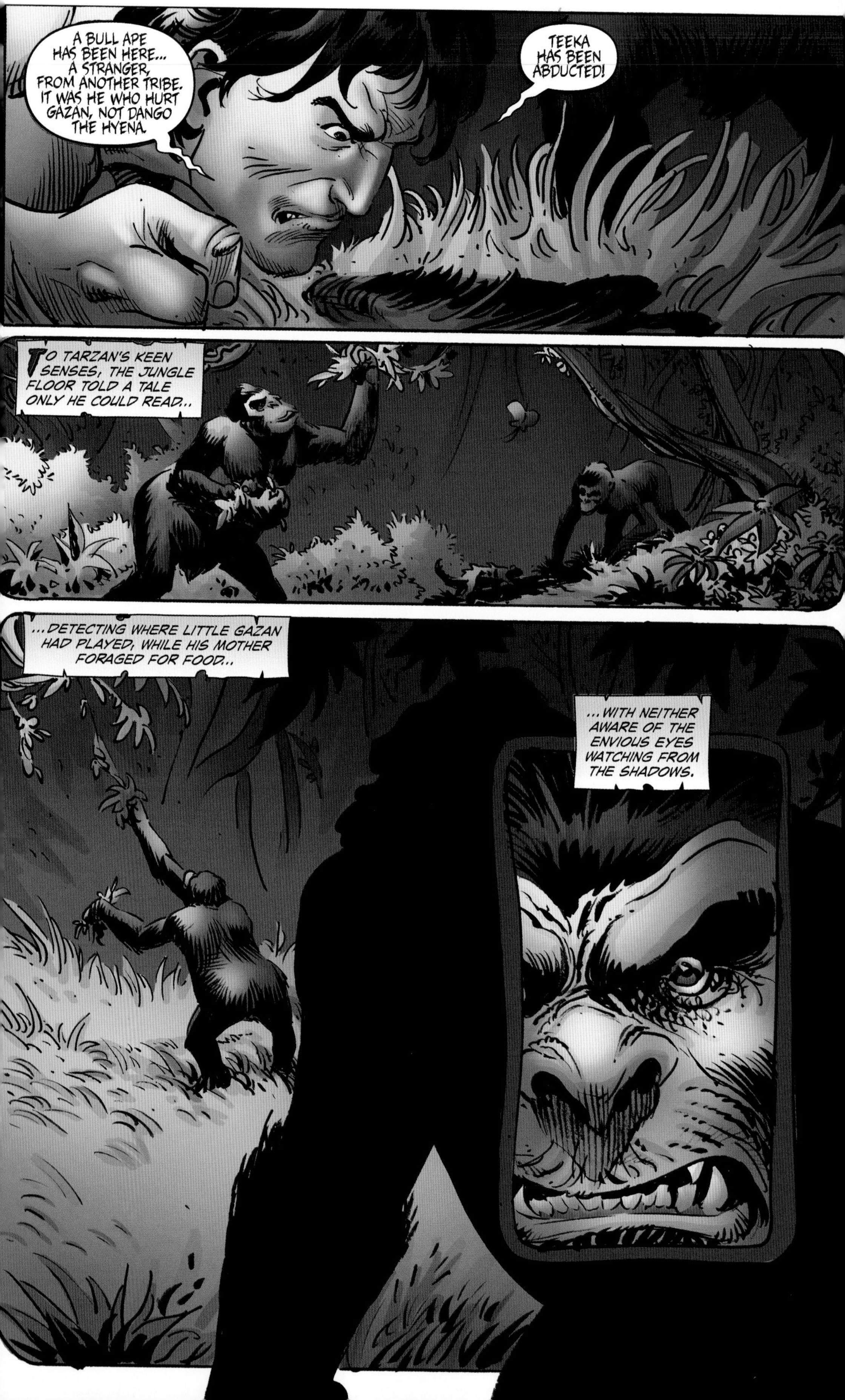
A BULL APE HAS BEEN HERE... A STRANGER, FROM ANOTHER TRIBE. IT WAS HE WHO HURT GAZAN, NOT DANGO THE HYENA.
TEEKA HAS BEEN ABDUCTED!
TO TARZAN'S KEEN SENSES, THE JUNGLE FLOOR TOLD A TALE ONLY HE COULD READ...
...DETECTING WHERE LITTLE GAZAN HAD PLAYED, WHILE HIS MOTHER FORAGED FOR FOOD...
...WITH NEITHER AWARE OF THE ENVIOUS EYES WATCHING FROM THE SHADOWS.

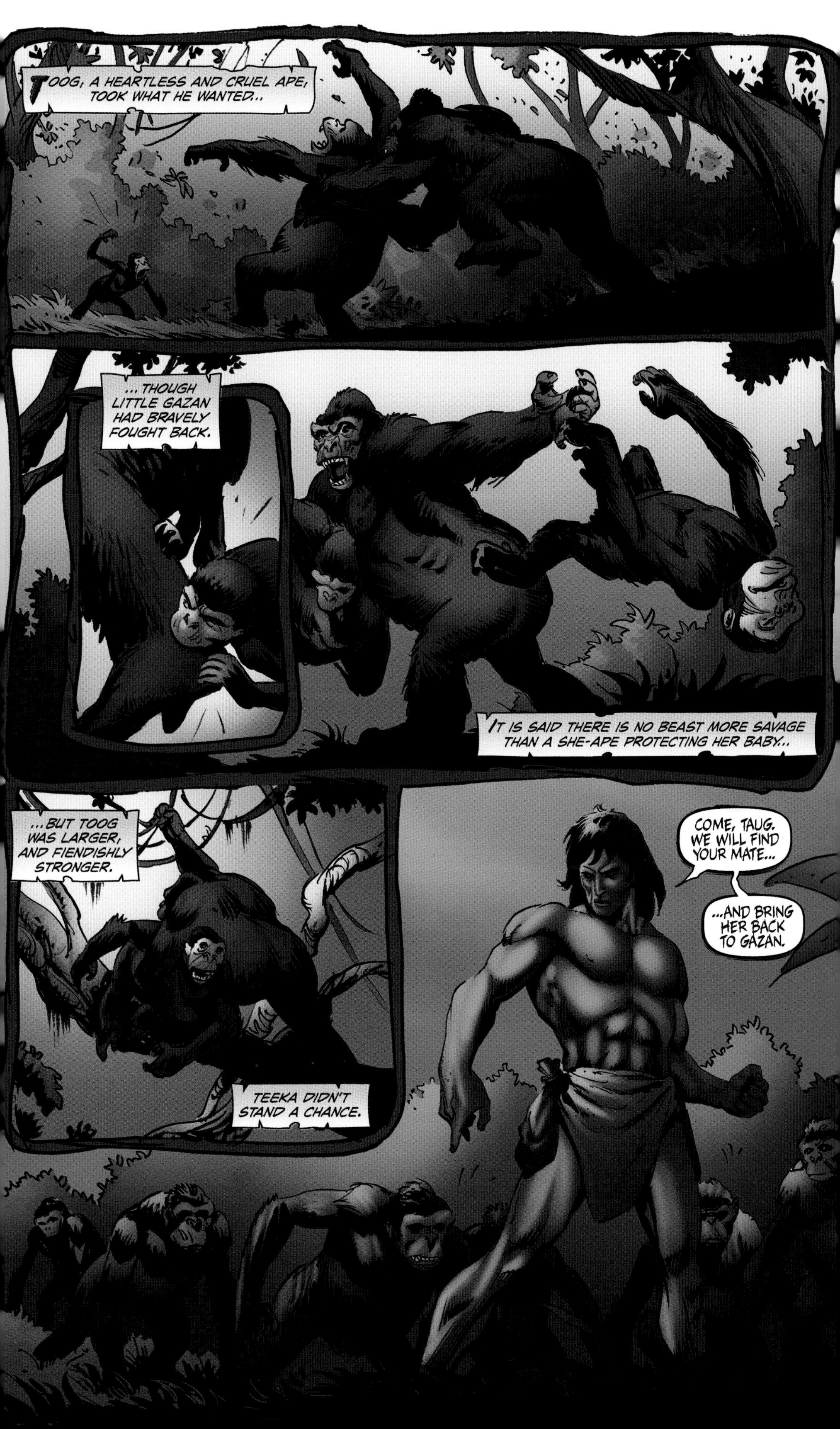
TOOG, A HEARTLESS AND CRUEL APE, TOOK WHAT HE WANTED...
...THOUGH LITTLE GAZAN HAD BRAVELY FOUGHT BACK.
IT IS SAID THERE IS NO BEAST MORE SAVAGE THAN A SHE-APE PROTECTING HER BABY...
...BUT TOOG WAS LARGER, AND FIENDISHLY STRONGER.
TEEKA DIDN'T STAND A CHANCE.
COME, TAUG. WE WILL FIND YOUR MATE...
...AND BRING HER BACK TO GAZAN.

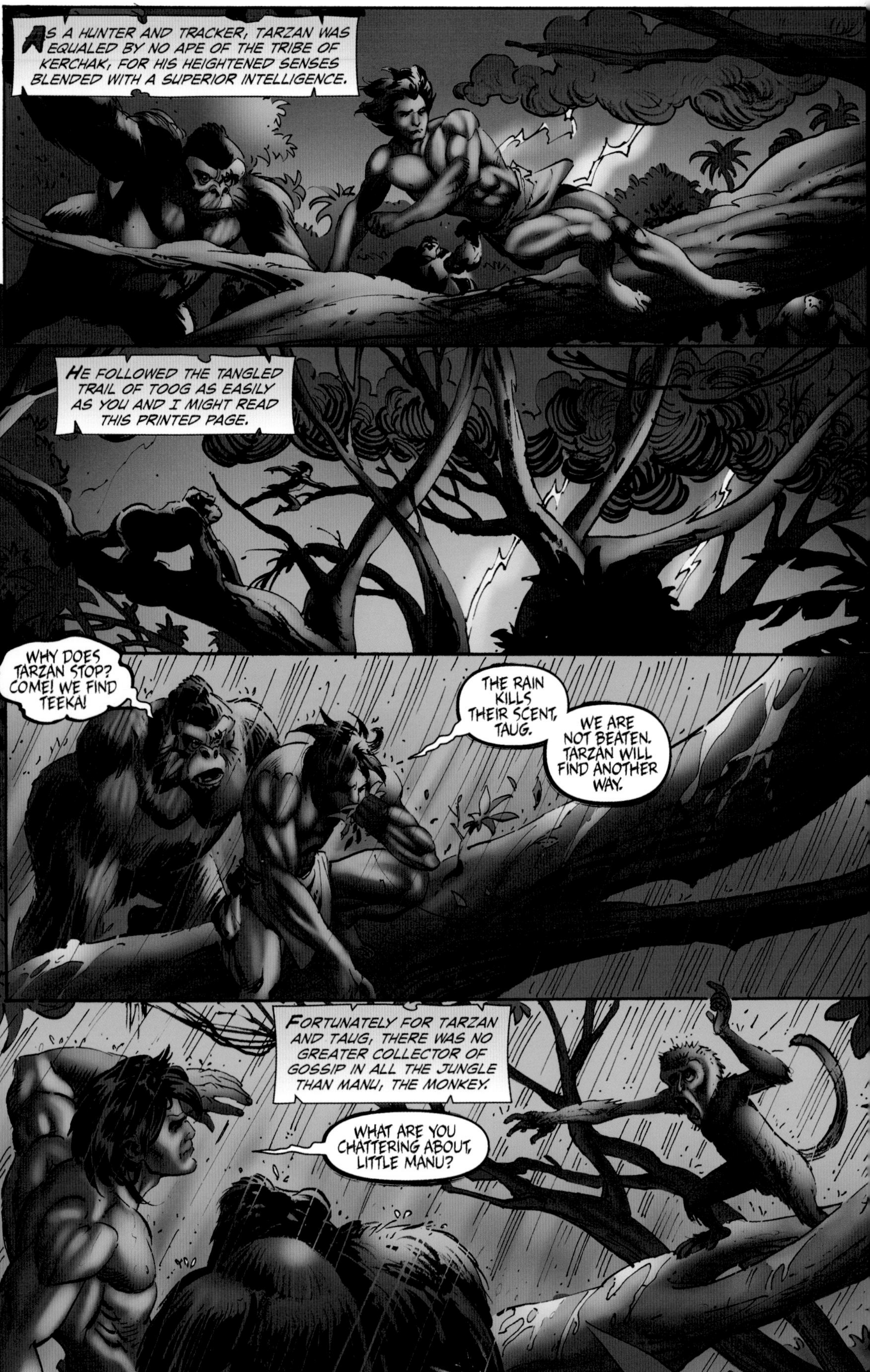
AS A HUNTER AND TRACKER, TARZAN WAS EQUALED BY NO APE OF THE TRIBE OF KERCHAK, FOR HIS HEIGHTENED SENSES BLENDED WITH A SUPERIOR INTELLIGENCE.
HE FOLLOWED THE TANGLED TRAIL OF TOOG AS EASILY AS YOU AND I MIGHT READ THIS PRINTED PAGE.
WHY DOES TARZAN STOP? COME! WE FIND TEEKA!
THE RAIN KILLS THEIR SCENT, TAUG.
WE ARE NOT BEATEN. TARZAN WILL FIND ANOTHER WAY.
FORTUNATELY FOR TARZAN AND TAUG, THERE WAS NO GREATER COLLECTOR OF GOSSIP IN ALL THE JUNGLE THAN MANU, THE MONKEY.
WHAT ARE YOU CHATTERING ABOUT, LITTLE MANU?

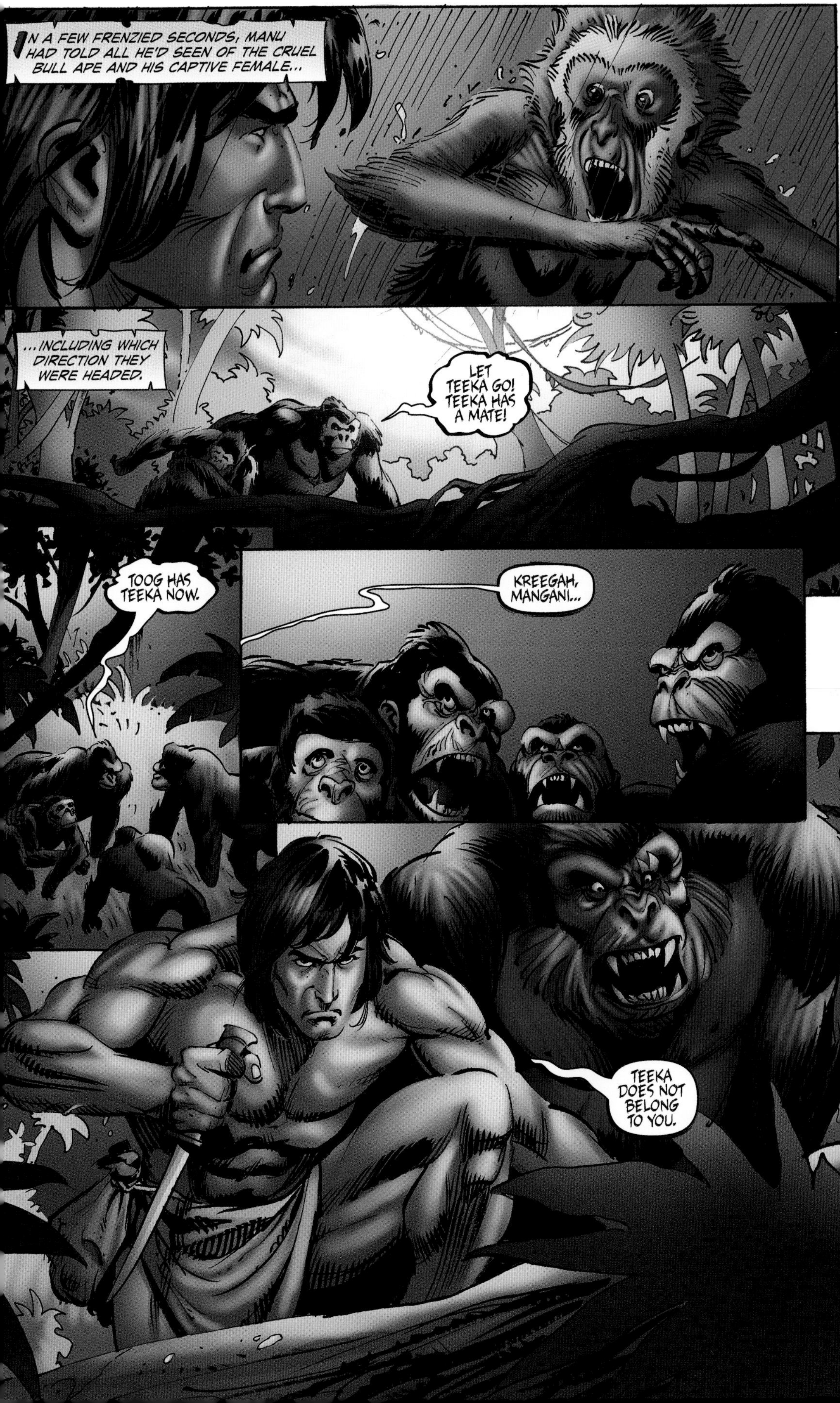
IN A FEW FRENZIED SECONDS, MANU HAD TOLD ALL HE'D SEEN OF THE CRUEL BULL APE AND HIS CAPTIVE FEMALE...
...INCLUDING WHICH DIRECTION THEY WERE HEADED.
LET TEEKA GO! TEEKA HAS A MATE!
TOOG HAS TEEKA NOW.
KREEGAH, MANGANI...
TEEKA DOES NOT BELONG TO YOU.

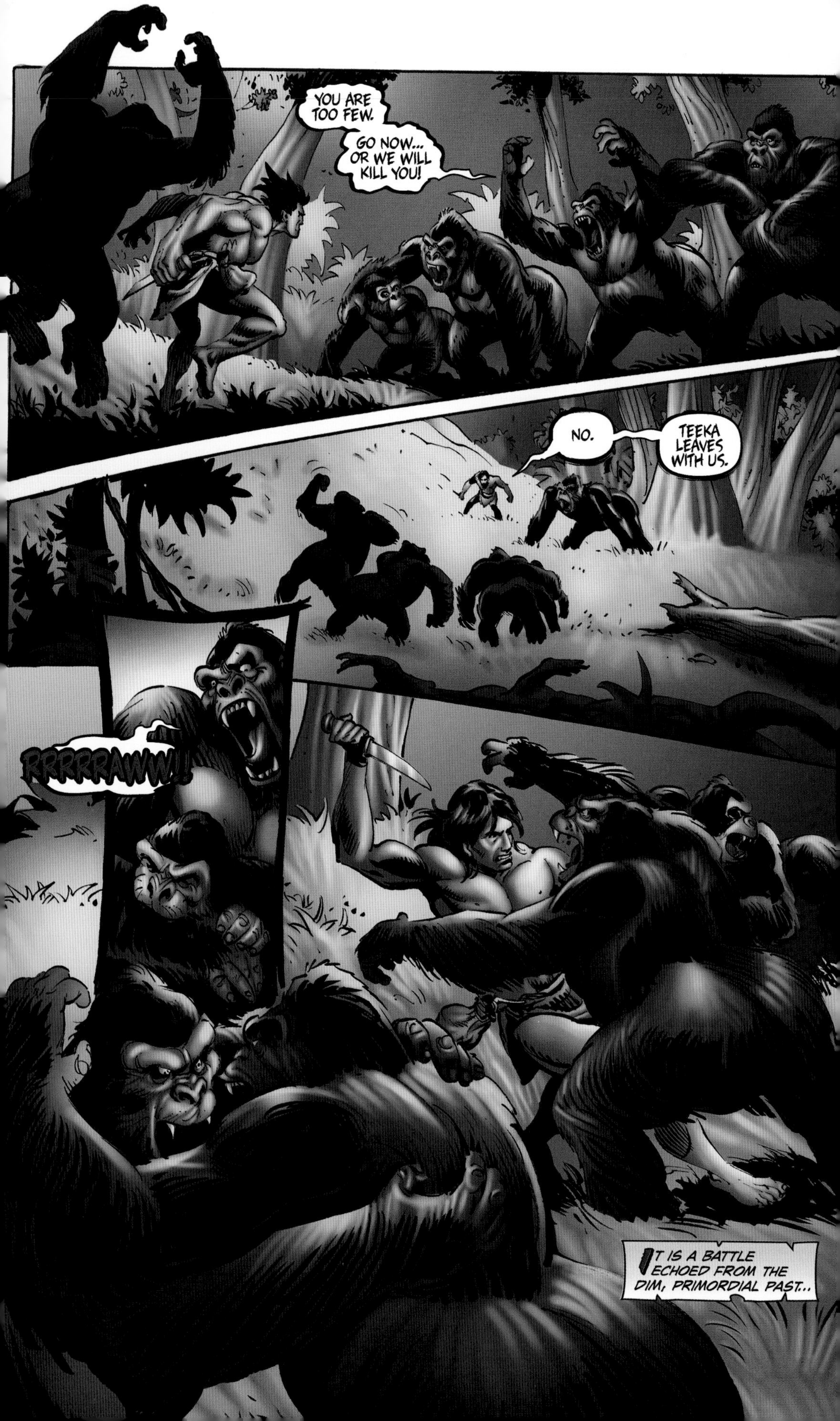
YOU ARE TOO FEW.
GO NOW... OR WE WILL KILL YOU!
NO.
TEEKA LEAVES WITH US.
RRRRRAWW!
IT IS A BATTLE ECHOED FROM THE DIM, PRIMORDIAL PAST...

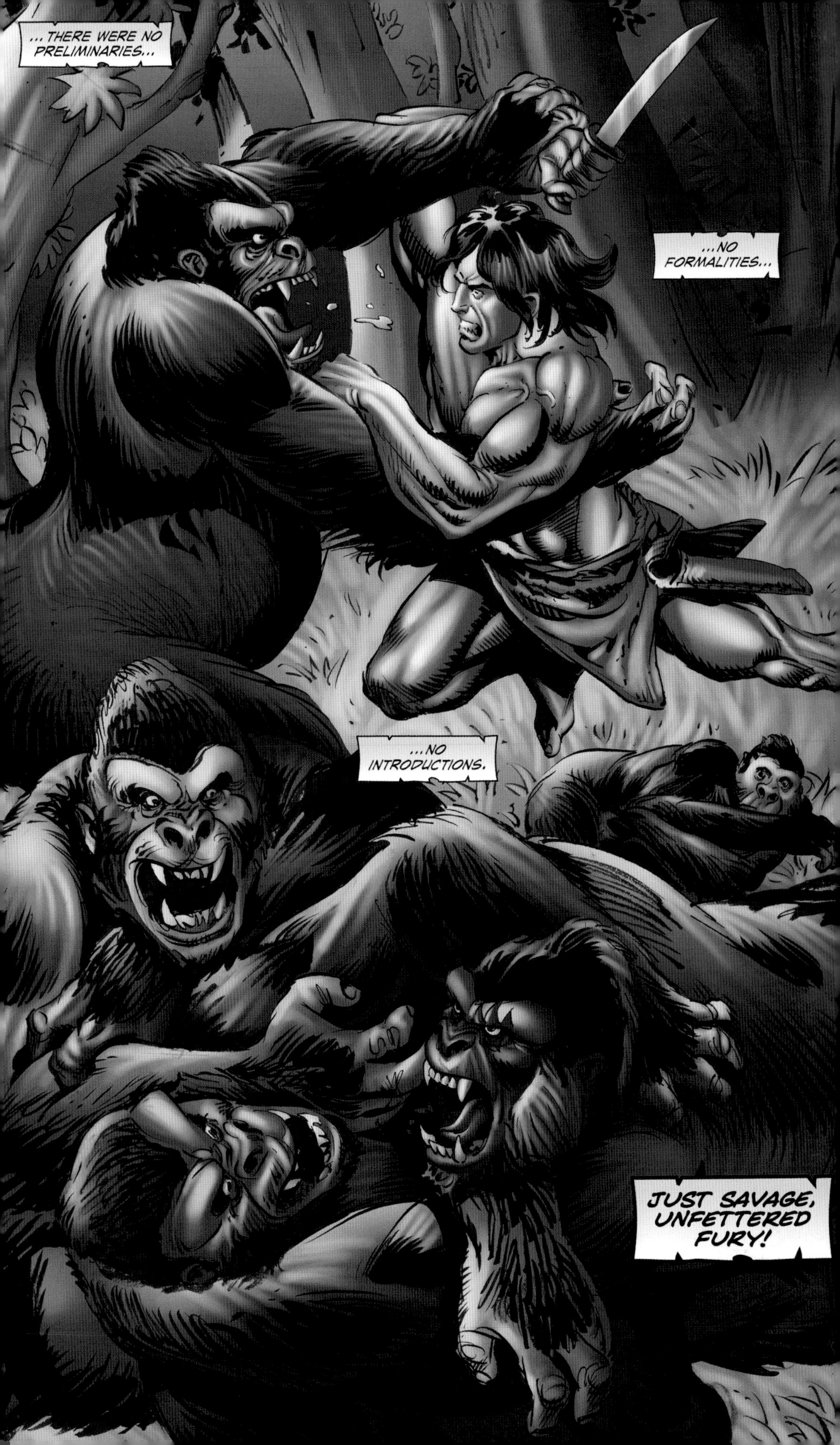
...THERE WERE NO PRELIMINARIES...
...NO FORMALITIES...
...NO INTRODUCTIONS.
JUST SAVAGE, UNFETTERED FURY!

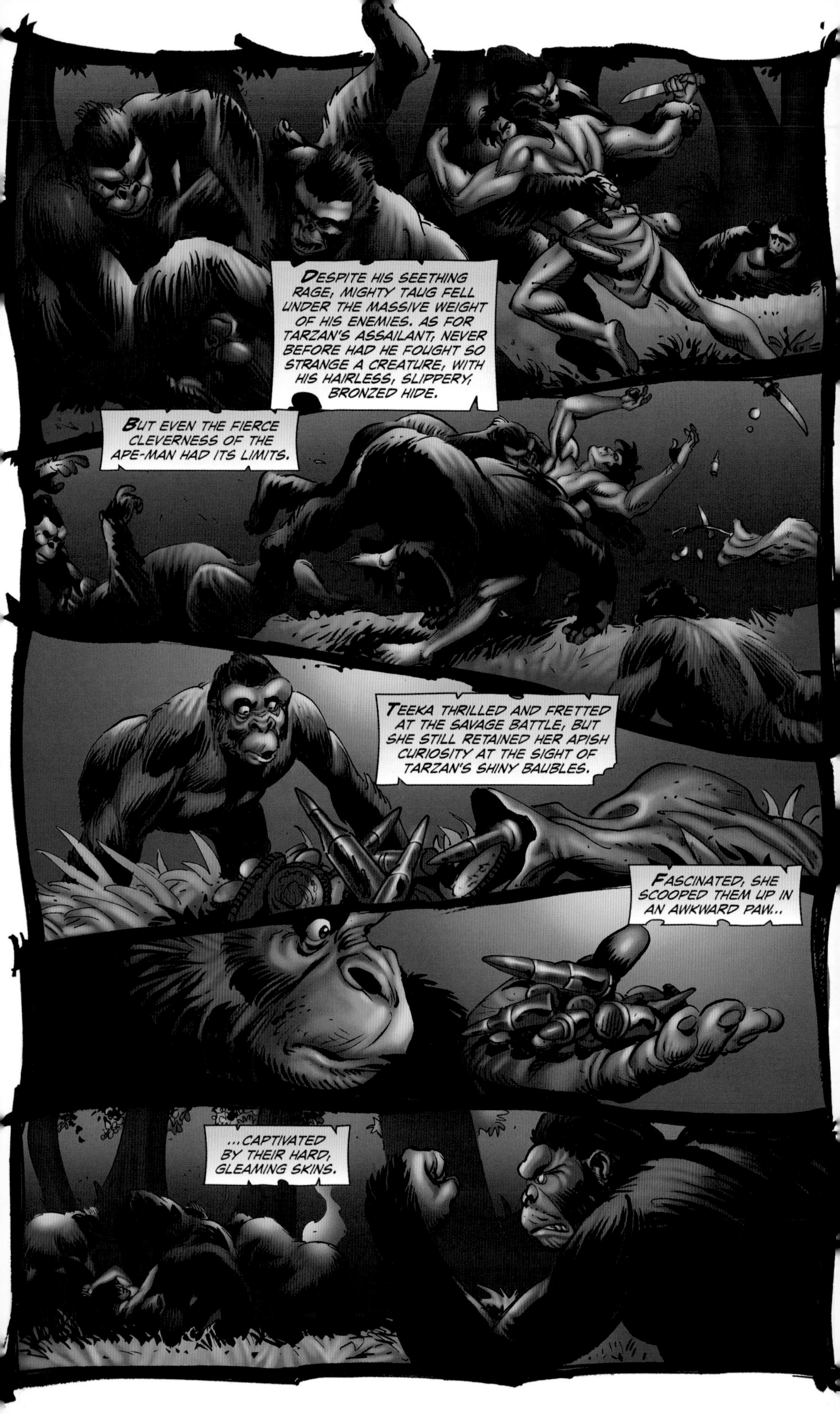
DESPITE HIS SEETHING RAGE, MIGHTY TAUG FELL UNDER THE MASSIVE WEIGHT OF HIS ENEMIES. AS FOR TARZAN'S ASSAILANT, NEVER BEFORE HAD HE FOUGHT SO STRANGE A CREATURE, WITH HIS HAIRLESS, SLIPPERY, BRONZED HIDE.
BUT EVEN THE FIERCE CLEVERNESS OF THE APE-MAN HAD ITS LIMITS.
TEEKA THRILLED AND FRETTED AT THE SAVAGE BATTLE, BUT SHE STILL RETAINED HER APISH CURIOSITY AT THE SIGHT OF TARZAN'S SHINY BAUBLES.
FASCINATED, SHE SCOOPED THEM UP IN AN AWKWARD PAW...
...CAPTIVATED BY THEIR HARD, GLEAMING SKINS.

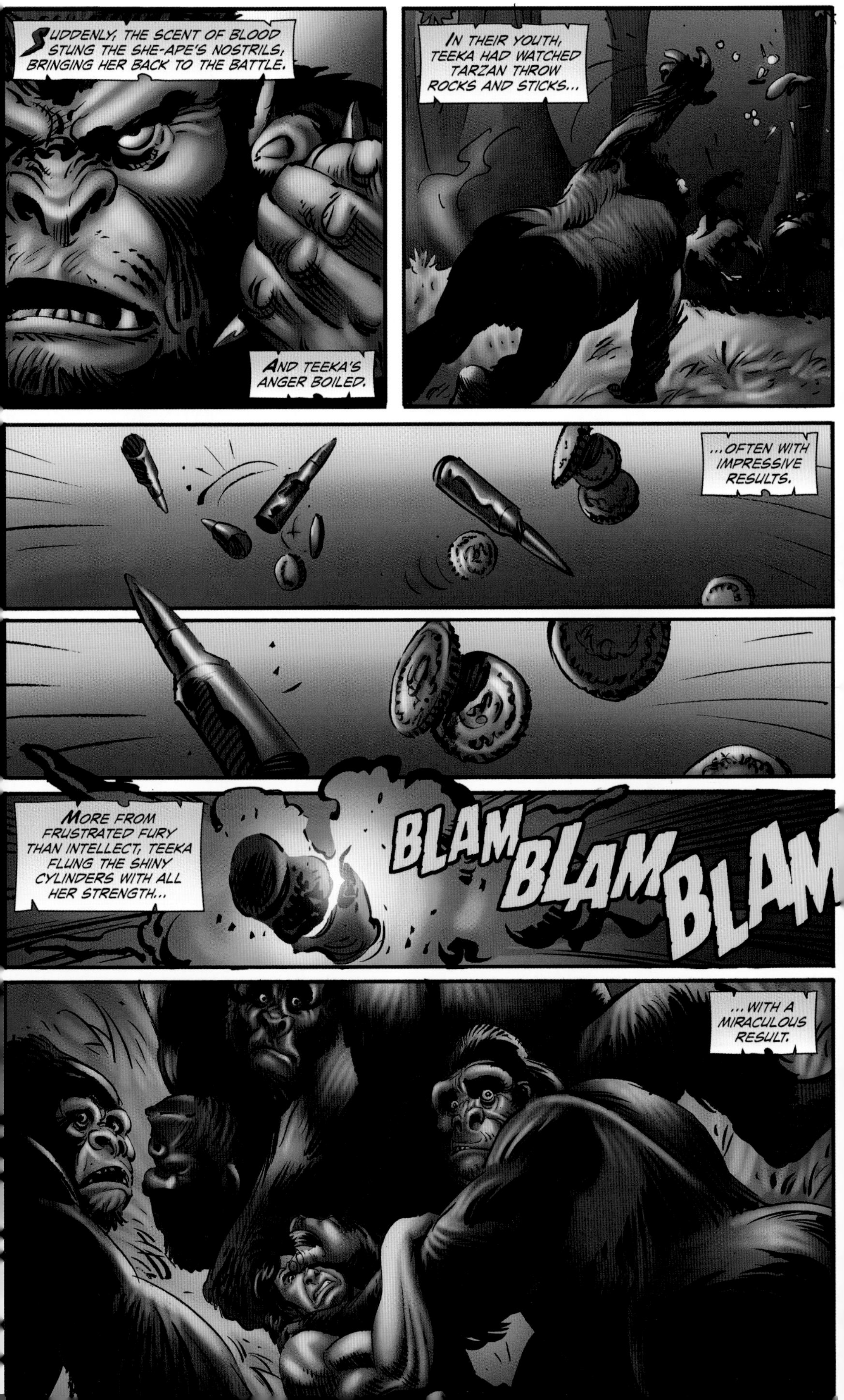
SUDDENLY, THE SCENT OF BLOOD STUNG THE SHE-APE'S NOSTRILS, BRINGING HER BACK TO THE BATTLE.
AND TEEKA'S ANGER BOILED.
IN THEIR YOUTH, TEEKA HAD WATCHED TARZAN THROW ROCKS AND STICKS...
...OFTEN WITH IMPRESSIVE RESULTS.
MORE FROM FRUSTRATED FURY THAN INTELLECT, TEEKA FLUNG THE SHINY CYLINDERS WITH ALL HER STRENGTH...
BLAM
BLAM
BLAM
...WITH A MIRACULOUS RESULT.

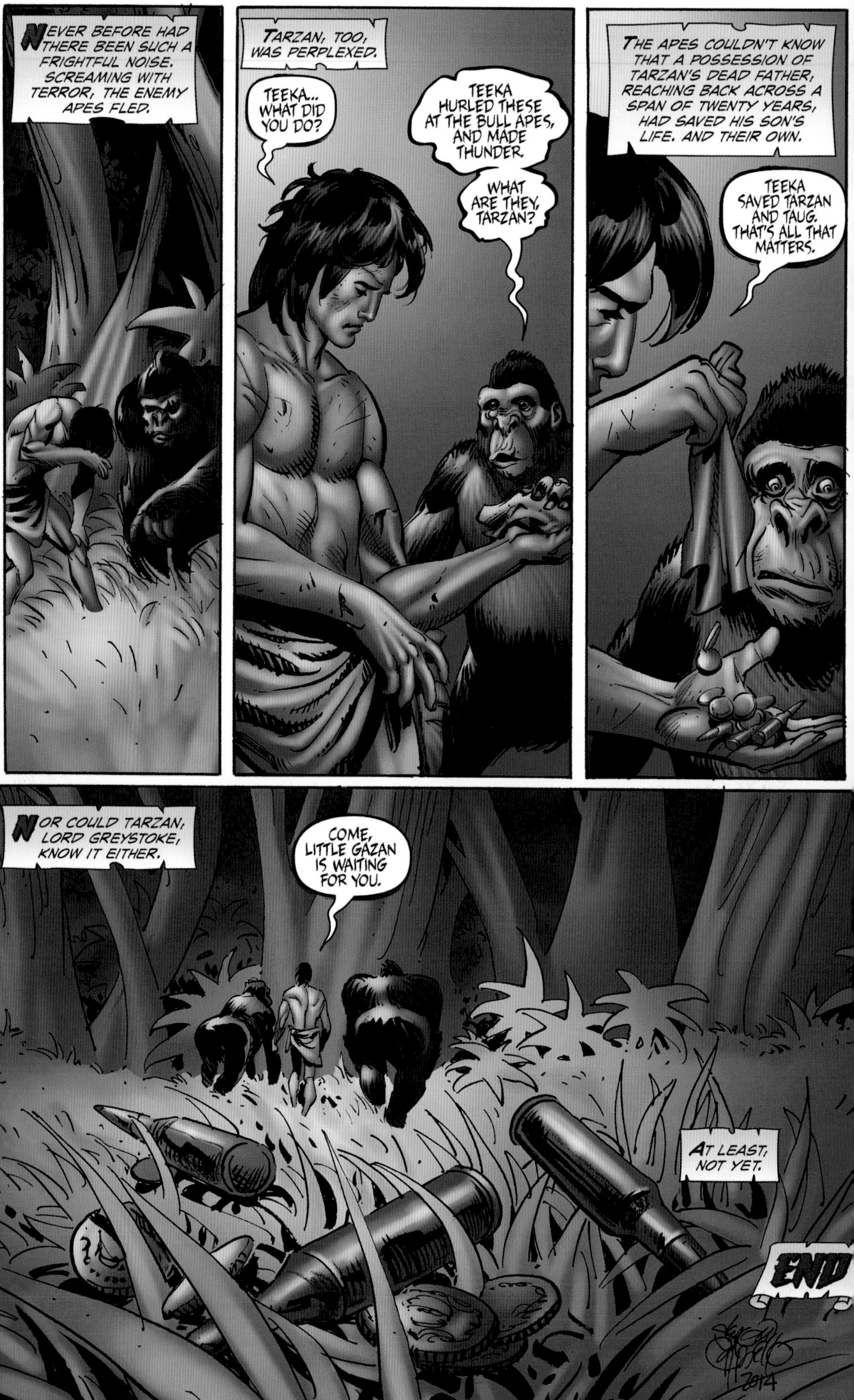
NEVER BEFORE HAD THERE BEEN SUCH A FRIGHTFUL NOISE. SCREAMING WITH TERROR, THE ENEMY APES FLED.
TARZAN, TOO, WAS PERPLEXED.
TEEKA... WHAT DID YOU DO?
TEEKA HURLED THESE AT THE BULL APES, AND MADE THUNDER.
WHAT ARE THEY, TARZAN?
THE APES COULDN'T KNOW THAT A POSSESSION OF TARZAN'S DEAD FATHER, REACHING BACK ACROSS A SPAN OF TWENTY YEARS, HAD SAVED HIS SON'S LIFE. AND THEIR OWN.
TEEKA SAVED TARZAN AND TAUG. THAT'S ALL THAT MATTERS.
NOR COULD TARZAN, LORD GREYSTOKE, KNOW IT EITHER.
COME, LITTLE GAZAN IS WAITING FOR YOU.
AT LEAST, NOT YET.
END
2014

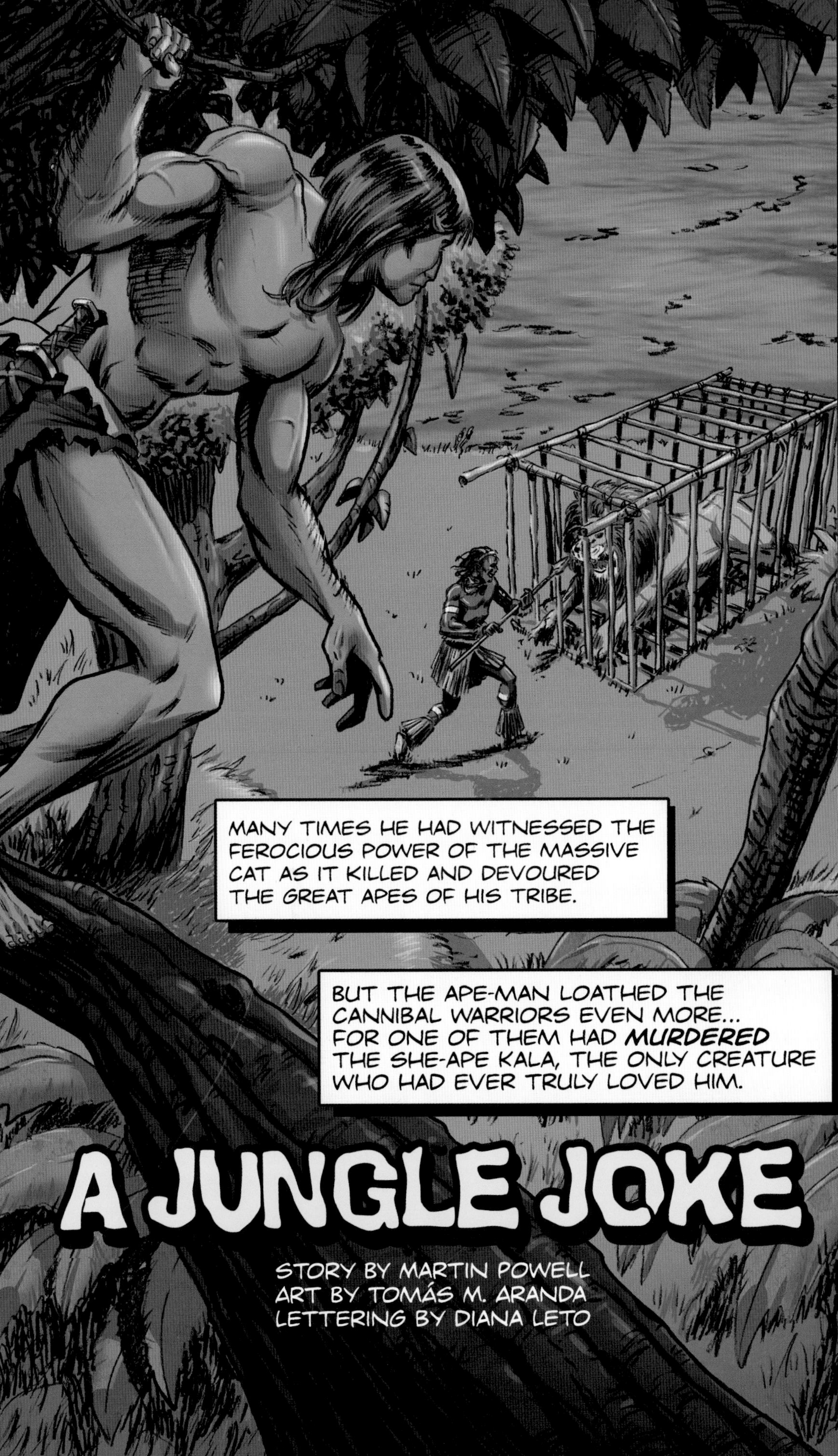
MANY TIMES HE HAD WITNESSED THE FEROCIOUS POWER OF THE MASSIVE CAT AS IT KILLED AND DEVOURED THE GREAT APES OF HIS TRIBE.
BUT THE APE-MAN LOATHED THE CANNIBAL WARRIORS EVEN MORE... FOR ONE OF THEM HAD *MURDERED* THE SHE-APE KALA, THE ONLY CREATURE WHO HAD EVER TRULY LOVED HIM.
A JUNGLE JOKE
STORY BY MARTIN POWELL
ART BY TOMÁS M. ARANDA
LETTERING BY DIANA LETO

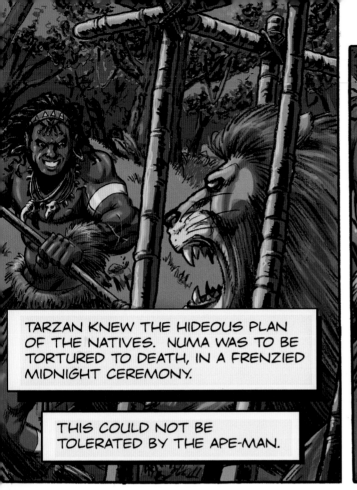

TARZAN KNEW THE HIDEOUS PLAN OF THE NATIVES. NUMA WAS TO BE TORTURED TO DEATH, IN A FRENZIED MIDNIGHT CEREMONY.

THIS COULD NOT BE TOLERATED BY THE APE-MAN.

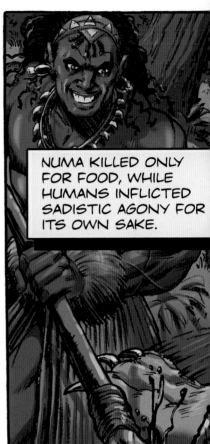

NUMA KILLED ONLY FOR FOOD, WHILE HUMANS INFLICTED SADISTIC AGONY FOR ITS OWN SAKE.

AN ENEMY AS NOBLE AS NUMA SHOULD NEVER SUFFER SUCH A FATE. NOT IF TARZAN COULD STOP IT.

AND STOP IT HE *COULD.*

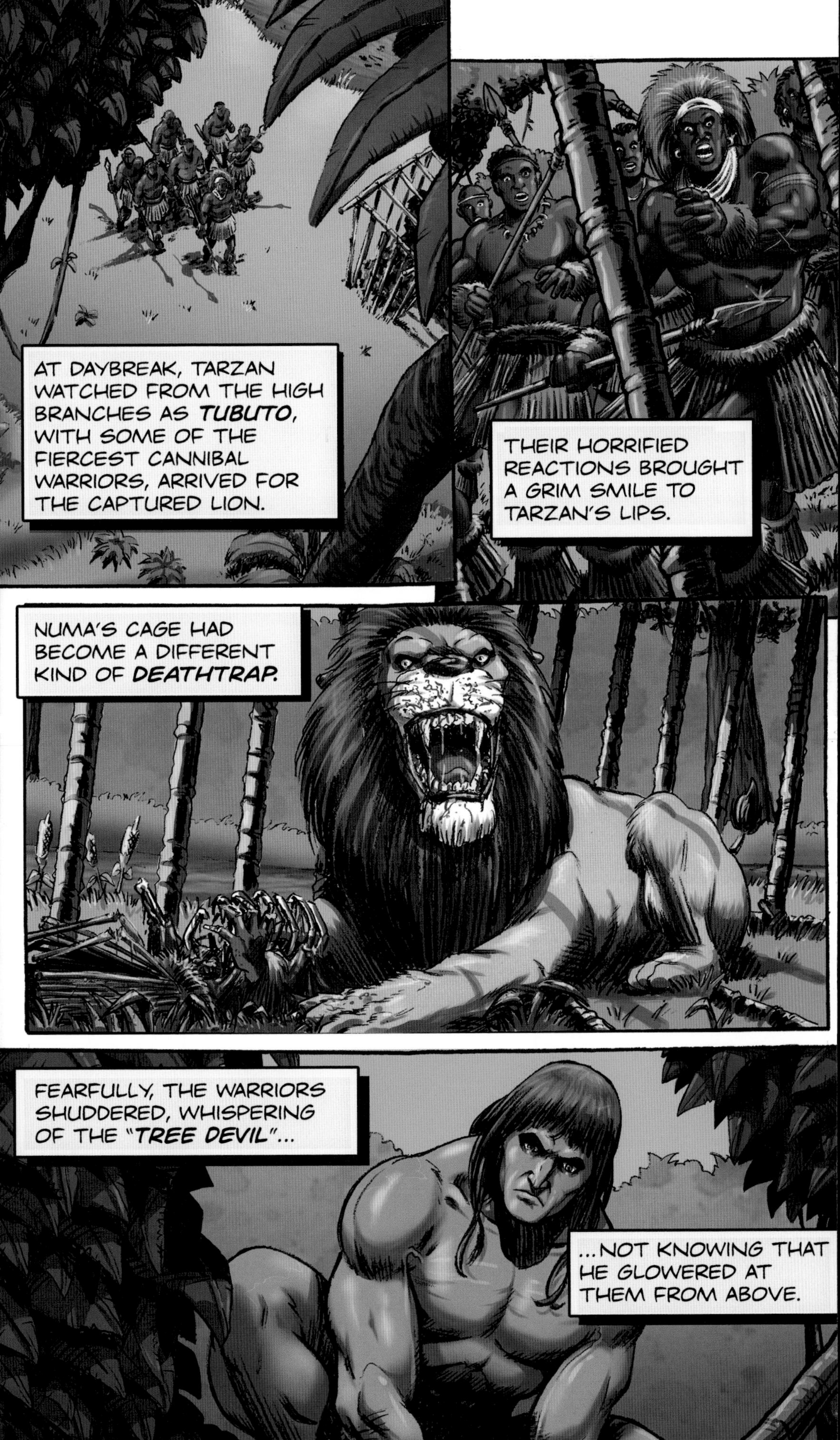
AT DAYBREAK, TARZAN WATCHED FROM THE HIGH BRANCHES AS TUBUTO, WITH SOME OF THE FIERCEST CANNIBAL WARRIORS, ARRIVED FOR THE CAPTURED LION.
THEIR HORRIFIED REACTIONS BROUGHT A GRIM SMILE TO TARZAN'S LIPS.
NUMA'S CAGE HAD BECOME A DIFFERENT KIND OF DEATHTRAP.
FEARFULLY, THE WARRIORS SHUDDERED, WHISPERING OF THE "TREE DEVIL"...
...NOT KNOWING THAT HE GLOWERED AT THEM FROM ABOVE.

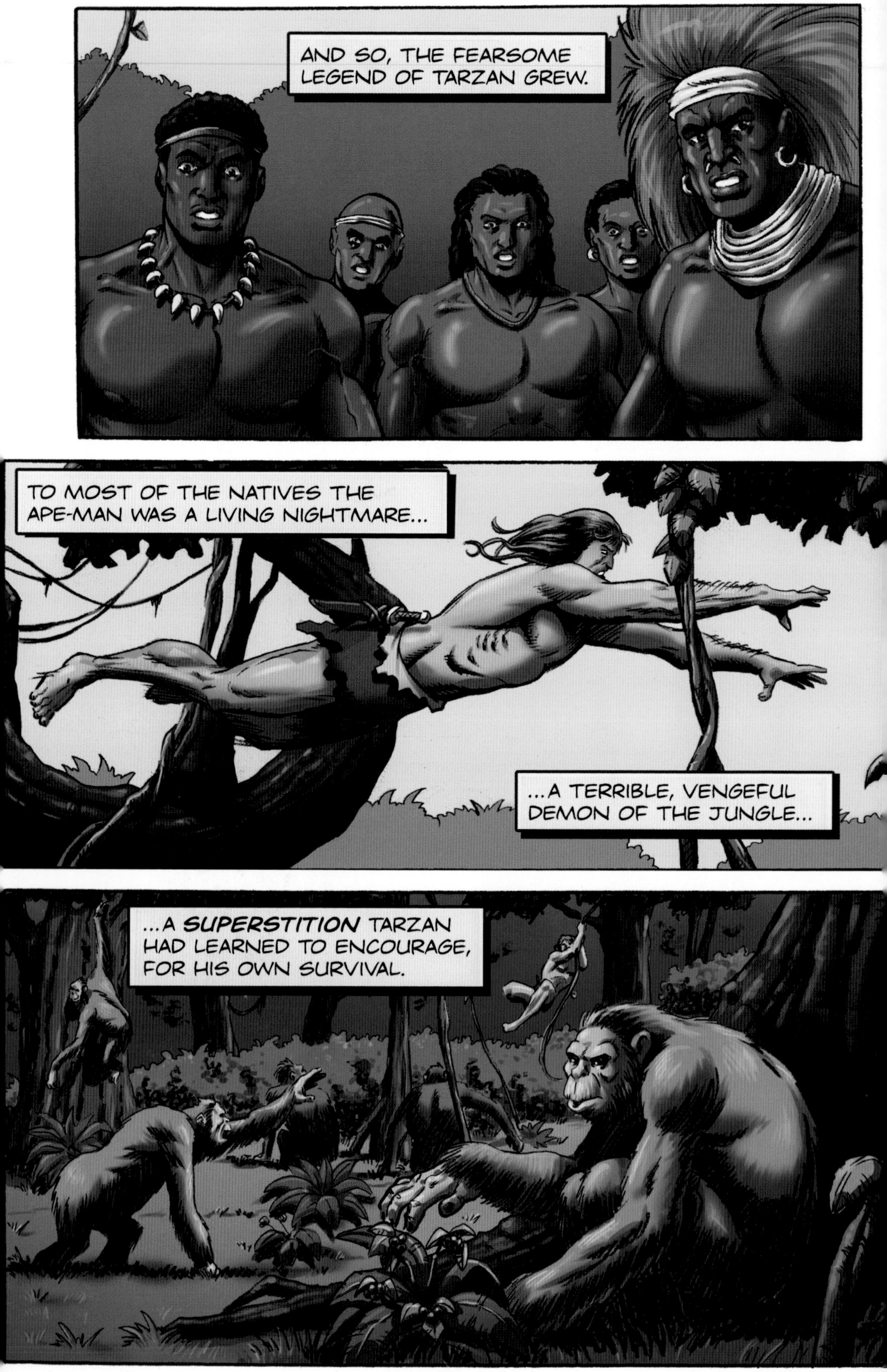
AND SO, THE FEARSOME LEGEND OF TARZAN GREW.
TO MOST OF THE NATIVES THE APE-MAN WAS A LIVING NIGHTMARE...
...A TERRIBLE, VENGEFUL DEMON OF THE JUNGLE...
...A SUPERSTITION TARZAN HAD LEARNED TO ENCOURAGE, FOR HIS OWN SURVIVAL.

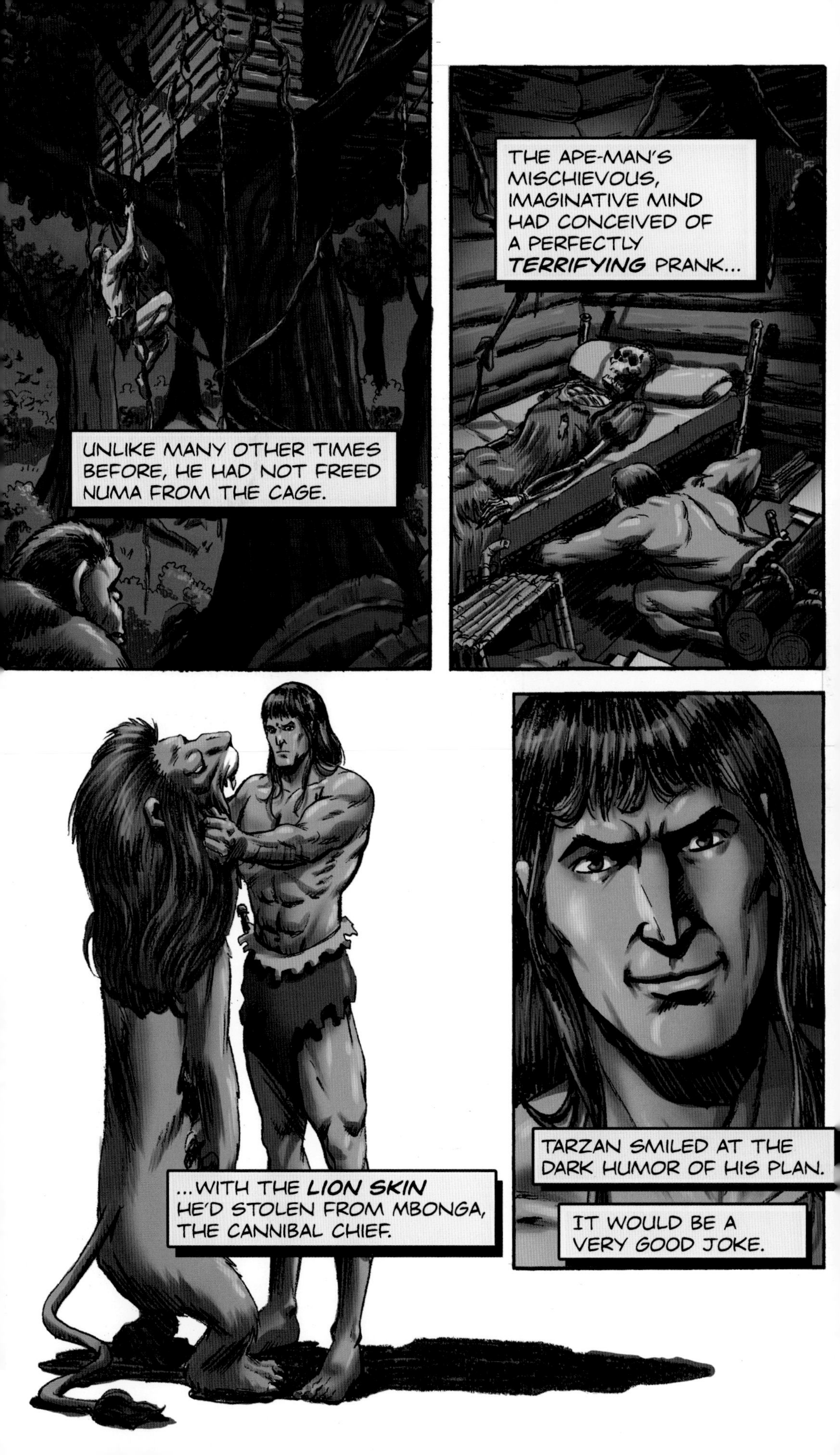
UNLIKE MANY OTHER TIMES BEFORE, HE HAD NOT FREED NUMA FROM THE CAGE.
THE APE-MAN'S MISCHIEVOUS, IMAGINATIVE MIND HAD CONCEIVED OF A PERFECTLY TERRIFYING PRANK...
...WITH THE LION SKIN HE'D STOLEN FROM MBONGA, THE CANNIBAL CHIEF.
TARZAN SMILED AT THE DARK HUMOR OF HIS PLAN.
IT WOULD BE A VERY GOOD JOKE.

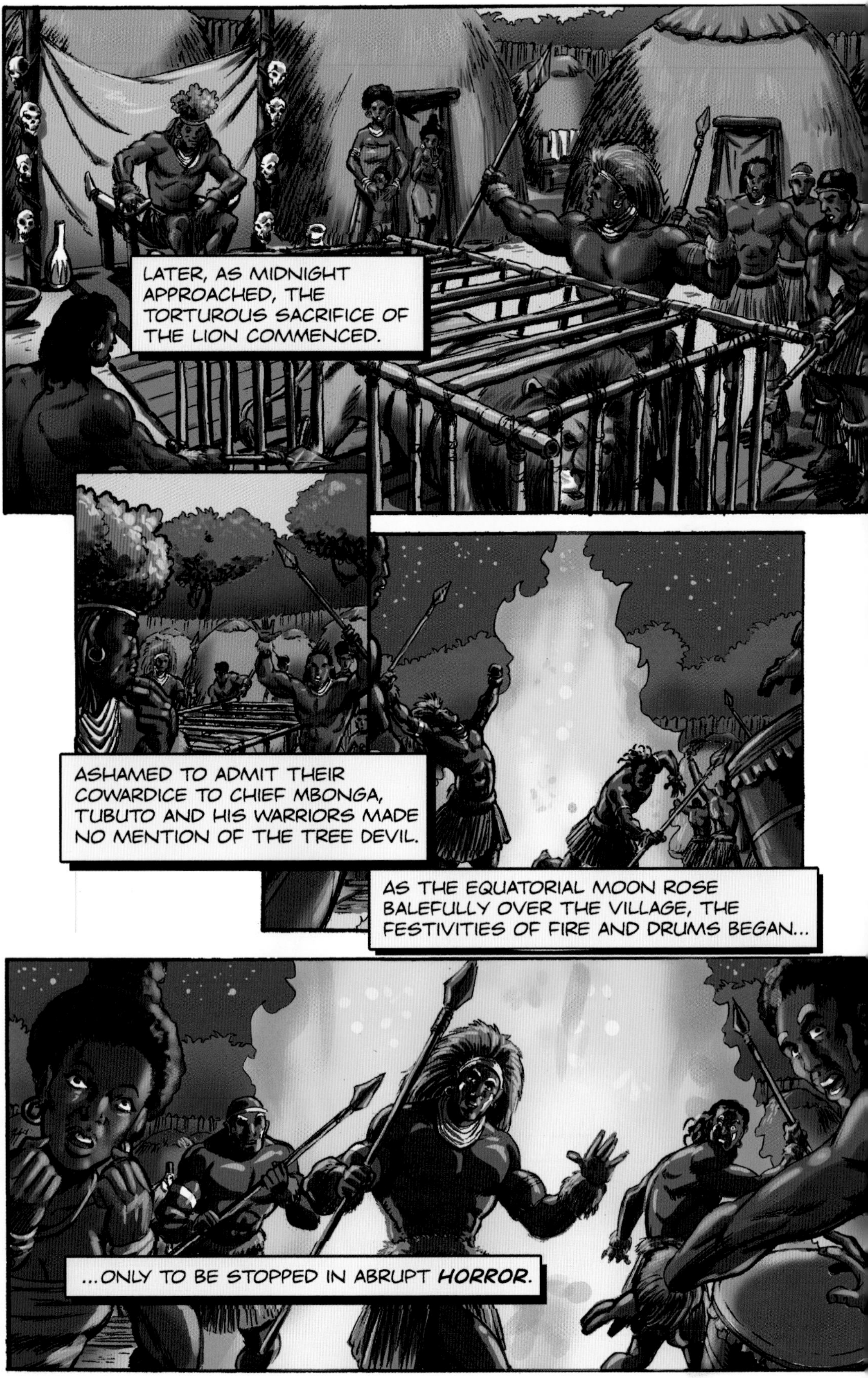
LATER, AS MIDNIGHT APPROACHED, THE TORTUROUS SACRIFICE OF THE LION COMMENCED.
ASHAMED TO ADMIT THEIR COWARDICE TO CHIEF MBONGA, TUBUTO AND HIS WARRIORS MADE NO MENTION OF THE TREE DEVIL.
AS THE EQUATORIAL MOON ROSE BALEFULLY OVER THE VILLAGE, THE FESTIVITIES OF FIRE AND DRUMS BEGAN...
...ONLY TO BE STOPPED IN ABRUPT *HORROR*.

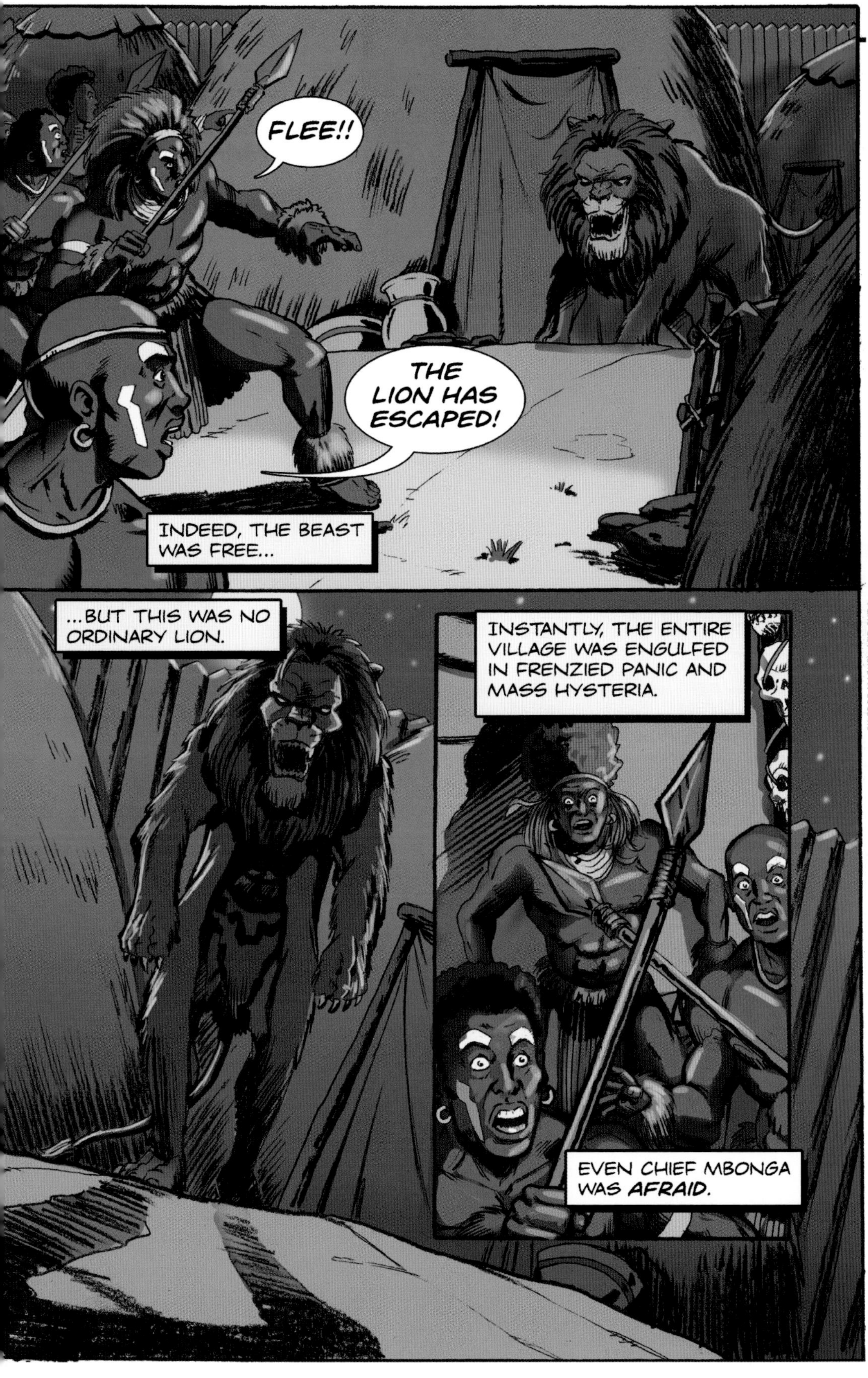
FLEE!!
THE LION HAS ESCAPED!
INDEED, THE BEAST WAS FREE...
...BUT THIS WAS NO ORDINARY LION.
INSTANTLY, THE ENTIRE VILLAGE WAS ENGULFED IN FRENZIED PANIC AND MASS HYSTERIA.
EVEN CHIEF MBONGA WAS *AFRAID*.

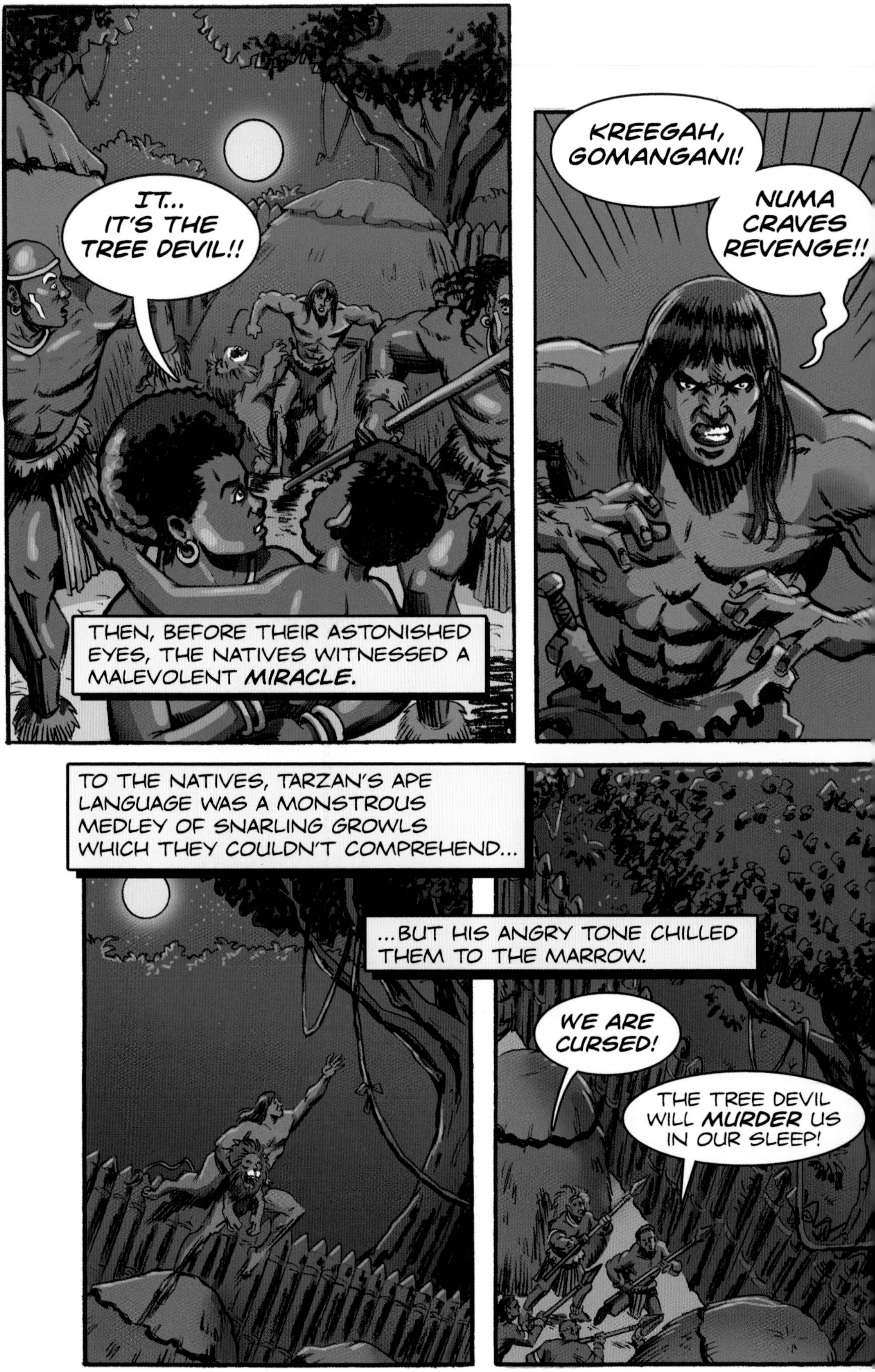
IT... IT'S THE TREE DEVIL!!
THEN, BEFORE THEIR ASTONISHED EYES, THE NATIVES WITNESSED A MALEVOLENT MIRACLE.
KREEGAH, GOMANGANI!
NUMA CRAVES REVENGE!!
TO THE NATIVES, TARZAN'S APE LANGUAGE WAS A MONSTROUS MEDLEY OF SNARLING GROWLS WHICH THEY COULDN'T COMPREHEND...
...BUT HIS ANGRY TONE CHILLED THEM TO THE MARROW.
WE ARE CURSED!
THE TREE DEVIL WILL MURDER US IN OUR SLEEP!

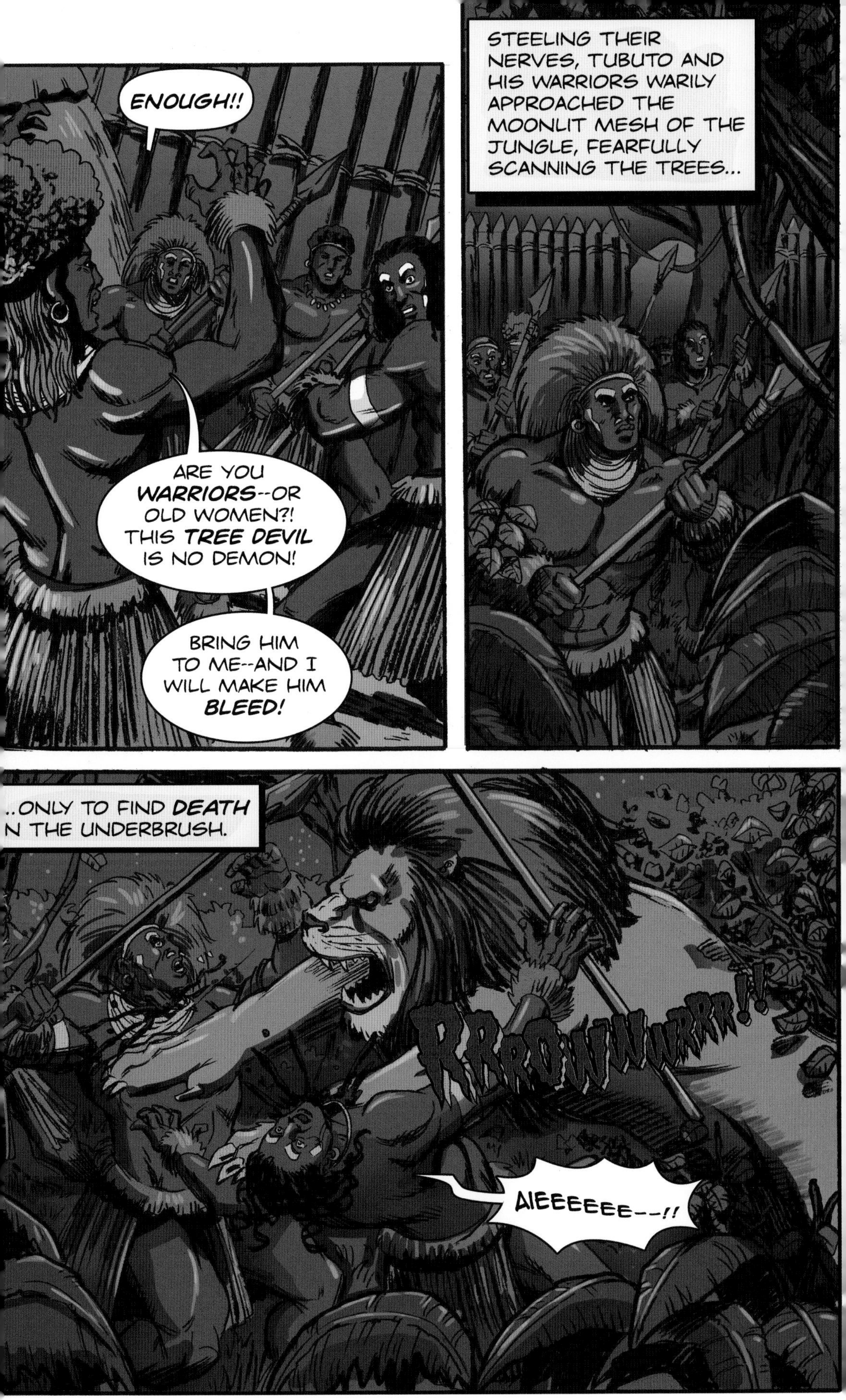
ENOUGH!!
ARE YOU WARRIORS--OR OLD WOMEN?! THIS TREE DEVIL IS NO DEMON!
BRING HIM TO ME--AND I WILL MAKE HIM BLEED!
STEELING THEIR NERVES, TUBUTO AND HIS WARRIORS WARILY APPROACHED THE MOONLIT MESH OF THE JUNGLE, FEARFULLY SCANNING THE TREES...
..ONLY TO FIND DEATH
N THE UNDERBRUSH.
RRROWWNWRRR!!
AIEEEEEEE--!!

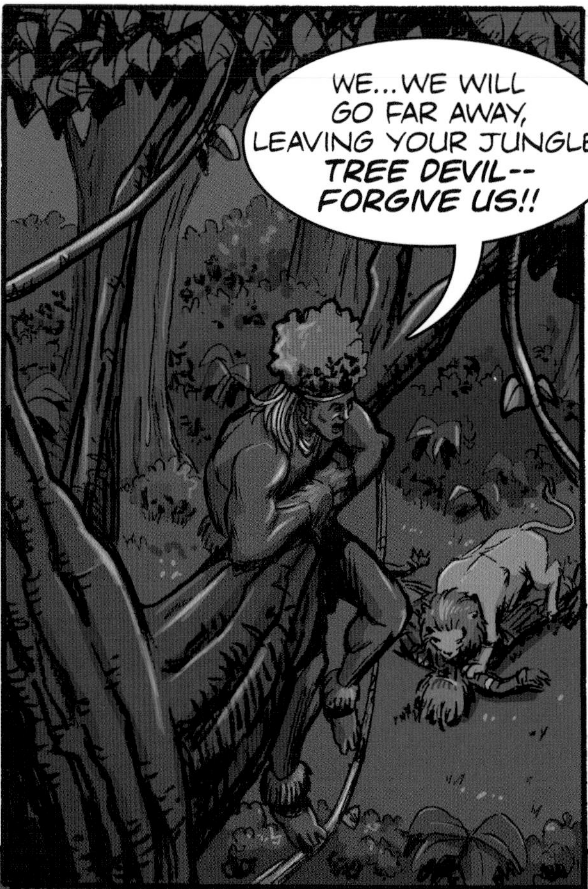
WE...WE WILL GO FAR AWAY, LEAVING YOUR JUNGLE! TREE DEVIL-- FORGIVE US!!
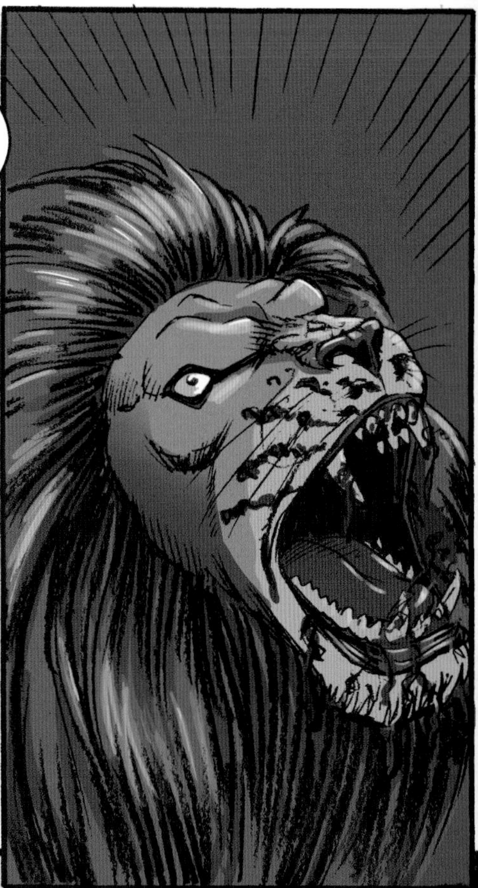
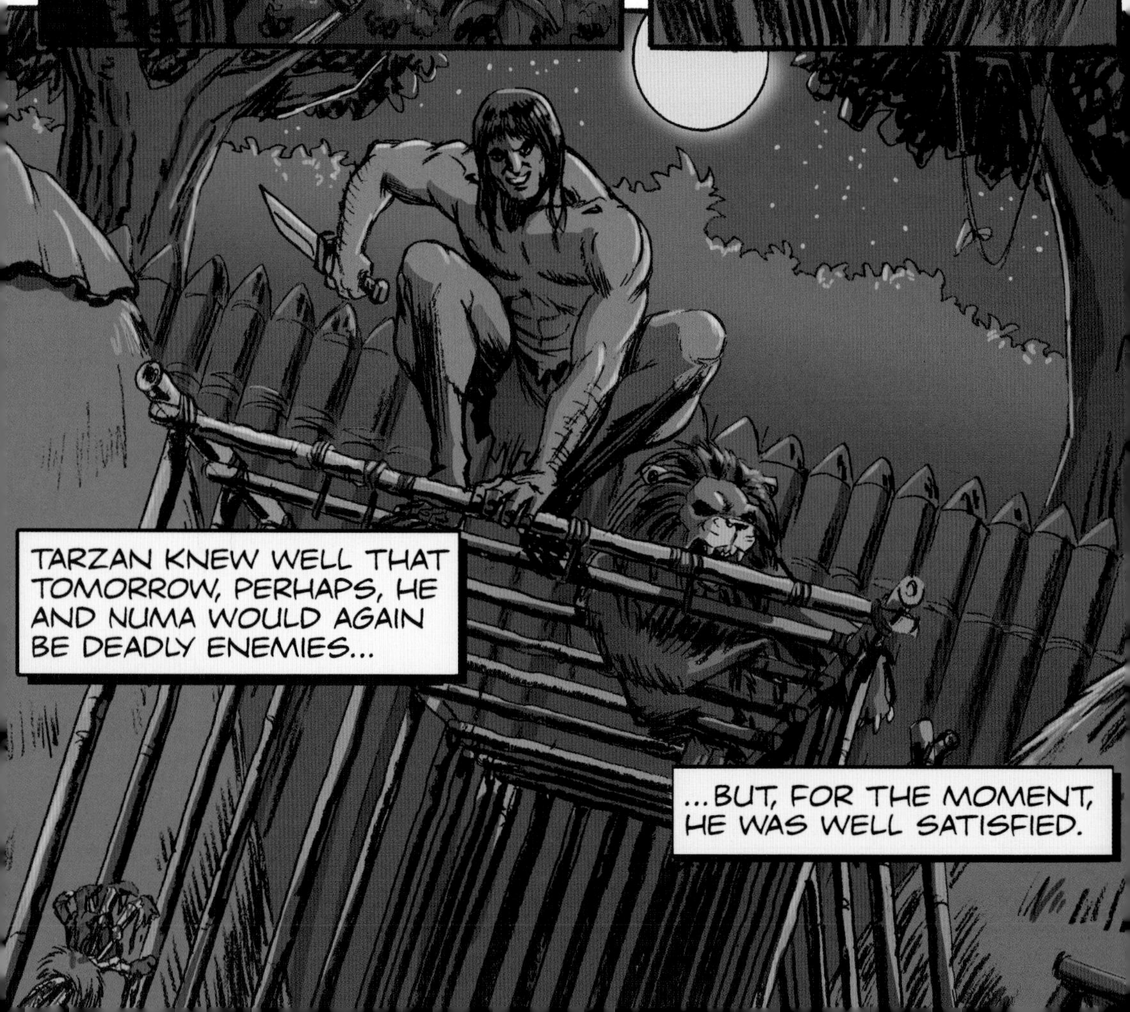
TARZAN KNEW WELL THAT TOMORROW, PERHAPS, HE AND NUMA WOULD AGAIN BE DEADLY ENEMIES...
...BUT, FOR THE MOMENT, HE WAS WELL SATISFIED.

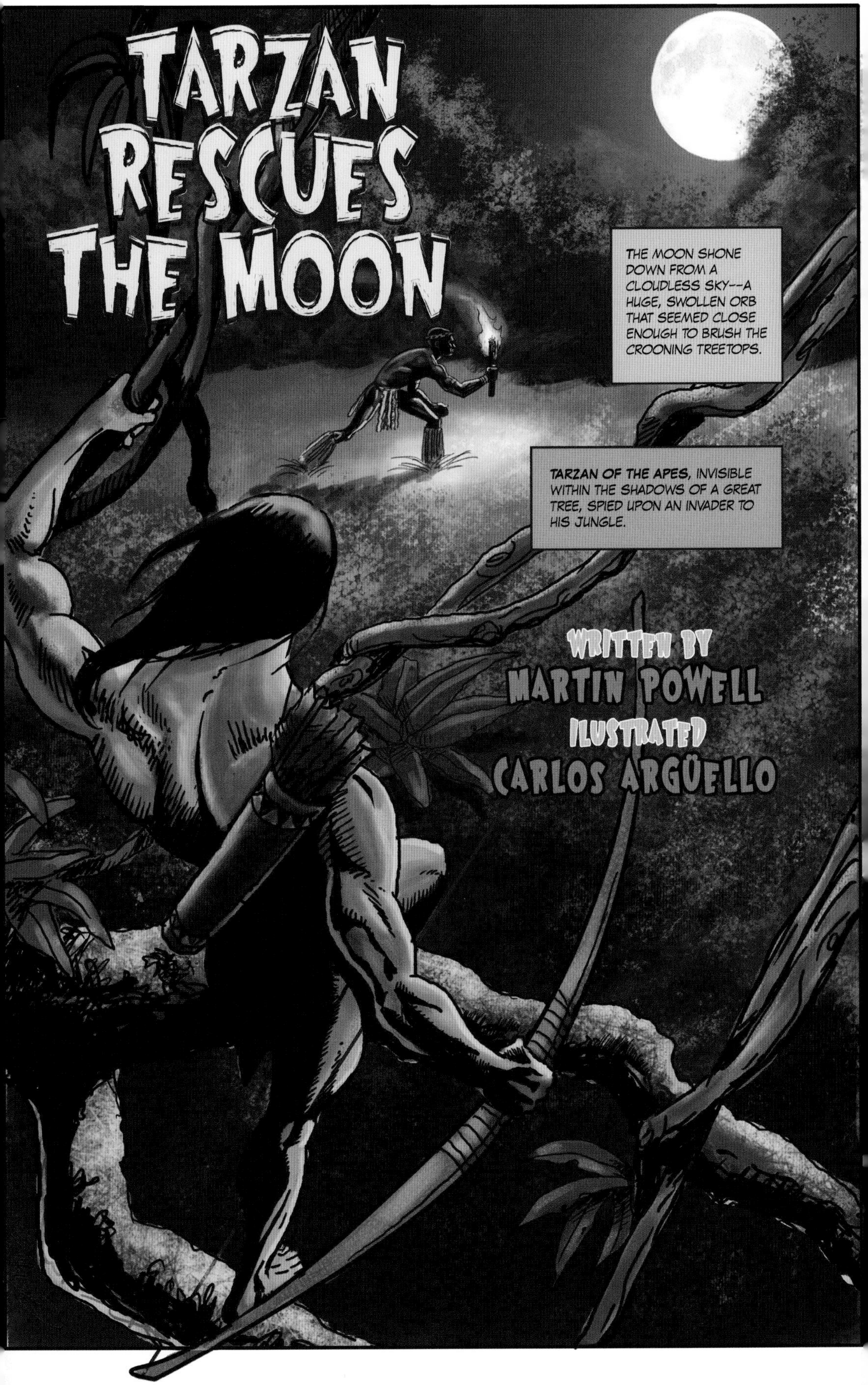
TARZAN RESCUES THE MOON
THE MOON SHONE DOWN FROM A CLOUDLESS SKY--A HUGE, SWOLLEN ORB THAT SEEMED CLOSE ENOUGH TO BRUSH THE CROONING TREETOPS.
TARZAN OF THE APES, INVISIBLE WITHIN THE SHADOWS OF A GREAT TREE, SPIED UPON AN INVADER TO HIS JUNGLE.
WRITTEN BY
MARTIN POWELL
ILUSTRATED
CARLOS ARGÜELLO

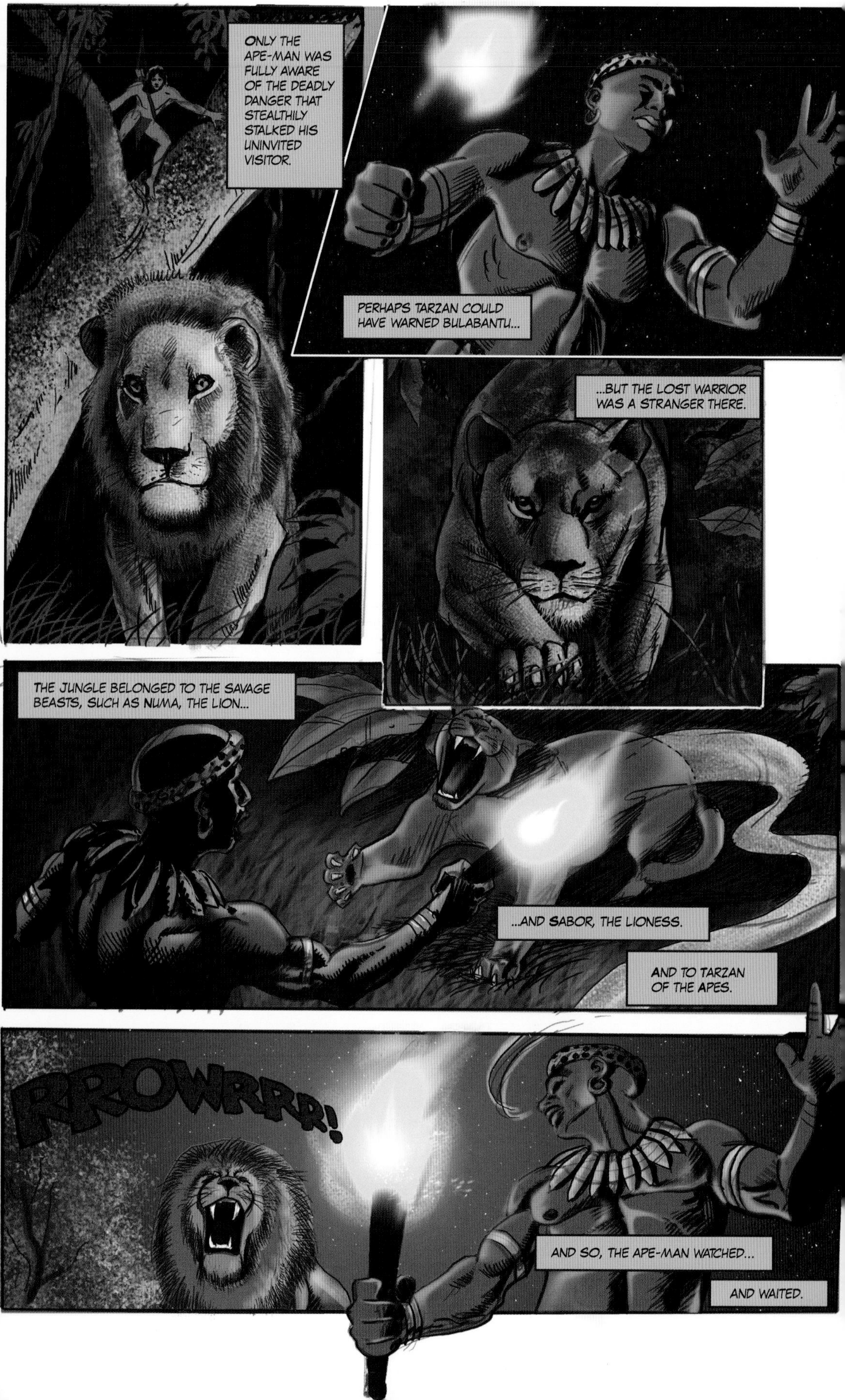
ONLY THE APE-MAN WAS FULLY AWARE OF THE DEADLY DANGER THAT STEALTHILY STALKED HIS UNINVITED VISITOR.
PERHAPS TARZAN COULD HAVE WARNED BULABANTU...
...BUT THE LOST WARRIOR WAS A STRANGER THERE.
THE JUNGLE BELONGED TO THE SAVAGE BEASTS, SUCH AS NUMA, THE LION...
...AND SABOR, THE LIONESS.
AND TO TARZAN OF THE APES.
RRROWRRR!
AND SO, THE APE-MAN WATCHED...
AND WAITED.

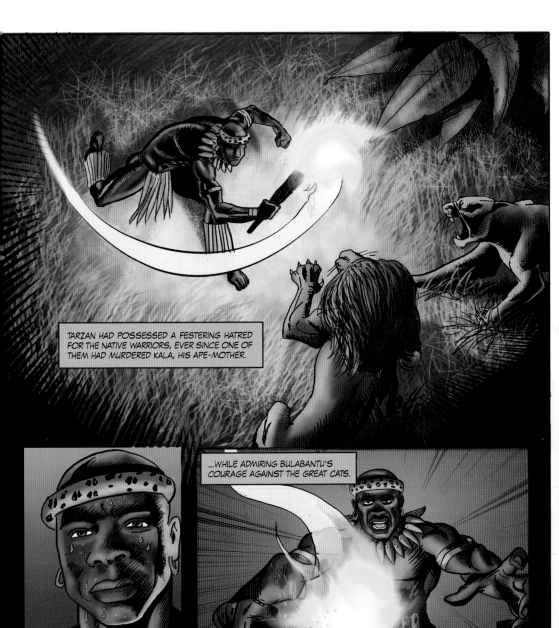

TARZAN HAD POSSESSED A FESTERING HATRED FOR THE NATIVE WARRIORS, EVER SINCE ONE OF THEM HAD MURDERED KALA, HIS APE-MOTHER.

...WHILE ADMIRING BULABANTU'S COURAGE AGAINST THE GREAT CATS.

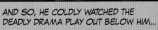

AND SO, HE COLDLY WATCHED THE DEADLY DRAMA PLAY OUT BELOW HIM...

WHEN THE BEASTS BOUNDED AWAY, IN SEARCH OF EASIER PREY, TARZAN SMILED.

ALTHOUGH HE DIDN'T EXACTLY UNDERSTAND WHY.

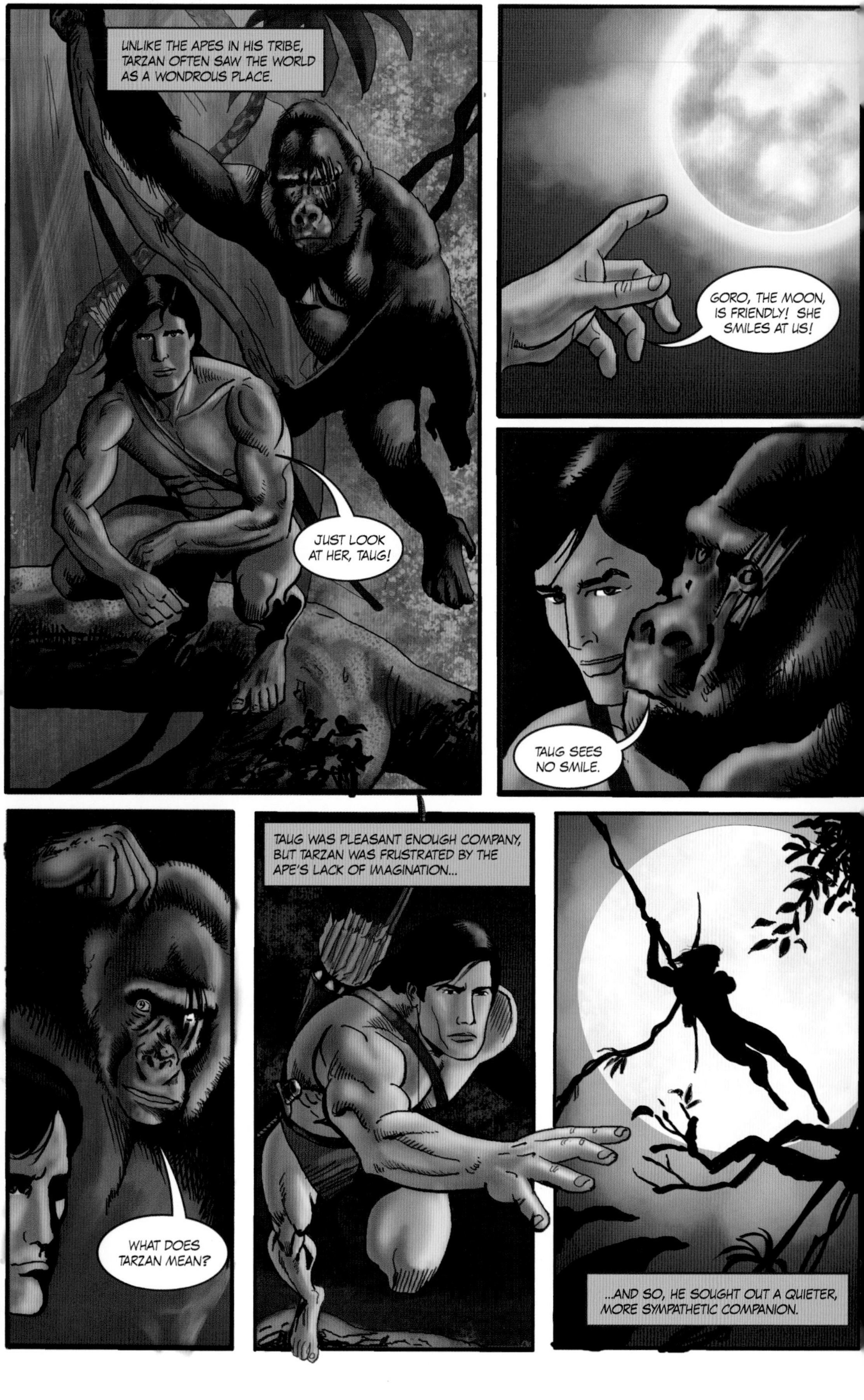
UNLIKE THE APES IN HIS TRIBE, TARZAN OFTEN SAW THE WORLD AS A WONDROUS PLACE.
JUST LOOK AT HER, TAUG!
GORO, THE MOON, IS FRIENDLY! SHE SMILES AT US!
TAUG SEES NO SMILE.
WHAT DOES TARZAN MEAN?
TAUG WAS PLEASANT ENOUGH COMPANY, BUT TARZAN WAS FRUSTRATED BY THE APE'S LACK OF IMAGINATION...
...AND SO, HE SOUGHT OUT A QUIETER, MORE SYMPATHETIC COMPANION.

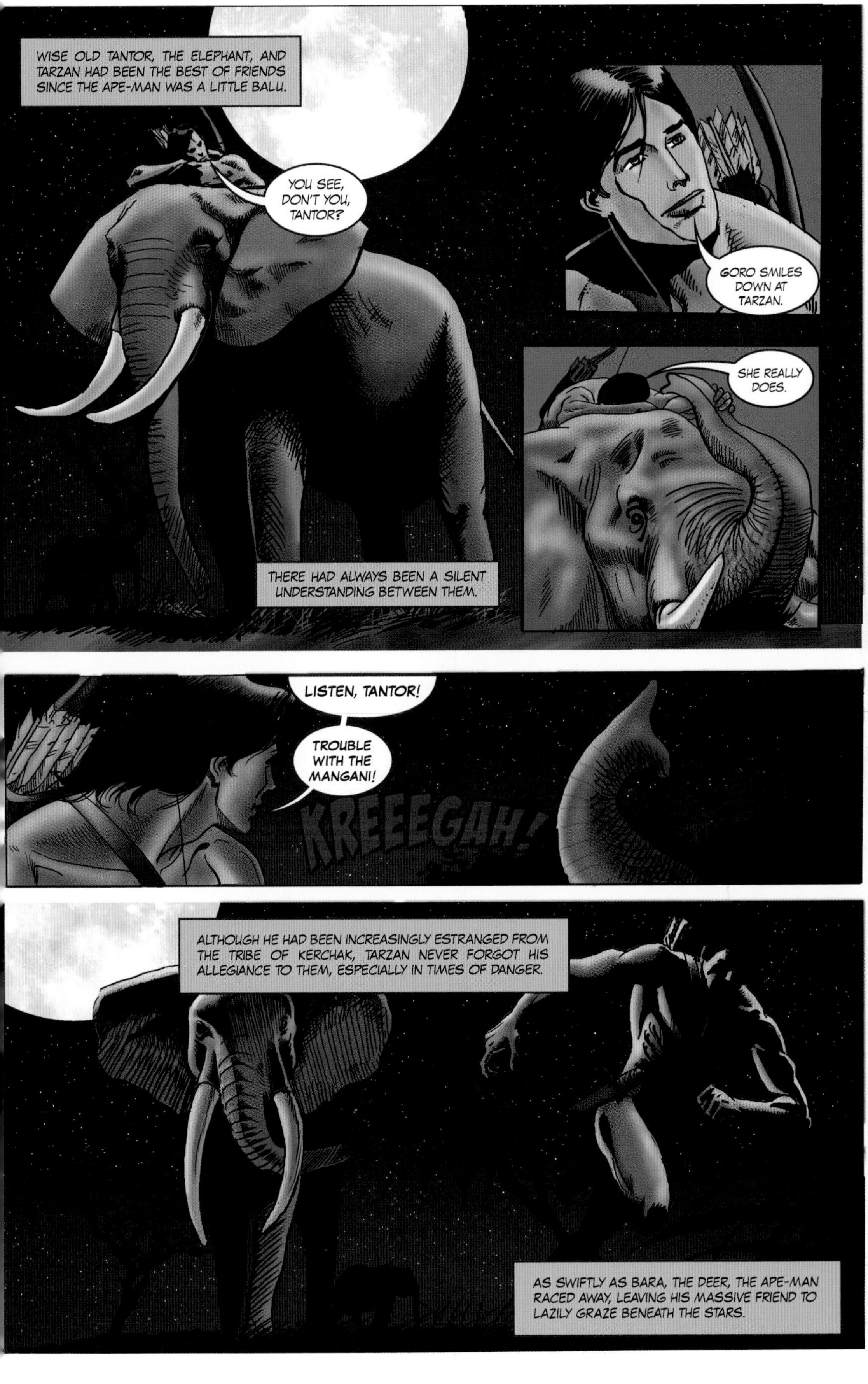
WISE OLD TANTOR, THE ELEPHANT, AND TARZAN HAD BEEN THE BEST OF FRIENDS SINCE THE APE-MAN WAS A LITTLE BALU.
YOU SEE, DON'T YOU, TANTOR?
GORO SMILES DOWN AT TARZAN.
SHE REALLY DOES.
THERE HAD ALWAYS BEEN A SILENT UNDERSTANDING BETWEEN THEM.
LISTEN, TANTOR!
TROUBLE WITH THE MANGANI!
KREEEGAH!
ALTHOUGH HE HAD BEEN INCREASINGLY ESTRANGED FROM THE TRIBE OF KERCHAK, TARZAN NEVER FORGOT HIS ALLEGIANCE TO THEM, ESPECIALLY IN TIMES OF DANGER.
AS SWIFTLY AS BARA, THE DEER, THE APE-MAN RACED AWAY, LEAVING HIS MASSIVE FRIEND TO LAZILY GRAZE BENEATH THE STARS.

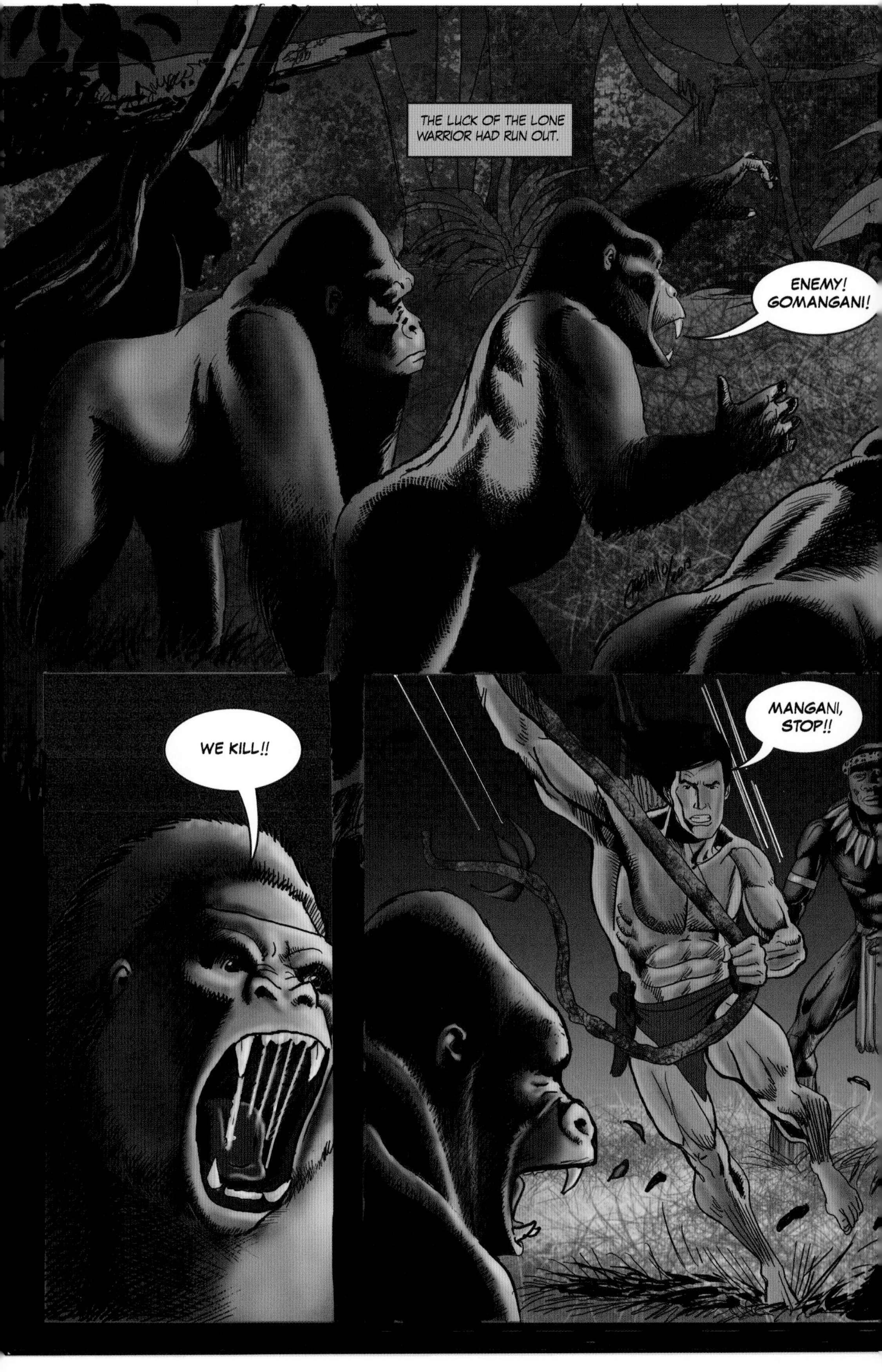
THE LUCK OF THE LONE WARRIOR HAD RUN OUT.
ENEMY! GOMANGANI!
WE KILL!!
MANGANI, STOP!!

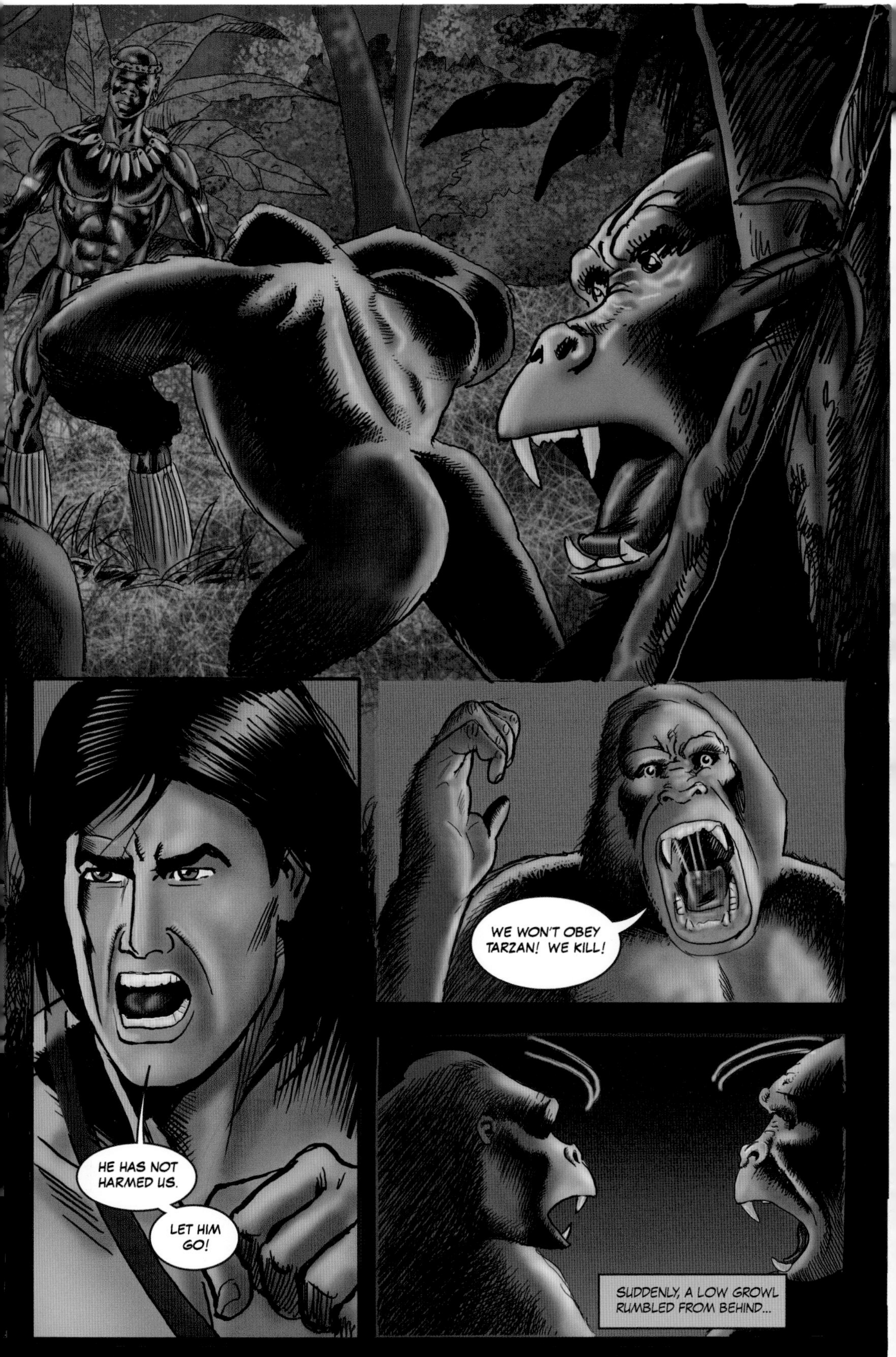
HE HAS NOT HARMED US.
LET HIM GO!
WE WON'T OBEY TARZAN! WE KILL!
SUDDENLY, A LOW GROWL RUMBLED FROM BEHIND...

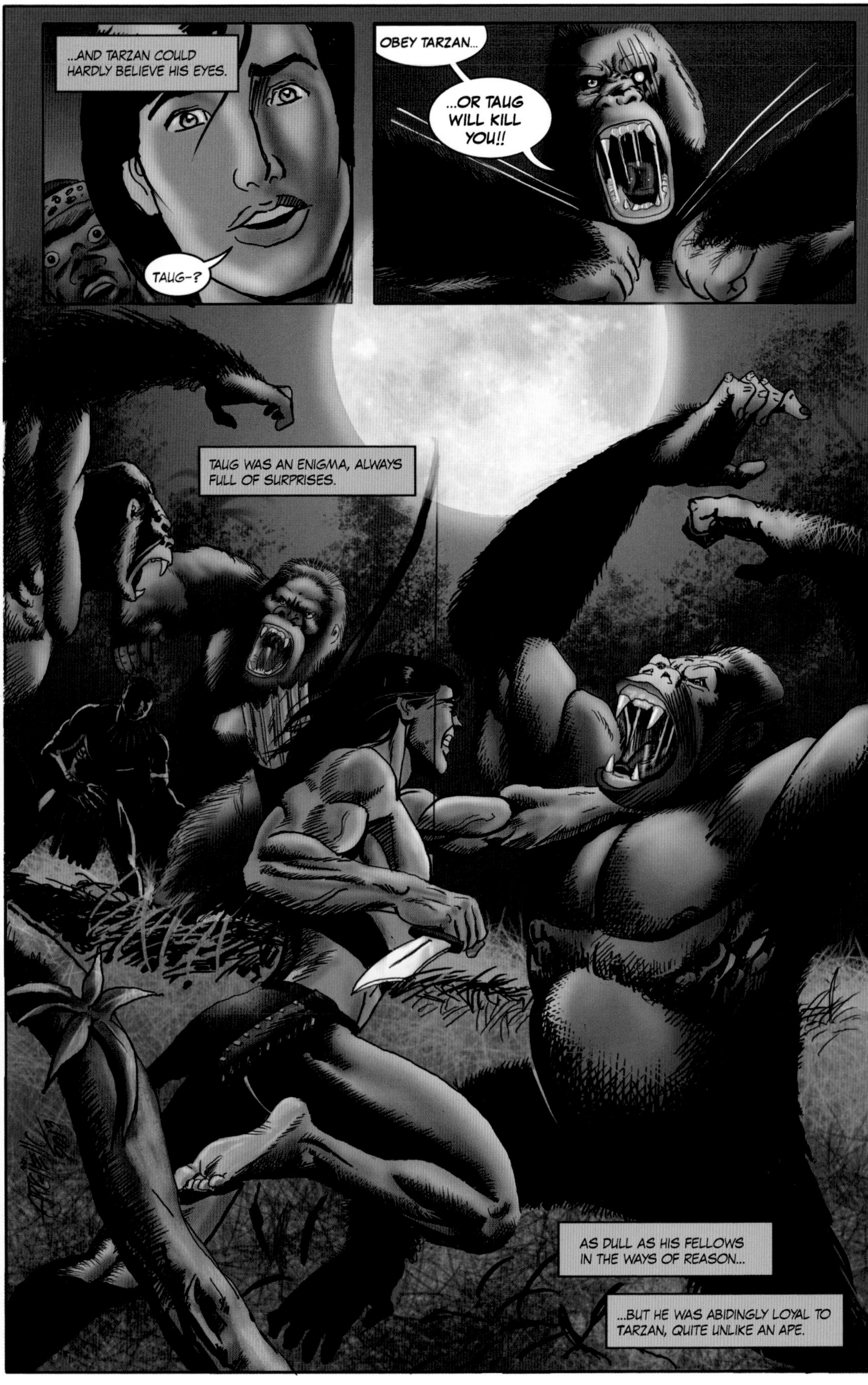
...AND TARZAN COULD HARDLY BELIEVE HIS EYES.
TAUG-?
OBEY TARZAN...
...OR TAUG WILL KILL YOU!!
TAUG WAS AN ENIGMA, ALWAYS FULL OF SURPRISES.
AS DULL AS HIS FELLOWS IN THE WAYS OF REASON...
...BUT HE WAS ABIDINGLY LOYAL TO TARZAN, QUITE UNLIKE AN APE.

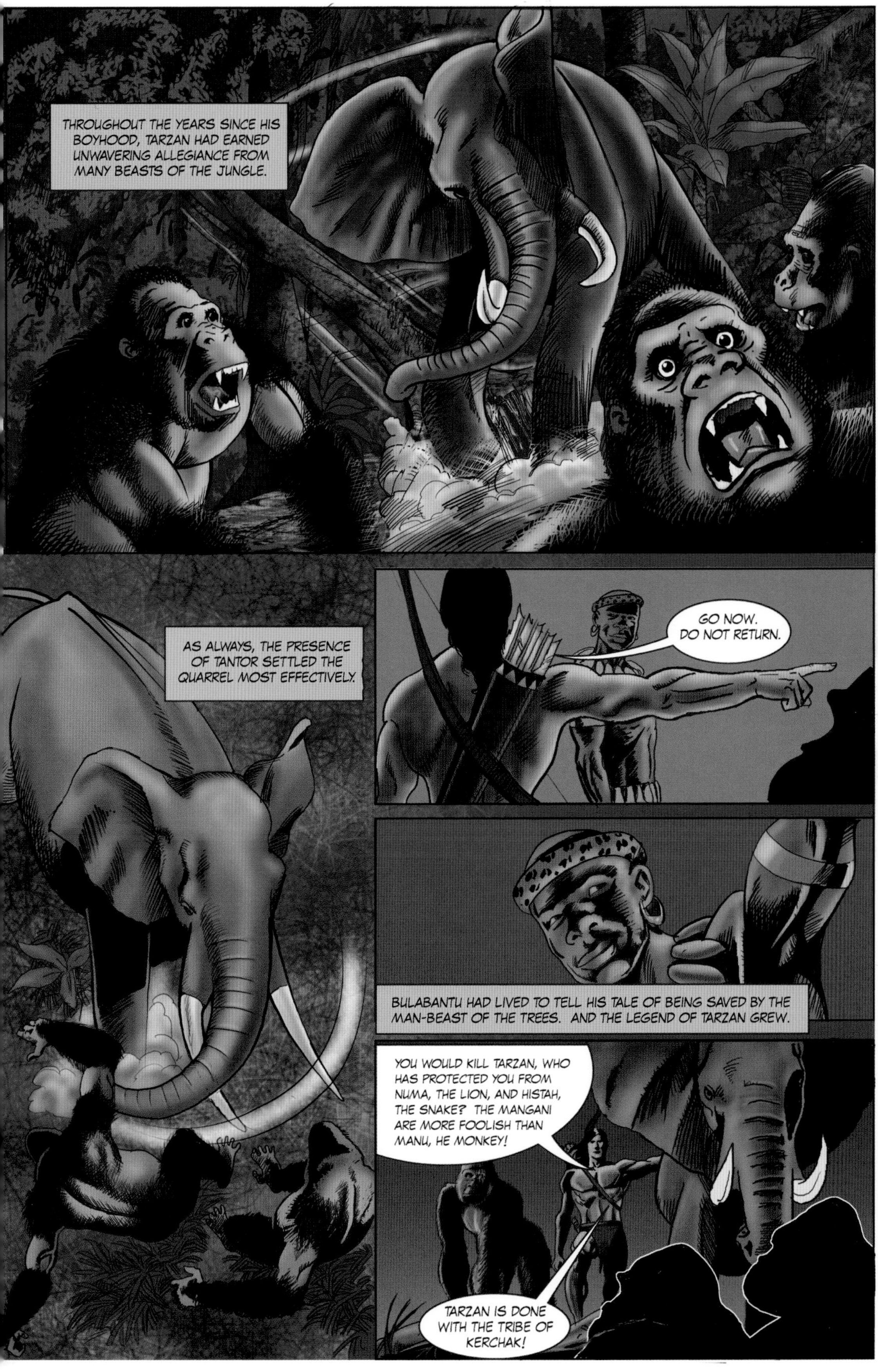
THROUGHOUT THE YEARS SINCE HIS BOYHOOD, TARZAN HAD EARNED UNWAVERING ALLEGIANCE FROM MANY BEASTS OF THE JUNGLE.
AS ALWAYS, THE PRESENCE OF TANTOR SETTLED THE QUARREL MOST EFFECTIVELY.
GO NOW. DO NOT RETURN.
BULABANTU HAD LIVED TO TELL HIS TALE OF BEING SAVED BY THE MAN-BEAST OF THE TREES. AND THE LEGEND OF TARZAN GREW.
YOU WOULD KILL TARZAN, WHO HAS PROTECTED YOU FROM NUMA, THE LION, AND HISTAH, THE SNAKE? THE MANGANI ARE MORE FOOLISH THAN MANU, HE MONKEY!
TARZAN IS DONE WITH THE TRIBE OF KERCHAK!

AND THEN, A STRANGE THING HAPPENED...

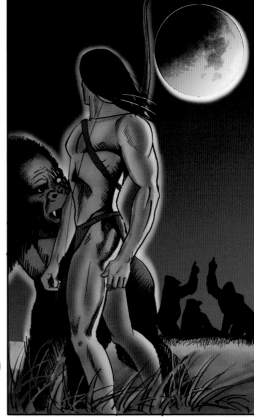

GORO, THE MOON, DOES NOT SMILE NOW.

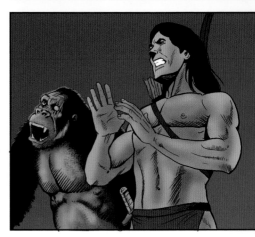

EVEN AS THE TRIBE LOOKED ON, AN EDGE OF THE MOON WAS GNAWED AWAY, BY SOMETHING BLACK AND MONSTROUS.

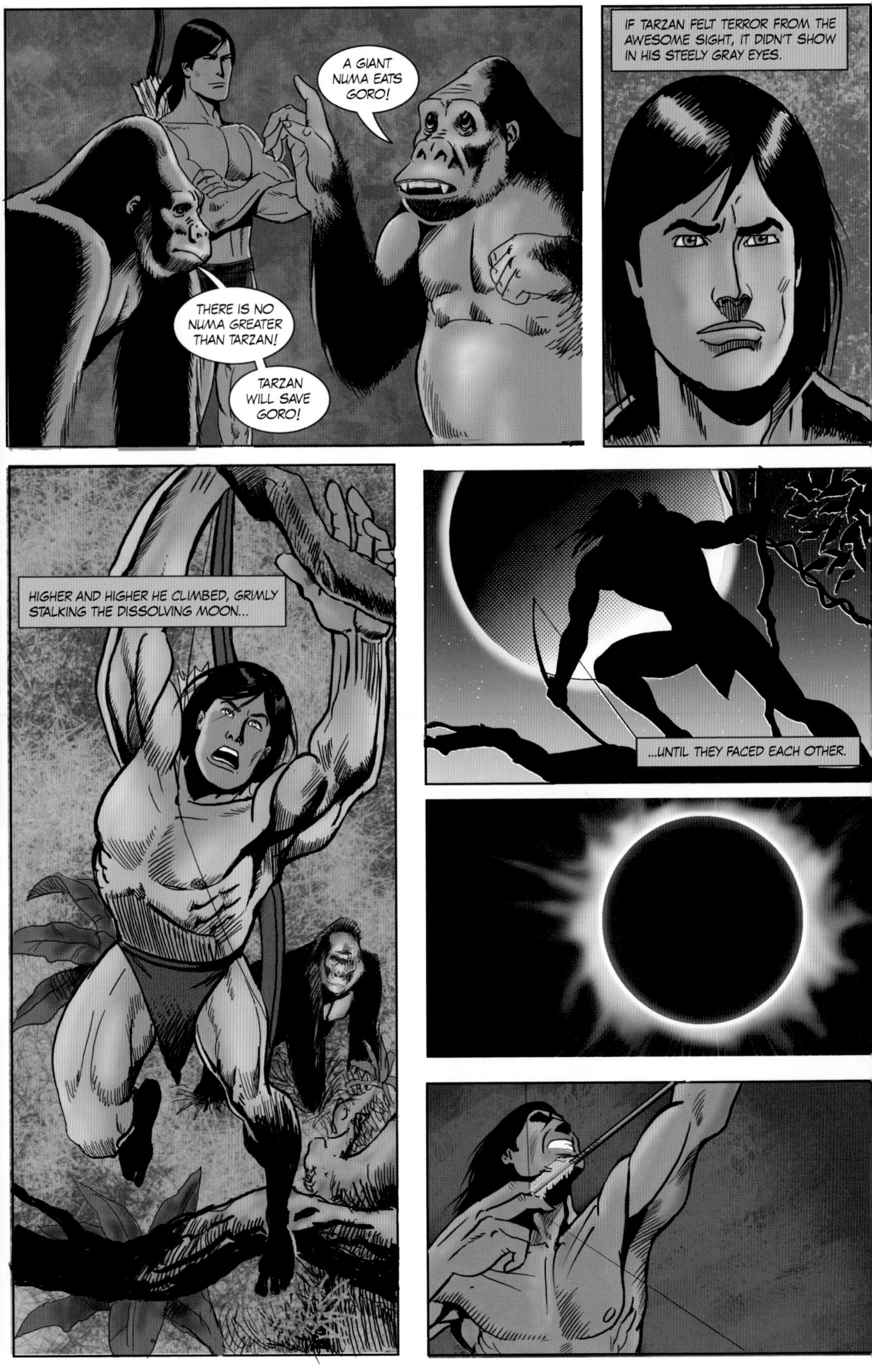
A GIANT NUMA EATS GORO!
THERE IS NO NUMA GREATER THAN TARZAN!
TARZAN WILL SAVE GORO!
IF TARZAN FELT TERROR FROM THE AWESOME SIGHT, IT DIDN'T SHOW IN HIS STEELY GRAY EYES.
HIGHER AND HIGHER HE CLIMBED, GRIMLY STALKING THE DISSOLVING MOON...
...UNTIL THEY FACED EACH OTHER.

THE APE-MAN AIMED AT THE IMAGINED HEART OF THE GREAT, BLACK NUMA, WHOSE WICKED EYES GLISTENED IN THE STARS. AND, SUDDENLY...

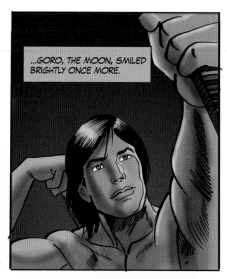

...GORO, THE MOON, SMILED BRIGHTLY ONCE MORE.

LOOK! LOOK! TARZAN HAS KILLED THE GREAT NUMA!

GORO RETURNS!

TARZAN OF THE APES CAME BACK TO THE TRIBE OF KERCHAK, TAKING A LONG STRIDE TOWARD KINGSHIP, WHICH HE ULTIMATELY WON.

AND GORO, THE MOON, CONTINUED TO SMILE.

The Legend Begins

"Even brave men . . . are sometimes frightened by solitude."

—EDGAR RICE BURROUGHS,
Tarzan of the Apes

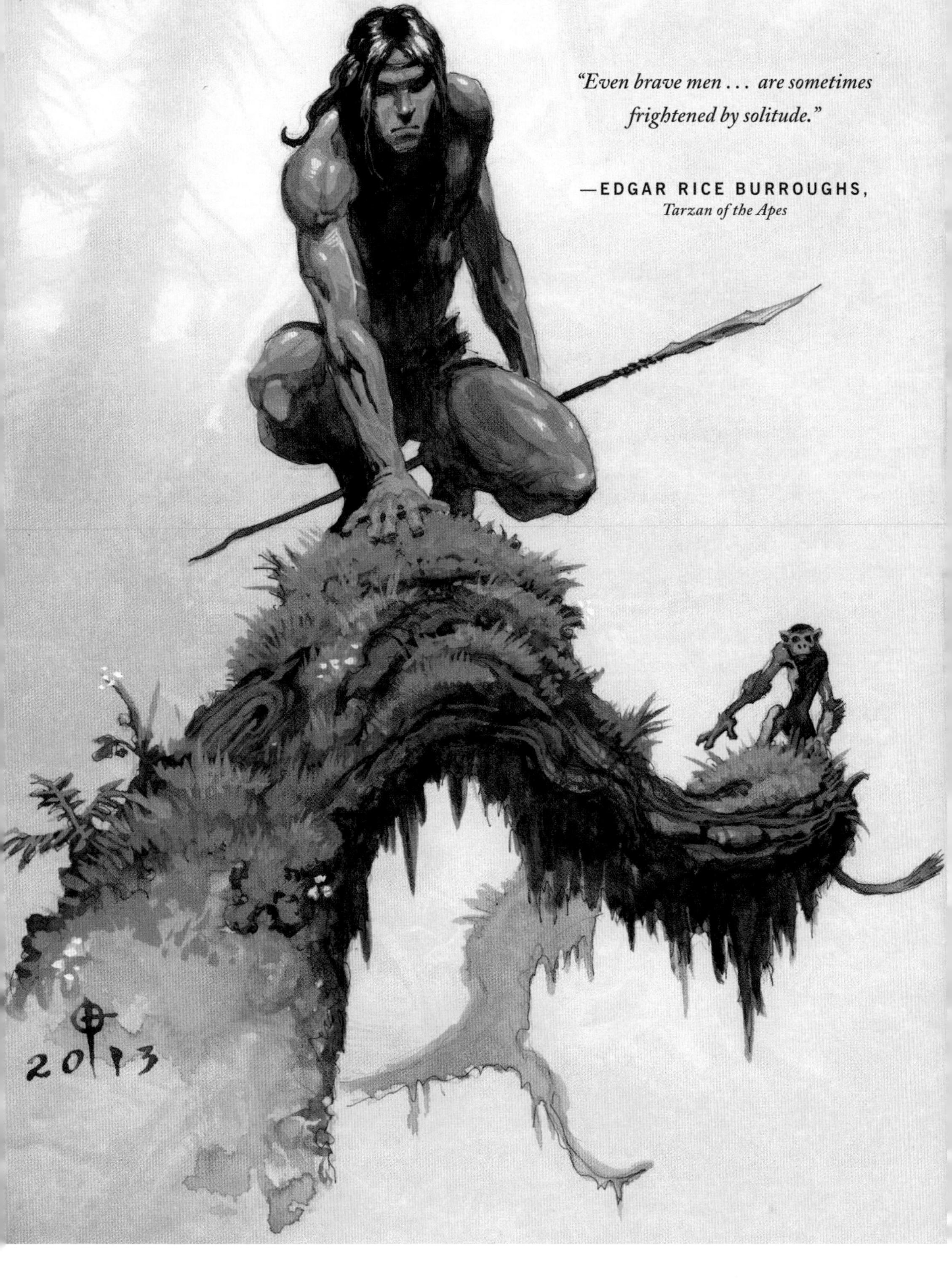

2013

ACKNOWLEDGMENTS

Very special thanks to Phil Currie, Tom Floyd, Scott Tracy Griffin, Bill and Sue-on Hillman, Robin Maxwell, George McWhorter, Rudy Sigmund, Jim Sullos, Jim Thompson, John Tyner, and Cathy Mann Wilbanks, for their warm and generous support. Also, I'm hugely grateful to L. R. Barrett-Durham, for her eagle-eyed proofreading of my scripts.

And I owe a tremendous debt of gratitude to Diana Leto. Without her valuable advice and tireless effort, this book would not have been possible.

—MARTIN POWELL

I wish to thank the Burroughs family, Scott Tracy Griffin, Jim Sullos, Michael Hudson, Cathy Mann Wilbanks, Rudy Sigmund, Patrick Thorpe, Mark Magner, and Martin Powell for making this book come to life. Their dedication to the writings of Edgar Rice Burroughs has been an inspiration to me, and I'm certain these stories will spark the imaginations of many others for generations to come.

—DIANA LETO

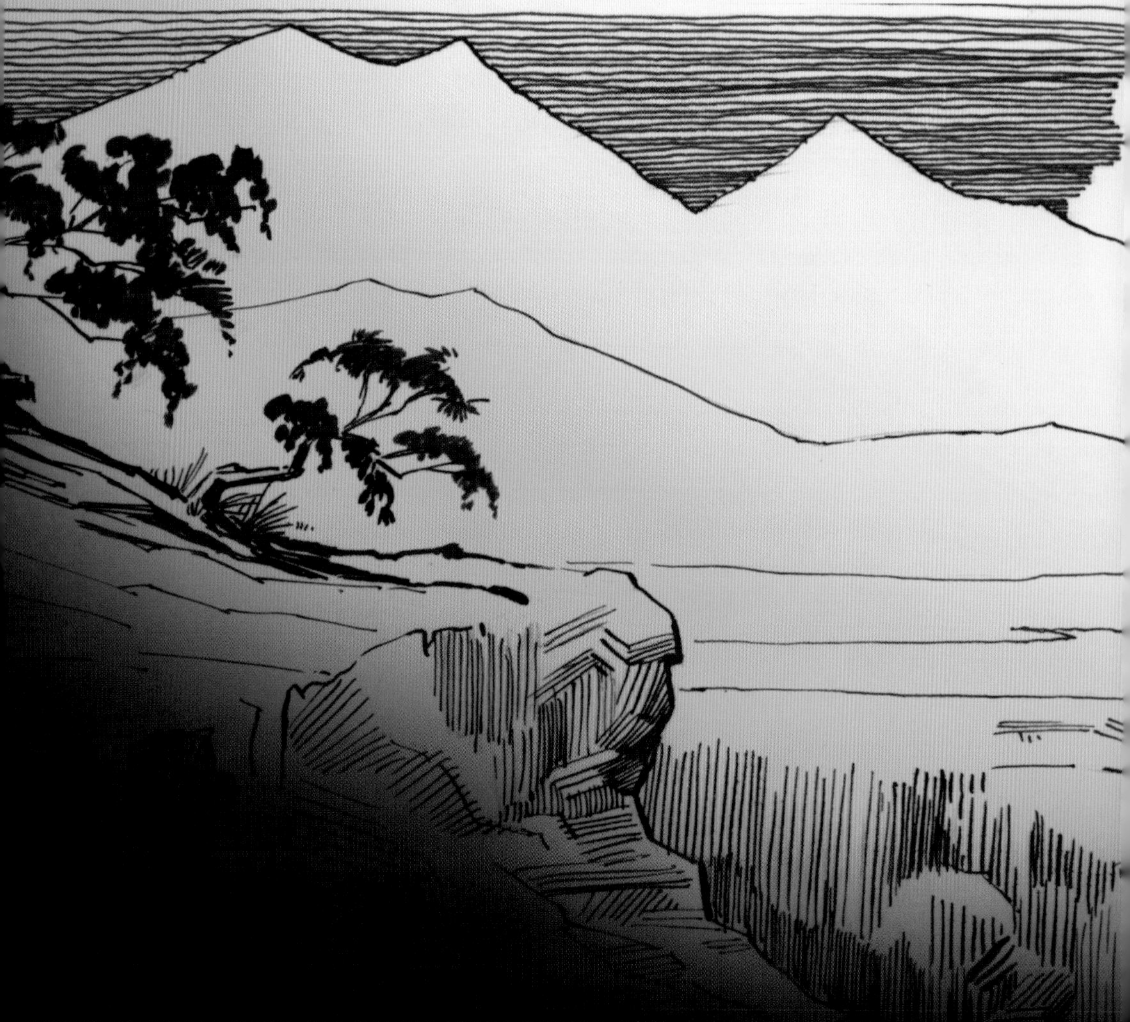

ARTWORK BY THOMAS FLOYD, ERB GOLDEN AWARD WINNER, 2010

I'd like to express my heartfelt appreciation and gratitude to each and every creator who had a part in this book. I am so proud of your work and the great accomplishment we all share in *Jungle Tales of Tarzan*. Diana Leto, thank you for your continuous mediation between creative parties and for your expertise in tying so many loose ends together into one cohesive unit.

Thank you, ERB, Inc., Jim Sullos, and Cathy Mann Wilbanks, for your support throughout this journey. To the worldwide Burroughs fan base: You've waited a long time for this book. Thank you for sticking with us. We all hope you enjoy our efforts. And a very special thank-you to Edgar Rice Burroughs for his creation of one of the most wonderful fictional characters that have ever graced the pages of a printed book (or e-reader, for that matter). May Tarzan and his world live on for as long as people seek the simple pleasures found in reading a good book.

—MICHAEL HUDSON

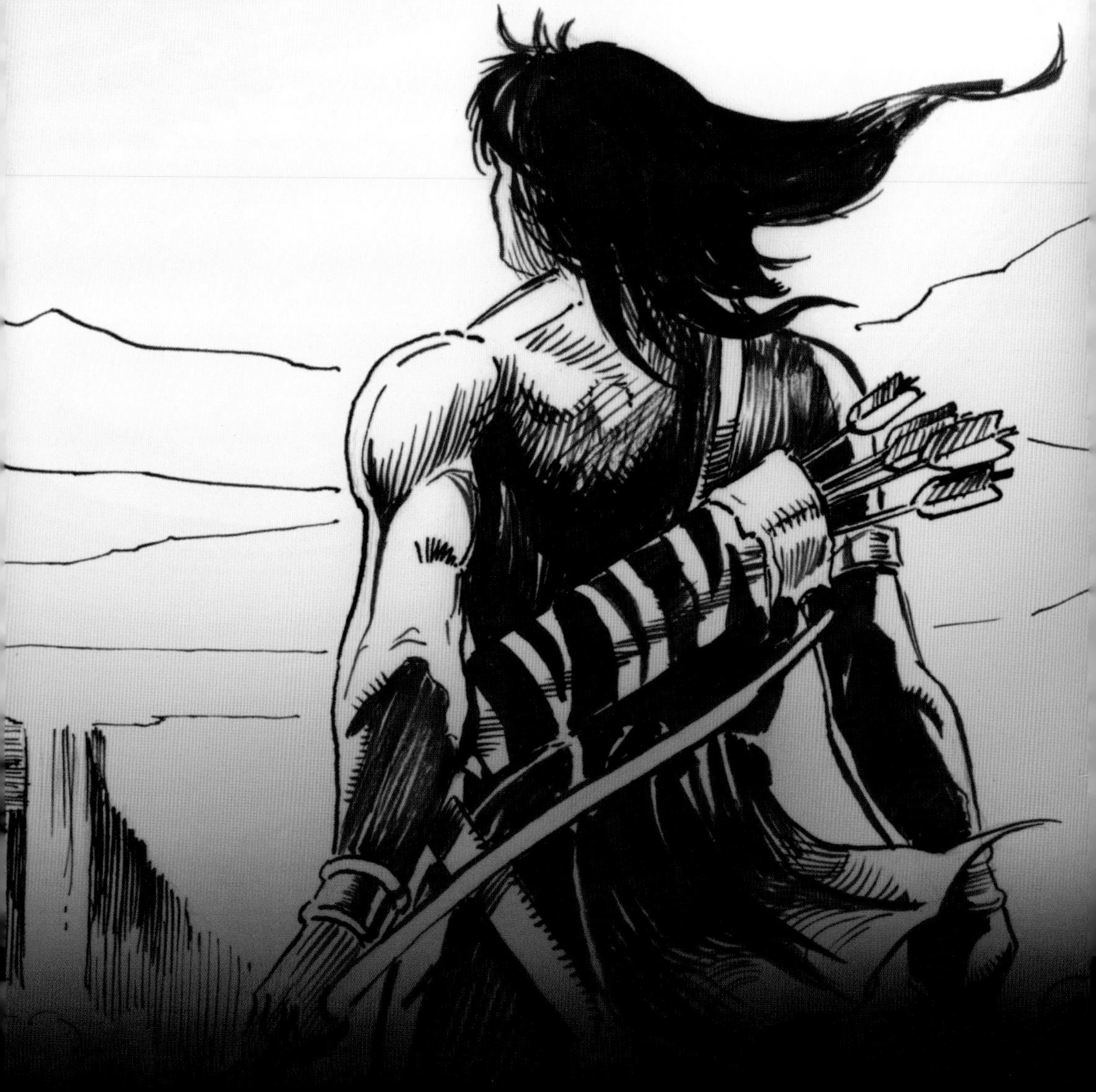

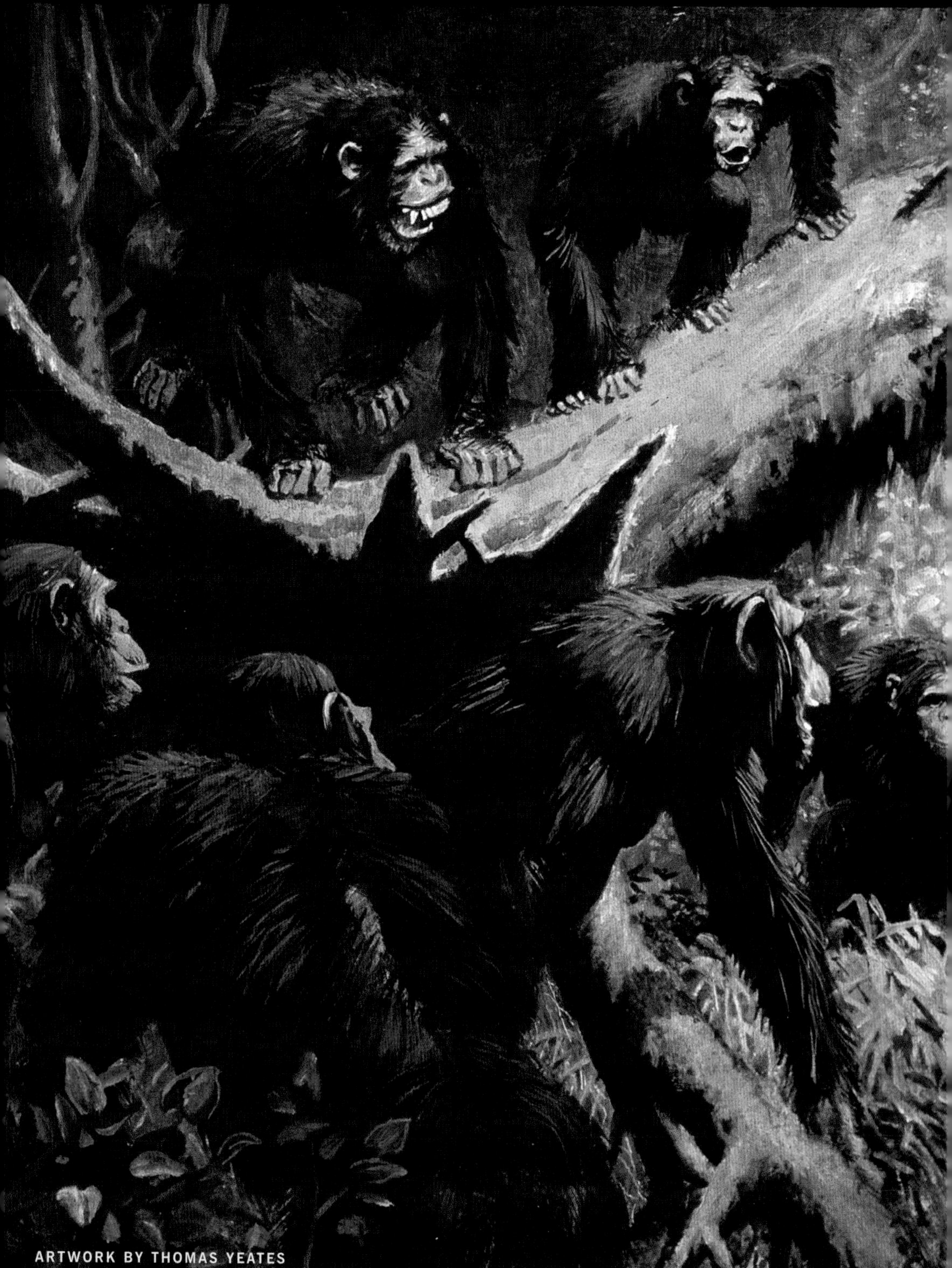
ARTWORK BY THOMAS YEATES

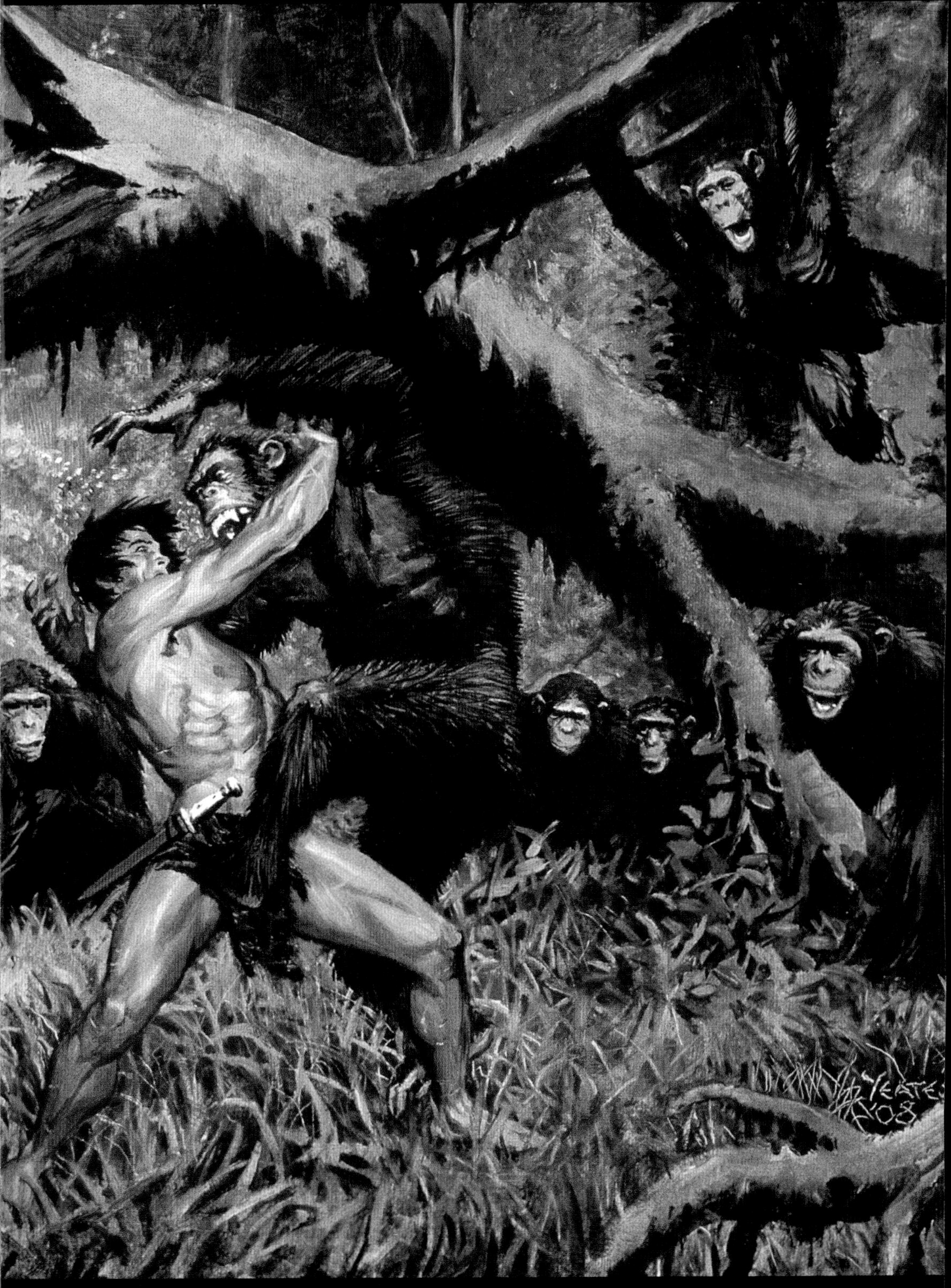
YEATES
'08

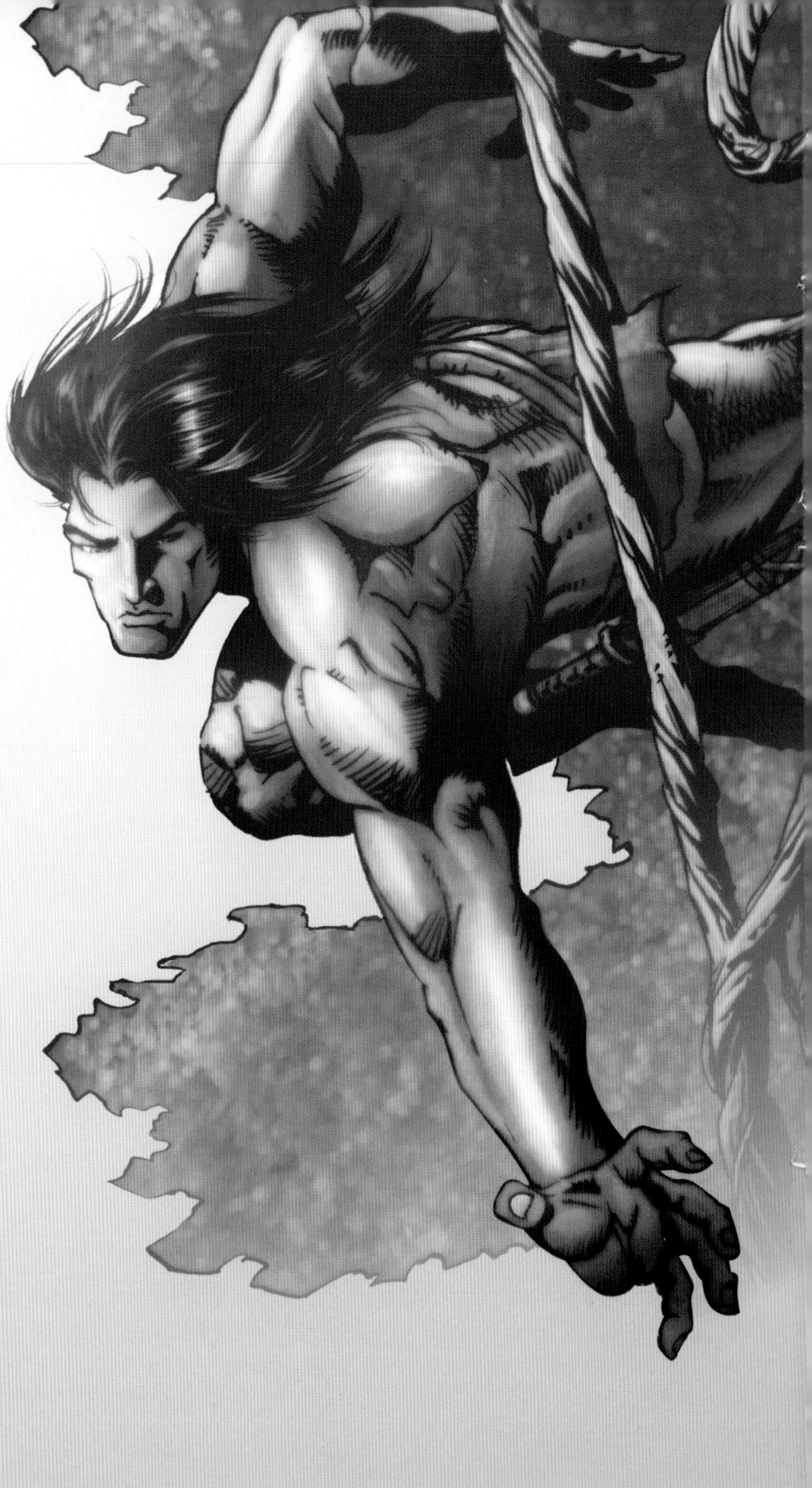

EDGAR RICE BURROUGHS'

Jungle Tales of **Tarzan**®